The
Modern
Prince

THE
MODERN
PRINCE

*What Machiavelli Can Teach Us
in the Age of Trump*

Carnes Lord

Encounter BOOKS

New York • London

First edition published in 2003 by Yale University Press.
Second edition published in 2018 by Encounter Books,
an activity of Encounter for Culture and Education, Inc.,
a nonprofit, tax exempt corporation.
Encounter Books website address: www.encounterbooks.com

Manufactured in the United States and printed on
acid-free paper. The paper used in this publication meets
the minimum requirements of ANSI/NISO Z39.48–1992
(R 1997) (*Permanence of Paper*).

SECOND AMERICAN EDITION

LIBRARY OF CONGRESS CATALOGING-IN-PUBLICATION DATA

Names: Lord, Carnes, author.
Title: The modern prince : what Machiavelli can teach us
in the age of Trump / Carnes Lord.
Description: Second Edition. | New York : Encounter Books, [2018] |
Includes bibliographical references and index.
Identifiers: LCCN 2018000965 (print) | LCCN 2018001568 (ebook) |
ISBN 9781641770118 (ebook) | ISBN 9781641770101 (hardcover : alk. paper)
Subjects: LCSH: Political leadership. | Elite (Social sciences) | Democracy.
Classification: LCC JC330.3 (ebook) | LCC JC330.3 .L67 2018 (print) |
DDC 320.1–dc21
LC record available at https://lccn.loc.gov/2018000965

Interior page design and composition: BooksByBruce.com

CONTENTS

PREFACE TO THE
SECOND EDITION

A decade and a half is a long time in politics, and much has happened in the world since this book first appeared. American politics in particular has been upended by the election of Donald Trump to the presidency in November 2016, which confounded the assumptions of most political observers and may well herald a strikingly new departure in the historical trajectory of the entire post–World War II era. Under these circumstances, what is to be gained by reissuing a study of leadership and statecraft rooted in a past that seems to be rapidly receding?

Two brief answers to this question may be offered. The first is that *The Modern Prince* is not a study of contemporary history but a treatise in political science. As such, it seeks to paint leadership and statecraft on a broad canvas, one that, while framed by the American experience, draws on examples from many states or societies and a wide range of classical as well as contemporary authors. These examples and sources have not aged over the last fifteen years. Second, and more to the point of the contemporary moment, if this book can be said to belong to the literary genre of "mirror of princes," no one today better resembles the face in that mirror than the forty-fifth president of the United States.

It is much too soon to predict what policies or actions the Trump administration will embrace, or what ultimate impact it will have on America or the world. It is not even clear whether these policies or actions will be conventionally "conservative," or whether the famously deal-making president will manage to forge a centrist coalition of a fundamentally new kind. The point is rather that Trump has ascended to the highest office in the land in the name of no established political party, but as an outsider determined to shake the pillars of the temple while offering a quasi-messianic vision of an America made "great" again. As one media commentator in the days following the inauguration said, only half in jest, Trump did not so much "*succeed* to power as *seize* power" in Washington.

To understand fully the meaning of this revolutionary turn in American politics, there is no better guide than *The Prince* of Niccolò Machiavelli (1513), the most famous treatise on political leadership of all time. Above all, Machiavelli wrote the playbook of the politician who takes power in a factionalized republic by siding with the common people against the dominant "elites." Machiavelli describes in the following words the challenge facing this "new prince," as he calls him:

> It should be considered that nothing is more difficult to handle, more doubtful of success, nor more dangerous to manage, than to put oneself at the head of introducing new orders. For the introducer has all those who benefit from the old order as enemies, and he has lukewarm defenders in all those who might benefit from the new orders. This lukewarmness arises partly from fear of adversaries who have the laws on their side and partly from the incredulity of men, who do not truly believe in new things unless they come to have a firm experience of them. Consequently, whenever those who are enemies have opportunity to attack, they do so with partisan zeal, and the others defend lukewarmly so that one is in peril along with them.[1]

This is precisely the situation facing President Trump in these early months of his tenure. Comparable moments in the history of the republic are rare. Perhaps only Jackson, Roosevelt, and Reagan went to the people in such a manner and faced such fierce political headwinds.

This new edition of *The Modern Prince* essentially reproduces the text of the 2003 version. The text has been edited primarily to fix chronological references and to update the endnotes. Later developments would have led me to revise my judgments in few if any cases; my relatively favorable treatment of Vladimir Putin, most notably, still seems reasonable in the context of that time, though my satisfaction at his treatment of the Russian so-called "oligarchs" I would perhaps soften in hindsight. My skepticism concerning the European Union has been amply validated by recent events. As regards the United States, I would only say that the practice of American statecraft has shown little improvement in the Bush and Obama eras, while the negative trends I identified in areas such as public administration, law, and education have worsened markedly. Indeed, they are a significant part of the explanation for the Trump revolution.

A final point bearing directly on the outlook of the new administration has to do with the too-long-neglected issue of economic statecraft. The stark decline of the working class in the United States under the impact of globalization is perhaps the single most important factor behind Trump's electoral victory, and underlines the importance of his departure from orthodox free-market economic assumptions dominant in the political class generally. At the same time, probably the most important positive development in American statecraft over the last fifteen years has been the radical improvement in the protocols governing economic sanctions. Arguably, this has opened the prospect of a very significant shift in the relative weight of the economic instrument in the toolkit of American statecraft. The Trump administration faces a great challenge—but also a great opportunity—to rethink in a fundamental way the proper role (and of course the limits) of federal intervention in the economic sphere.[2] How well it manages this challenge could spell success or failure for the overall Trump enterprise.

PREFACE

The theory of democracy tells us that the people rule. In practice, we have leaders who rule the people in a manner not altogether different from the princes and potentates of times past. This paradox seems for the most part cheerfully accepted by contemporary electorates. That it remains problematic nevertheless is evident. What exactly is the nature of political leadership today? How to account for the persisting if not growing importance of executive as distinct from other forms of political leadership? How can it be justified and accommodated within the framework of contemporary democracy? What are its characteristic weaknesses? And what if anything can be done to fix them? These are the fundamental issues this book sets out to address.

The central importance of leadership in our democratic age is nowhere clearer than in times of war. The ability of a supreme leader to inspire confidence in the nation at large and communicate resolution and seriousness to allies and adversaries is as vital to success in war today as it ever was. Neither the sophisticated weaponry nor the vast and complex organizations of a modern military establishment nullify the need for such leadership—a lesson the United States once learned to its great cost in the jungles of Southeast Asia. Not so long ago, it seemed unthinkable that the United States—or for that matter the other democracies of the newly enlarged West—would be faced in the imaginable future with a prolonged conflict that might test its national leadership in comparable ways. The global war on terror should force us to rethink at a fundamental level what we want and need in our political leaders.

But the leadership requirements of democracies today are by no means limited to foreign or military affairs. Among other things, Americans look to their leaders—particularly to their presidents—to ensure that the nation's mighty economic engine remains in good repair and that its benefits are distributed with tolerable fairness to all. They also look to presidents as guardians of the laws and symbols of national values. In these and other respects, they look to presidents not only for competent management of the nation's affairs, but for justice and a measure of inspiration. This is why the character of presidents matters. Indeed, given the ethos of instant gratification that pervades popular culture throughout much of the West today, personal integrity in our leaders seems both more fragile and more necessary than ever.

In the United States today, the idea of "leadership" is very much in vogue. This is in part because of its growing prominence in the world of American business, where it has been touted as an essential supplement to traditional business "management" in an era of rapid technological change and global competition. But the phenomenon is a much wider one. Leadership has become a watchword of public discourse in contemporary America because (or so one might speculate) it provides a value-neutral and therefore generally acceptable way to build character and foster civic responsibility in younger Americans at a time when these qualities are felt to be in decreasing supply.

All of this is no doubt to be welcomed, but it has a certain sedative effect when it comes to serious analysis of the role of leadership in politics. "Leadership" in such contexts is something almost wholly benign. It is seen as an exquisitely democratic activity, one in which the interests of leaders and the interests of followers mostly coincide, leaders are keenly sensitive to the needs and wants of followers, and decision-making is highly consensual. As such, it is a fundamentally apolitical concept, one that ignores central concerns of political leadership such as power and authority. It has succeeded in making leadership entirely respectable, not to say "politically correct," but at the price of a loss of clarity about the problematic aspects of leadership in democratic as well as other societies.

Some forty years ago, in his pioneering work on this subject, James MacGregor Burns could write, "The crisis of leadership today is the mediocrity or irresponsibility of so many of the men and women in power, but leadership rarely rises to the need for it. The fundamental crisis underlying mediocrity is intellectual. If we know all too much about our leaders, we know far too little about *leadership*. We fail to grasp the essence of leadership that is relevant to the modern age and hence we cannot agree even on the standards by which to measure, recruit, and reject it."[3] These words remain true today. There can be little question that the contemporary world is experiencing an acute leadership deficit, and that much of the reason for this is the lack of appropriate intellectual preparation for leadership functions in the political class. While in no way denying the importance of the psychological and moral dimension of leadership, I will concentrate on exploring the fundamental—and rarely posed—question: What is it exactly that politicians today must know in order to lead effectively? The answer has little do with the tactics and techniques of winning elections or maintaining a strong position in opinion polls, although these things are of course a major preoccupation for most democratic leaders today. Rather, it has to do with knowledge of what I shall call—using a patently old-fashioned but nevertheless indispensable term—"statecraft."

Leadership is less necessary in times and places where state and society are in good working order. In times of economic prosperity and international stability, the issue of leadership tends to recede still further in the general consciousness. It is reasonable to assume that the advanced democracies today are less in need of strong leadership than are the emerging or would-be democracies of the former Communist bloc, or for that matter the democracies, nominal democracies, and traditional and autocratic regimes of the developing world. There is no cause to be complacent, however, about leadership in the democracies of the West. This is particularly so in the case of the United States, given its key international role (especially pronounced now in the context of the global war against terrorism) and what will be very generally agreed to be the flawed performance of its national leadership during much of its recent history. Partly for these reasons, partly because the American model of democratic leadership seems increasingly to set the tune for the world at large, but partly also because the history of American statecraft is uniquely transparent and well-documented, the United States will be featured prominently in my discussion.

Yet leadership and statecraft will appear throughout on a larger stage. Both contemporary and historical examples from different sorts of societies will be used to illuminate the distinctiveness of the American experiment and of constitutional democracy more generally. Within the contemporary world, special attention will be given to the instructive extremes of Japan (chapter 9) on the one hand and France and Singapore (chapter 10) on the other. Some may find it odd that a study of modern leadership makes occasional use of examples from the ancient world; the explanation is that the character of modern leadership reveals itself fully only from a vantage point beyond itself. In any event, I believe it is wrong to ignore or dismiss older models of leadership, as writers on this subject commonly do today—"as if heaven, the sun, the elements, men, are different in their motion, order and powers from what they were in ancient times."[4]

This project is admittedly an audacious one, and all the more so because of the standard of comparison it invokes. Machiavelli's *Prince* (1513) is the most famous treatise on political leadership ever written. It is not obvious that a book composed over five hundred years ago should have much of interest to say to leaders or anyone else today. Yet *The Prince* continues to be widely read and admired, in spite or indeed because of the stark realism and questionable morality of the guidance it provides to princes or potential princes, and has inspired more than one contemporary treatise on political or business leadership.[5] As will become apparent, this study does not necessarily endorse all of Machiavelli's ideas, and it does not attempt in any systematic way to update them for contemporary readers. Still less does it try to provide an adequate interpretation of this controversial and frequently misunderstood author. Rather, it uses *The Prince* selectively, both as a point of reference for understanding the particular character and (especially) the limitations of leadership today and as a tool for shaping the elements of an art of politics to suit the needs of contemporary leaders. I will contend that Machiavelli remains of great interest for anyone approaching politics in this perspective rather than under the guidance of the conventions of the academy or the pieties of regnant political opinion. *The Prince* also serves as a literary model of sorts, with its brisk, colloquial, and irreverent style designed, among other things, to deflate the pretensions of intellectuals and catch the attention of busy men.

This book, like *The Prince* itself, is a critical assessment of contemporary leadership, not a celebration of it. It is deeply concerned with the growth of executive power and the trend toward plebiscitary leadership in the advanced democracies, and related phenomena such as the weakening of parties and the erosion of constitutional forms and the rule of law. At the same time, it indicts contemporary leaders for their failure to provide essential checks on powerful and democratically unaccountable institutions such as the judiciary, the bureaucracy, and the media, as well as the elites that dominate them. Contemporary leadership, I shall argue, combines strength and weakness in a peculiar and unsatisfactory way, one that ill serves the cause of constitutional democracy and should make us fear for its future.

Executive power in modern democracies generally can be understood as a peculiar and in some sense unnatural combination of strength and weakness. What is the origin of this notion? An excellent case can be made that it derives from a fundamental rethinking of the requirements of political leadership undertaken in the sixteenth century by a single individual—Niccolò Machiavelli. If this is correct, as I believe it is (see the discussion in chapter 8), there is little need for a more elaborate justification for placing Machiavelli at the center of a book about modern leadership. It also helps explain what some might otherwise regard as the excessive attention given to the history of political philosophy in a book that purports to be a practical guide to statecraft. This study remains firmly grounded in the premise that ideas have important consequences in the real world.

One of the purposes of this book is to show that the practice of statecraft today suffers from the absence of an adequate theory of statecraft. As I will argue (chapter 3), the science of politics as studied in our universities is not such a theory, nor, given its fundamental premises, is it capable of providing one. I will suggest that traditional political science, especially in its original incarnation in the thought of the Greek philosopher Aristotle, comes closer to providing, if not a full-blown theory of statecraft, at any rate a conceptual foundation for one that is in important respects more satisfactory and better suited to contemporary requirements. In this regard, I make a sustained if necessarily limited effort to mine the insights of a variety of older writers on politics and statecraft, both well known (Alexis de Tocqueville, Carl von Clausewitz, or the authors of *The Federalist*) and relatively obscure (the nineteenth-century British political writer Walter Bagehot, among others).

It is to be hoped that this effort will be received in the spirit in which it is offered. I make no attempt to develop this critique of contemporary political science in more than a partial, tentative, and suggestive fashion, something that in any event would be difficult or impossible even in a very long book. Works referenced are in general those from which I have learned something of interest rather than those that simply do scholarly duty. Certain points forcefully made in the interests of clarity (or intellectual provocation) would no doubt require extensive defense or qualification in a more conventionally academic presentation. Moreover, everything I have to say on individual leaders or the states or regimes over which they preside is necessarily incomplete. Above all, I have made no effort to pass comprehensive judgment on particular political leaders. This is a book less about leaders than about leadership and statecraft. Particular statements about contemporary leaders must be understood in the context in which they appear and in the light of the argument of the work as a whole. Those who find a lack of charity (or for that matter an uncritical enthusiasm) in my treatment of particular politicians will have missed the point of the exercise.

What should leaders today know? In the first place, their own political environment—states and regimes or forms of government, and the national elites that both enable and limit their power. It is surprising to what extent these elemental realities are not fully grasped even by sophisticated modern politicians. (They are discussed in chapters 4–6.) In the second place, the goals that states and their leaders pursue—these too can be opaque to leaders schooled in the narrowly rationalistic outlook of contemporary political science (chapter 11). Further, the tools or instruments available to leaders in pursuit of their goals. These tools of statecraft, spanning the full spectrum of domestic as well as foreign policy-making, are inseparably bound up with the various institutions that make up the modern administrative state and the bureaucratic subcultures that shape them. Contrary to a view that is too common even among experienced politicians, these institutions are rarely supple and responsive instruments for leaders. Rather, they tend to resist strategic direction by national policy makers, obeying instead their own institutional imperatives and professional deformations. (The tools of statecraft are discussed in chapters 12–20.) Partly for this reason, but partly too because of the unique conceptual challenges involved, the requirements of decision-making by today's leaders are more demanding than is sometimes imagined. Political leaders are not infrequently the lonely guardians of national strategy, and face fearsome responsibilities in undertaking strategic action in crisis situations (chapters 21–22). They face baffling difficulties in structuring mechanisms for advice and decision, as well as in shaping the political environment to support their policy goals (chapters 23–24). And for all of these reasons, they rise with difficulty, if indeed at all, to the fundamental challenges of our times.

I

WHY LEADERSHIP IS STILL POSSIBLE

It is not obvious that leadership is actually possible in contemporary democracies. Constitutional democracy is supposed to rely on the rule of law rather than the rule of men. Because its fundamental law is laid down in a written document, opportunities for even the greatest statesmen to effect major change are severely restricted. Constitutional democracy rests on powerful institutions, not individuals, both to give it direction and to curb its excesses through a process of mutual checking and balancing. But more than that, the very commitment to liberty that is at the heart of the idea of democracy in modern times greatly limits the sway of politicians over the wider society.

Over the course of America's history, many of its presidents have behaved as if they agreed with this view, deferring to Congress for policy leadership and in other respects playing a relatively passive or instrumental part in the machinery of government. Nowadays, for reasons we shall explore shortly, Americans have gotten used to the idea that presidents are all-powerful figures, princes in all but name. It is certainly convenient for presidents if people think this. But is it true? Or is democratic leadership, in the United States or elsewhere in today's world, perhaps a kind of illusion, a sleight of hand perpetrated by politicians desperate to assert their own importance and justify their role?[1] Are there broader trends at work that frustrate effective leadership?

A plausible argument can be made to this effect. Marxists have long held that the real rulers of capitalist states are not the politicians but the owners of the means of production. In spite of the obvious flaws in this notion, it would be hard to deny that democratic politicians today are extraordinarily sensitive to the needs of major corporations and other critical cogs in the machinery of the national economy. Other domestic interest groups (labor unions or trial lawyers, to name a few) can also wield substantial power, often because they contribute disproportionately to the coffers of political parties and candidates. It is hard to overstate the challenge some democratic leaders face in contending with the daily realities of party government. And virtually all democratic leaders today must defer to one degree or another to the wishes of deeply entrenched bureaucracies. In extreme cases (Japan, notably), leaders have little ability to contest policy positions developed within the state bureaucracy.

Especially but not only in the developing world, political leaders today complain that their freedom of action at home is increasingly constrained by global economic and technological trends. Global interdependence, so long talked about, is now a reality. And the growth of transnational regimes and institutions of all kinds limits what leaders can do at home as well as abroad. The United Nations has less patience than in the past with absolute claims of national sovereignty, and in Europe, a vast rule-making bureaucracy threatens to usurp the traditional powers of legislators and politicians.

Then, there is the near-crippling impact on leadership in some advanced democracies of the news media and the political culture. A culture of extreme egalitarianism of the sort now found throughout the English-speaking world as well as much of northern Europe tends to be hostile to the pretensions of politicians and unforgiving of their flaws and errors. This tendency is aggravated by the emergence of a mass media that is independent of government and, indeed, views the exposure of its shortcomings as a measure of merit and one of its primary functions. All of this has contributed to a decline in public respect for the political class throughout the West, and it has fostered a wider alienation from politics that is reflected in reduced voter participation and a generalized cynicism concerning the motives and accomplishments of political leaders. Given such attitudes, it would be hardly surprising if even the most effective political leaders found it difficult to generate public interest or confidence in their programs or to mobilize the political support essential for implementing them.

What is true now of the West may be true soon enough throughout the rest of the world. If or to the extent that democracy is destined to sweep the globe, as argued not many years ago by Francis Fukuyama in a work of impressive historico-philosophical analysis, the legitimacy of leadership will be increasingly in doubt. The "end of history" of the philosophers has little place for leadership in the traditional sense of the word—leadership on behalf of great causes or ideals. The conquest of nature by modern technology, the unprecedented prosperity it has brought and the resulting growth of a democratically minded middle class, and the rarity if not the disappearance of great wars—all this threatens to make politics unimportant and leaders dispensable. To borrow the well-known Marxist prediction about the post-revolutionary future: the government of men will be replaced by the administration of things. Yet that is not all. The radically egalitarian culture that looms on the historical horizon may destroy the very psychological conditions necessary for the nurturing of leaders.[2]

There is something to all this—certainly more than is generally recognized. Such a vision of the end of history is no doubt off the mark in foreseeing the virtual disappearance of politics and international conflict, and overly optimistic in assessing at least the near-term prospects for democracy throughout the world. It is more compelling in its sketch of the trajectory of democratic ideology and culture. There can be little question that the egalitarian turn in world history marked by the American and French revolutions has fundamentally altered the way many if not most human beings alive today view social hierarchy and political authority. Nor can it be doubted that the democratic idea has an internal dynamic of its own, one that continues to play itself out in our own times. Slavery in the United States proved itself incompatible with the principles of the Declaration of Independence and the Constitution. By the early twentieth century, indirect election of the Senate had lost democratic legitimacy. Women eventually acquired the right to vote. In consequence of the Great Depression of the 1930s and the political realignment it brought about, the interests of the "common man" trumped those of America's traditional elites, and the welfare state was born. Today's political movements on behalf of the rights of minorities and women continue this trend, while radicalizing it in significant ways.

Most important here is the rise of the feminist movement, and the increasing sensitivity of American politics to the concerns and outlook of women in general. Feminism of course takes many forms, but it tends to unite in questioning the legitimacy of traditional male leadership, whether in the public arena or the home. In such a view, the leading role assumed by men in virtually all societies in the past—"patriarchy"—is inherently oppressive, failing to acknowledge both the fundamental equality of women and their specific nature and needs. Feminism's milder variants tend to minimize male-female differences and focus on policy issues that are thought to empower women in the workplace and their private lives generally and thereby restore gender equality. More radical versions, on the other hand, make a more provocative claim—that women are in fact better suited to the exercise of political power than men. This is because women are allegedly less competitive or aggressive than men, more compassionate, and better at understanding and accommodating the needs of others. At the extreme, the argument is sometimes made that women should be welcomed as political leaders, for nations then would never go to war.[3]

Such beliefs may not be widely accepted, in America or elsewhere; but they have made their mark on politics and the wider global culture. Politicians, mindful of the voting strength of women, cater to their interest in issues such as education or health care. They tend to shy away from discussing policy matters women supposedly find frightening, particularly national defense. And they craft their own political personalities to be "unthreatening," caring, and compassionate. Hence the tendency in the United States for politicians to couch all public policy issues in terms of their impact on children.

Is all of this simply a passing cultural style? Or does it reflect a more fundamental shift in the character of contemporary politics—a kind of "feminization" of democratic leadership? It is not necessary to decide this question to wonder whether leadership can really be leadership if it is wholly lacking in such traditionally manly qualities as competitiveness, aggression, or for that matter, the ability to command. Women of course have no monopoly on compassion; it is a distinctive feature of our politics generally. It is the democratic virtue par excellence.[4] The problem is that it is not a political virtue and, in fact, tends to be at cross purposes with the requirements of prudent and effective political leadership. Leadership that is not prepared to disadvantage anyone is hardly leadership at all.

Contemporary circumstances undoubtedly make leadership harder. Do they make it impossible? A backward glance over the last quarter of a century reveals surprising, if not conclusive, grounds for optimism.

By the late 1970s, it had become fashionable in the West to lament the "ungovernability" of contemporary democracies.[5] Rising popular expectations of the welfare state were proving difficult for political leaders to meet in an economically responsible manner. President Jimmy Carter, frustrated by his inability to win public or congressional support for his reform initiatives, famously invoked a national "malaise" in assigning blame for this state of affairs. On top of that, the democracies seemed increasingly in the grip of an institutional crisis of governance. In the United States, questions began to be raised about the fundamental adequacy of the nation's traditional political structures. The deepening antagonism between the executive and legislative branches of the government, it was alleged by some, had led to a kind of political paralysis that could only be broken by far-reaching constitutional reforms to restore the possibility of effective political leadership.[6] Others doubted whether Western leaders had the political will to confront the challenge of rising Soviet military power and global ambitions.

With the arrival of conservative governments in Washington and London at the end of the decade, such talk soon faded. Indeed, a new era seemed at hand. Ronald Reagan and Margaret Thatcher led a revolution in economic policy and (more important) in popular attitudes toward free markets and the role of government in their respective countries. No one should have been unduly concerned at the feminization of contemporary leadership during Margaret Thatcher's tenure as prime minister of Britain. Thatcher's successful assault on the power of the labor unions early in her term stunned the entire political class and established her personal authority to push forward an agenda of free-market reform; and her conduct of the Falklands War of 1982 demonstrated courage and strategic leadership of a high order. Reagan, his successor George Bush, Thatcher, Pope John Paul II, Helmut Kohl, and Yasuhiro Nakasone in various ways brought extraordinary leadership skills to bear on the key global geopolitical challenge of the day, the tottering Soviet empire. In the Gulf War of 1990–1, President Bush gave a further demonstration of political and military leadership in the decisive victory won by the United States and its allies in the largest international armed conflict in four decades. The collaboration of Nelson Mandela and F.W. de Klerk that led to the peaceful dismantling of the apartheid regime in South Africa is an extraordinary story of moral leadership and skillful political engineering. Moral leadership was a critical ingredient of the transition to democracy in central Europe—in the role played by Václav Havel and other former dissidents in circumstances of tremendous stress and uncertainty. In Russia, Boris Yeltsin's courageous defiance of a coup attempt in August 1991 by forces loyal to the old Soviet order will also be remembered as a decisive act of contemporary leadership.

From the perspective of the present, however, such optimism may seem misplaced. Most of the leaders of the 1980s and early 1990s are long departed; few found worthy successors. At the same time, the achievements of the outstanding leaders of those years were rarely unalloyed or, for that matter, lasting. Thatcher was unceremoniously ousted as party leader and prime minister, thus ending the conservative resurgence in Britain. Nakasone's energetic leadership broke on the rock of Japanese political culture (for reasons we shall shortly explore). Revelations of financial improprieties and autocratic behavior threatened to eclipse Kohl's achievement in reunifying Germany. The first generation of Eastern Europe's new democratic leaders foundered in various ways on the wreckage left by the old order, opening the way for a return to power of former Communist apparatchiks. In Russia, Yeltsin failed spectacularly to manage the transition to stable democratic institutions and a free-market economy; rather than the "normal" Western country most Russians wanted and expected, what they got instead was a bizarre system of personalistic rule that was nonetheless unable to curb the rising power of the new barons of finance and the media or reverse the leakage of Moscow's authority to regional bosses or the collapse of its military power. Yeltsin's successor, Vladimir Putin, has recentralized the power of the Russian state and revitalized its military, while at the same time reducing Russian democracy to a mere façade.

Much could be said in criticism or praise of these figures and their successors. For our purposes, though, the case of Reagan is critical. Reagan has been much criticized in the United States and elsewhere both for the policies he pursued and for his governing style. At the extreme, his apparent accomplishments (particularly the fall of Soviet Communism) have been chalked up to mere luck, and his presidency seen as little more than an actor's performance scripted by others. There can be little question that such a view is fundamentally wrong. Reagan certainly relied heavily on words as an instrument of governance, but he showed (by contrast with Carter) how presidential rhetoric could be used effectively to rally the nation behind a political agenda. The enactment of Reagan's reform economic program in 1981 was a classic instance of presidential leadership both of the country as a whole and of a politically divided Congress. Reagan's personal conviction that tax cuts combined with a severely anti-inflationary monetary policy could restore the American economy to health—a conviction shared by virtually no one else in his own administration, let alone by outside economists—proved essentially correct and laid the groundwork for the unprecedented prosperity of the later 1980s and beyond. Also unlike most of his advisers and conservative supporters, Reagan sensed the vulnerability of the Soviet Union to economic and political challenge. He consistently pursued a two-track policy of rearmament and negotiation with the Soviets that satisfied few of his critics or supporters, yet proved in the end decisive in bringing a bloodless end to the Communist experiment. In fact, Reagan's presidency as a whole proved the most successful since at least that of Dwight D. Eisenhower in the 1950s. Of the gallery of twentieth-century presidents, his achievement can be compared only to that of his original political hero, Franklin Delano Roosevelt.[7]

It is true that the lessons of the Reagan years are not without ambiguity. Reagan's personality and leadership style were key elements in his dominance of the political arena and helped to obscure or compensate for problems encountered in other areas. Reagan's relation to the Republican political establishment was tenuous, and he never succeeded in shaping the party sufficiently in his own mold to ensure the political survival of conservative ideas. In spite of an unprecedented effort to control the federal government through presidential appointments, the bureaucracy remained a significant obstacle to the implementation of the president's program, as indeed did the Congress; and in other respects Reagan's intragovernmental leadership left much to be desired.[8] Finally, the hostility of the media and the nation's cultural and intellectual elite sharply limited what he and his closest advisers proved willing to undertake (this was the primary factor behind the issueless reelection campaign of 1984). These problems all contributed significantly to the administration's mishandling of its Central America policy and Reagan's political near-death experience in the Iran-Contra scandal. None of them could easily have been remedied.

In spite of all this, however, there is a sense in which Reagan's achievement surpasses even FDR's. In 1932, almost everyone agreed the nation faced a dire economic crisis, that strong measures were needed to deal with it, and that such measures had to involve a greater degree of government intervention in the economy than seen before in the United States. Reagan, by contrast, lacked a clear popular mandate for fundamental change and was navigating into a strong headwind of political and intellectual resistance. Listen to Machiavelli:

> It should be considered that nothing is more difficult to handle, more doubtful of success, nor more dangerous to manage, than to put oneself at the head of introducing new orders. For the introducer has all those who benefit from the old order as enemies, and he has lukewarm defenders in all those who might benefit from the new orders. This lukewarmness arises partly from fear of adversaries who have the laws on their side and partly from the incredulity of men, who do not truly believe in new things unless they come to have a firm experience of them. Consequently, whenever those who are enemies have opportunity to attack, they do so with partisan zeal, and the others defend lukewarmly so that one is in peril along with them.[9]

This perfectly describes Reagan's relationship with the American political and media establishment. If the achievement fell short in various ways, what is surprising is that he could do so much.

The twentieth century has been called the century of the common man. It was also a time marked by uncommon leaders. Some of these were revolutionaries who set out to advance utopian projects or agendas of national liberation. Others sought to save democracies from their enemies—or themselves. In the United States, three great reforming presidents—the two Roosevelts and Woodrow Wilson—made industrial capitalism safe for democracy and ensured democracy's survival in a world increasingly hostile to it. Great wartime chiefs in Britain and France—Churchill and de Gaulle—provided inspiration that overcame defeatism and strategic leadership that secured victory. And after World War II, two more American presidents defeated challenges in Europe and the Far East and laid the groundwork for the unprecedented peacetime alliance that held the ring against Soviet Communism until its final collapse; they were aided in this endeavor by a generation of farsighted leaders throughout what would become known as the free world. This story is of course so familiar that it ceases to amaze—or instruct. Yet the forces arrayed against the democracies were formidable indeed, and their internal weaknesses profound. That they prevailed is a powerful commentary on what democratic leaders can accomplish.

But revolutionaries and democrats do not exhaust the spectrum of contemporary leadership. Machiavelli takes it for granted that republics as well as principalities are in need of a founding prince.[10] The great state-builders and modernizers of this century may be ambiguous figures in the annals of democracy; nevertheless, their peculiar greatness and lasting impact should not be underestimated. Kemal Atatürk built a modern, secular Turkey on the ruins of the Ottoman Empire—a state that has inspired fierce loyalty in its citizenry and endures today. In the course of his long reign, King Hussein of Jordan crafted a nation from unpromising materials, defended it adroitly against powerful domestic and foreign adversaries, and created the framework of parliamentary democracy in a part of the world not noted for it. Lee Kuan Yew did the same for Singapore.

None of this is to suggest that the characters or actions of any contemporary leaders are without blemish. Indeed, one of the most striking things about outstanding leaders in any historical period is the extent to which the failed or incomplete aspects of their political projects may be traced to flaws in their personalities, rather than to any inexorable constraints imposed by the age. If Ronald Reagan was a democratic visionary, he was also a gentleman who shunned personal confrontation and thought only the best of his associates and staff; admirable as these traits may be, they contributed to much unnecessary infighting and confusion within his administration. Thatcher, by contrast, never known for her modesty, argued vehemently with her cabinet and sometimes humiliated them in public; not surprisingly, the resentments this caused led directly to her downfall.

It seems safe to conclude that the scope for effective leadership in today's world, though no doubt diminished in significant ways compared to earlier times, remains ample enough. Yet it is well to remember that leaders are fragile instruments. As in classical tragedy, their very virtues often contain the seeds of failures and disasters; and self-knowledge is not generally their strongest suit. If this is so, however, it is worth asking whether, other things being equal, leadership is something contemporary societies should actually want. In particular, we need to explore further the question of the relationship between leadership and democracy.

II

WHY LEADERSHIP IS STILL NECESSARY

That we should want strong leaders is something most people today—if they are citizens in a democracy at any rate—simply assume. This assumption comes particularly naturally to Americans. The citizens of the world's oldest constitutional democracy have long been accustomed to the idea of a presidential office that is institutionally separate from the legislative branch of government; and for a century or more, they have lived under presidents who regularly assume an independent role as tribunes of the people and leaders of the nation in peace as well as war. Elsewhere in the world, the American model seems increasingly to represent the norm—if not of formal institutional arrangements, which by and large continue to favor British-style parliamentarianism, at any rate of the informal understandings that shape the actual exercise of executive power in democracies. In Britain itself, former prime minister Tony Blair freely appropriated American leadership styles and practices, as have other near-contemporary parliamentary leaders such as Yasuhiro Nakasone in Japan, Silvio Berlusconi in Italy, and Benjamin Netanyahu in Israel.

Yet not everyone feels comfortable with leadership in this sense. Consider the case of Germany. The German word for "leader" (*Führer*) is indelibly stained for contemporary Germans by its association with Adolf Hitler and Nazism. Hitler, one should recall, came to power in 1933 through popular election. His wide political appeal and personal magnetism soon enabled him to overthrow the weak parliamentary regime of the Weimar Republic. In a certain sense, Hitler embodied the vision of "plebiscitary" leadership that had been championed after World War I by the distinguished sociologist Max Weber as a key feature of Germany's new parliamentary democracy. Though Weber would undoubtedly have been horrified by the Third Reich, his emphasis on the importance of extraparliamentary leadership in modern democracies is merely an embarrassment for Germans today.[1]

Japan is another interesting case. The failure of the relatively cautious political and institutional reforms pushed by Prime Minister Nakasone in the 1980s underscores how much the personalistic leadership style characteristic of contemporary American politics has remained an alien import in the self-effacing, consensus-oriented culture of the Japanese. Mention should also be made of the Swiss, who change their presidents every year and decide major policy issues by referendum. In the premodern tradition of democratic or republican government, executive power was similarly suspect. Athenians distrusted their leaders and sought to control them through devices such as term limits and short tenures in office. The Romans (it was said) hated the name of king and for many centuries firmly subordinated their chief magistrates to the authority of the Senate. The eventual overthrow of the Roman republic by ambitious magnates who put themselves at the head of private armies was a lesson not lost on those who sought to re-create republican government in modern times.[2]

Even from an American perspective, however, matters are not so simple. The United States came into being in the eighteenth century by way of a self-conscious rejection of British constitutional monarchy and the principle of strong executive governance it embodied. American political culture was a natural outgrowth of the Whig or "Country" opposition in England, which favored parliamentary supremacy and stricter constraints on the political, fiscal, and military prerogatives of the king. The struggles between popularly elected colonial legislatures and the royal governors set over them by London had pushed Americans yet further in the direction of pure republicanism and created a powerful distaste for executive leadership. The American Revolution was run, after all, not by George Washington but by committees of a Congress representing the various colonies (Washington was not even given sole command of

American forces). The manifest inadequacies of the colonial governments as well as the Continental Congress itself persuaded many of those who gathered in Philadelphia in 1787 to frame a new national government that there had to be a place in its fundamental law for a unitary and relatively powerful executive. Even after the venerated Washington had become the nation's first president, however, there were some who feared that this office would be a springboard for the reintroduction in the United States of an English-style monarchy or military dictatorship (such as the one set up by Oliver Cromwell during the English civil war). Presidents themselves were long reluctant to make the sorts of claims for their authority—or to engage in many of the political practices—that are today taken for granted in American politics.[3]

It is easy enough to dismiss the worst fears that were expressed about the presidential office at the time of the founding. This was, after all, a period in American history when national institutions had not yet taken root, and there were few attractive models of a strong republican executive. It is less easy to dismiss the underlying concern about presidential leadership that serious-minded Americans have harbored throughout much of the nation's history—that presidents will play the "demagogue."

Demagoguery—let us define it as the art of political pandering—is as old as democracy itself (the word comes from a classical Greek term meaning simply "leader of the people"). Critics of the Athenian democracy of the fifth and fourth centuries BC thought it dangerously vulnerable to unscrupulous politicians who played on the hopes and fears of the people in order to advance their own careers. Such people were usually highly effective orators who could arouse passions and sway decisions in large popular assemblies. These rhetorical skills helped them to gain public office and sometimes (like Hitler) to usurp legitimate processes of democratic decision-making and set themselves up as tyrants. The American founding fathers, searching far afield for useful models for republican government, were thoroughly familiar with this history. It continued to color American perceptions of political leadership at least through the presidency of Franklin Delano Roosevelt—who inspired precisely these fears in more than a few Americans in the 1930s.

It is hard to deny that political pandering has entered fully into the fabric of the contemporary American presidency. Political campaigns increasingly rely on extravagant if not simply fraudulent promises to various (and often competing) constituencies. (As late as a century ago, by contrast, it was considered barely appropriate for a presidential candidate to make any specific promises to the voters.)[4] This development might be dismissed as the price that must be paid for politicians to gain access to an office which they will thereafter use in the disinterested pursuit of the national interest. In fact, what we have experienced in very recent years is a tendency for our leaders to view governance as merely an extension of political campaigning. It is hardly surprising that the result has been a marked decline in trust in government—and not only in America. The combination of overpromising and underperforming by governments and their leaders is a problem throughout the advanced democracies today, and raises serious questions about the attachment of ordinary citizens to democracy over the long run.[5]

Demagoguery is a challenge, among other things, to the rule of law. The fundamental problem with demagoguery in the ancient democracies was its tendency to undermine settled law and policy by encouraging the direct exercise of supreme authority by the people. In a revealing speech early in his career, Abraham Lincoln warned of the danger of supremely talented politicians who might be tempted to seek their own advancement through championing illegal measures such as the emancipation of slaves.[6] To be sure, there is a respectable defense to be made of the exercise of executive "prerogative" in cases where the law is silent or inadequate, or in times of national emergency (this is an issue we shall return to). Lincoln, for one, did not hesitate to wield such powers during the national crisis that marked his presidency. Still, the principle of the rule of law is clearly in tension with the principle of the sovereignty of the people, and democratic leaders who identify their political fortunes with gratification of the people's will are unlikely to be scrupulous champions of the rule of law.

The temptation for leaders to place themselves above the law is one that should not be underestimated. The fortunes amassed by the world's autocrats often seem to serve little purpose other than the thrill of stealing them. But the democracies are not always much better. Slush funds of illegal contributions for party-building purposes, some of them directly administered by heads of government, have been a regular source of scandal in Western Europe and Japan in recent years. But consider the staggering peculations, innocent of any public purpose, of politicians like Joseph Estrada in the Philippines, who was eventually driven from power when caught in a massive gambling kickback scheme, not to mention the egregious Imelda Marcos. Consider, too, the lawyerly evasions of the American justice system by President Bill Clinton in his effort to avoid being held to account for his reckless personal behavior. The much increased transparency of democratic politics today might be thought to provide a sufficient check on executive malfeasance of this nature. Unfortunately, this too often seems not to be the case. Leaders often behave as if the very fact of holding power somehow makes them invisible.

In the United States, celebration of presidential power has been a staple feature of liberal political doctrine since the heyday of the Progressive Era at the turn of the last century. In the Progressive vision, the president is uniquely representative of the people as a whole, and the sole force for real change in a system in which the people's elected representatives tend to be the prisoners of party bosses, special interests, and local or regional perspectives. To play this role, however, presidents needed to become more directly concerned with the acquisition and exercise of personal power than they had in the past. To begin with, they needed to become masters rather than creatures of a party. They needed to develop their own program, take the initiative in placing it on the legislative agenda, and use the resources of their office and prestige to influence congressional action in support of it. And they needed to strengthen and extend the reach of the instruments of governance most readily available to them—presidential rhetoric and the federal bureaucracy.

The working out of this vision is the history of the American presidency in the twentieth century. The two Roosevelts and Woodrow Wilson laid the foundation for this new presidential edifice; subsequent presidents, particularly but not only of the Democratic Party, have inhabited it. The edifice remains standing today. It has, however, sustained major structural damage in recent decades. With Lyndon B. Johnson, the Progressive presidency visibly sagged under the weight of an overly ambitious domestic agenda and a disastrous foreign war that was fought—with supreme political misjudgment—as an executive sideshow. With Richard Nixon, who threatened to employ the new powers of the office recklessly or for dubious ends, the fundamental logic of the Progressive presidency began to unravel. The Watergate scandal and the various congressional investigations of the executive branch to which it led created a climate in which Progressive liberals were decrying a suddenly "imperial" presidency and rediscovering the constitutional prerogatives of the Congress. The relative decline in the prestige and power of the presidency in the 1970s that resulted from these developments soon became apparent. Congress reasserted itself institutionally through a dramatic increase in congressional staffs and in efforts to impose permanent constraints on executive authority in areas such as intelligence and war powers. It was largely unresponsive to the reform agenda of a president—Jimmy Carter—of the same party that controlled both its houses.[7]

If Congress plays its part adequately, is there really a need for activist presidents in the Progressive mold? This question is rarely asked anymore, even by those who complain of contemporary presidential leadership—these people hold their tongue in anticipation of what they might want to do when their own party controls the office.[8] When the leaders of the Republican Party in the House of Representatives created a common platform for Republican candidates (the "Contract with America") in the 1994 elections, then took control of the House and proceeded to implement most of what had been promised, they were directly challenging the president's status as the sole "national" elected official; and it looked for a time as if Congress as a whole might be able to wrest the national policy agenda from a president badly weakened by various missteps at the beginning of his term. This would have been an instructive experiment in returning legislative leadership to what might be thought to be its proper home.

The resourceful Clinton of course managed to prevent such a development. He did so, however, only through a strategy of political trimming ("triangulation") that transformed his presidency into little more than an opportunistic vehicle of personal aggrandizement. In this and other respects, the Clinton years represent the nadir of the modern American presidency. The president's frenetic activism was a sad parody of the dynamism of a Wilson or a Franklin Roosevelt. His relentless pursuit of political approval through the doling out of small favors to a large number of constituencies, aided by a personality that could ingratiate itself with the public in ways that proved impervious to scandal (or indeed, impeachment), made him a highly popular figure. In the process, he demonstrated clearly the fundamental validity of traditional American fears of presidential demagoguery. Clinton's was not, fortunately, a demagoguery of soaring ambition, like that of which Lincoln had warned. But in some ways it was worse. It trivialized the office, lowered public expectations of presidential behavior, and debased the coin of presidential speech.[9]

The chief lesson of this history is that our need for strong presidents—leaders in the Progressive mold—should not simply be taken for granted. In the first place, the need for such leaders has to be balanced against the risks of overreliance on them. There is much to be said for the old republican antipathy toward kings, however benevolent they may be. Second, and less obviously, the need for such leaders cannot be adequately assessed without paying some attention to the alternative leadership resources available to democratic societies at a given time. These resources fall into two categories. To the first belong the other institutional structures that make up the modern state—the legislature, the judiciary, the administrative bureaucracy. To the second belong the various elites who staff these institutions and dominate other key sectors of civil society—the higher civil service, the military, lawyers and judges, the captains of industry, commerce, and finance, journalists of the national media, and the higher professoriate, to name the most important.

As a general proposition, where the institutional structures of any state function competently and are not tainted by corruption or private influences, strong executive leadership is less necessary. And where a nation's elites are well educated, imbued with professionalism and public spirit, and reasonably united in political outlook, political leadership altogether is likely to be less necessary. The trick, of course, is to devise ways to make useful judgments about these matters. The lack of transparency of most of the institutions and professional bodies just mentioned, even in the open and information-rich United States, severely complicates any such calculus. Still, it is important to make the effort. The fundamental point is that leadership in any society should not be conceived as the responsibility only of heads of state or government or, more broadly, as simply a governmental function. Elites too have a significant leadership role. One of the costs of a one-sided emphasis on the leadership of individual politicians is that it tends to devalue the contribution of elites (not to speak of elected legislators) and undermine their sense of political responsibility. History shows that marginalized elites—consider the French aristocracy of the eighteenth century—can be hazardous to the health of regimes.

Another basic point needs to be made here. In its most expansive sense, leadership is about ruling. It describes relations of initiative and response, of authority and subordination, of command and obedience, that are common to societies throughout history. But the term *leadership* is also used in a more restricted sense to refer to a particular type or style of rule, one relying on persuasion or example rather than coercion or command; leadership of this type is at home especially in democracies or republics. Yet this still fails to capture fully the positive flavor of leadership as a term of art today. In politics as well as in business, leadership is associated above all with energetic individuals who seek to impose their own "vision" on an organization and to initiate or oversee "change" in pursuit of that vision. True leadership, to use the terms popularized by James MacGregor Burns, is "transformational" rather than "transactional"—leadership that seeks to change the rules of the game and perhaps the course of history, not the messy bargaining and accommodation that is what most political leaders do most of the time.[10]

The fundamental problem with this approach is that it fails to take account of changing historical circumstances. Leadership requirements vary according to differences in what Machiavelli calls "the times." A student of the presidency of the second Roosevelt, Burns manifestly models his idea of leadership on FDR and the progressive conception of the role of the presidency. Burns's approach seems validated by the Reagan presidency, which displayed the same kind of transformative activism as FDR's, though in a different cause. Whatever one thinks of the way Roosevelt or Reagan handled the challenges facing them, however, they were very different from the challenges facing, for example, Harry Truman or Dwight D. Eisenhower, though both of these men also have strong claims to exemplary presidential leadership. The case of Eisenhower in particular raises the obvious yet neglected question whether great leadership cannot also be exercised in a more passive, defensive, or historically (as distinct from ideologically) conservative mode than Burns allows. Winston Churchill, by common consent the greatest statesman of the twentieth century, was, by inclination as well as by circumstance, a conserver rather than a transformer. The same could be said of Disraeli and Salisbury, arguably the most outstanding British prime ministers of the nineteenth century.[11]

Do we need leadership? The answer to this question has to be yes.

Plainly, the fact that leadership has its dark side is not an effective argument against it. The dangers of demagoguery, corruption, and tyrannical ambition cannot be avoided in any political system if leadership is to be given reasonable scope. As Aristotle once said, all good things can be misused, except virtue. Leadership is a good thing, and it is worth putting up with the risks it poses.

It is good in the first place for symbolic reasons. As Walter Bagehot argues in his forgotten classic *The English Constitution*, the governing arrangements of every regime include a "dignified" element that sustains national identity and provides a focus of popular loyalty, and an "efficient" element that actually governs.[12] This formulation is designed to explain the logic of the constitutional monarchy of nineteenth-century England; but its application is broader. The leaders of contemporary democracies—whether they are heads of state or of government or both—all perform symbolic functions of considerable political significance, and they do so precisely as individuals who personify the majesty of the state or the unity of the nation. Historically, political leaders have often been at the same time the high priests of a national religion. Political leaders can set the moral tone for a nation, either in positive (Queen Victoria) or negative (Bill Clinton) fashion.

Second, leadership is good because it provides an essential locus of authoritative decision-making. All societies need some mechanism for arbitrating disputes among powerful interests and distributing scarce resources. Even—or rather precisely—in societies lacking a coercive state apparatus, such as primitive bands or tribes, this is the primary function leaders are called on to perform at most times and the factor most responsible for the emergence of permanent leaders and leadership institutions. Leaders gain authority from the impartiality and wisdom of their decisions, and this authority in turn helps to overawe the losing parties and keep social peace. In more highly developed states, this function underlies and legitimizes the exercise of both judicial and executive power.[13]

Third, leadership is good because it is indispensable in times of trouble. Leadership certainly involves democratic-style persuasion, but it also involves command—in democracies as in other regimes. In wartime, it is virtually a requirement of command in the strict sense of the term that it be exercised by a single individual. Heads of state or government in democracies invariably exercise at least nominal command of the nation's armed forces, and in any event are held directly responsible for their wartime performance. Yet it is not only in wartime that the command function of leadership can come into play. Crises or emergencies of various kinds call forth and legitimize a kind of leadership that differs sharply from democratic leadership in ordinary times.

Finally, leadership is good because leaders are a vital mechanism for bringing political knowledge to bear on the business of politics. Since this proposition is in a sense obvious, yet in another sense wildly implausible, it needs some elaboration. This is our next task.

III

LEADERSHIP AND STATECRAFT

What is the essence of leadership? That the answer to this question could be knowledge in any form seems implausible in the first place because we tend today to equate knowledge with expertise. Politicians are not experts, and we do not expect them to be experts. What they do have that sets them apart from ordinary people seems rather a kind of personal dynamism, an ability to inspire trust in their integrity and confidence in their ability to perform. A convenient term for this personal quality or set of qualities is *charisma*.

The notion of charismatic leadership derives from the German sociologist Max Weber's well-known distinction between "traditional," "rational-legal," and "charismatic" forms of governance. According to Weber, the distinctive feature of modern society is its increasing domination by complex organizational structures governed by impersonal rules ("rational-legal" governance). Though in most respects a historical advance over "traditional" governance by socioeconomic elites, this process of bureaucratization—a phenomenon Weber saw operating in government and business alike—also poses potential dangers. It regiments people and stifles individual initiative. In the worst case, it threatens to abolish politics altogether as traditionally practiced, leaving government in the hands of mere administrators who lack creativity, vision, and passion. The antidote to all of this, in Weber's view, was the deliberate promotion of politics as a "vocation" and of a political class schooled to exercise popular leadership. In order to be effective, such leadership would require an independent ground or source of appeal to the people. This Weber found in charisma. The model for Weber's charismatic leader was the religious prophet, whose personal authority is uniquely compelling because it seems to derive from a source beyond himself.[1]

That Weber points to an important dimension of political reality is undeniable. Those who come face to face with politicians are often struck by their extraordinary energy and vitality. Many politicians have a highly intuitive sense of people and the issues of concern to them. And some have a capacity to mobilize and inspire others that often has little to do with any actual record of achievement. On the other hand, charisma has its limits. Speaking of prophets who found states, Machiavelli famously observes that "all the armed prophets conquered and the unarmed ones were ruined. For . . . the nature of peoples is variable; and it is easy to persuade them of something, but difficult to keep them in that persuasion. And thus things must be ordered in such a mode that when they no longer believe, one can make them believe by force."[2] Whatever the merits of this last remark, the point has a broader validity. The problem with prophets in politics is that they do not reliably deliver the goods. Politicians, particularly but not only in democracies, must demonstrate to the people that they have a grasp of political reality and are capable of performing concrete political tasks. Talk, no matter how inspiring, is a wasting asset.

The theory—and, indeed, much of the practice—of leadership today brings to mind Aristotle's observation about the ancient "sophists" who tried yet failed to invent the discipline of political science. "For the most part," he says, "they do not even know what sort of thing it is or what things it has to do with, for otherwise they would not have laid down that it is the same as rhetoric or even inferior to it, or believed it is easy to legislate by collecting the most renowned laws—they think it possible to select the best laws, as if the very selection were not a matter of understanding, and correct judgment were not the most important thing here."[3]

The identification of leadership with charisma or rhetorical ability reinforces the demagogic tendencies in contemporary politics and causes us to lose sight of what is arguably at its core—a certain kind of reasoned knowledge or expertise. This kind of knowledge is not what might be called policy knowledge. In contemporary politics, the language of policy is spoken universally. But this is a language easily learned and just as easily unlearned, one that is in constant flux as issues are thrust forward into a leader's awareness, get resolved, recede in political importance, and are eventually forgotten. It is, to pursue the metaphor, a language that a user can make very serviceable without mastering its grammar. Even politicians who speak it fluently need not master its grammar fully; indeed, to the extent that they are politically successful, they tend to lose the incentive to do so. The grammar of leadership is "statecraft."

Though far from absent in the language of contemporary political discourse, the concept of statecraft is rarely analyzed carefully or brought into relationship with the idea of leadership. Even its basic meaning is not especially clear. The term is now used almost exclusively to refer to diplomacy or the conduct of foreign policy in a broad sense.[4] Yet it is also widely recognized that the foreign policy behavior of states cannot be adequately understood if they are treated as indistinguishable billiard balls colliding on the international stage according to a set of predictable laws. Domestic politics and the cultural and ideological imperatives that shape and motivate the decisions of leaders are frequently as important as external factors in determining their behavior, if not indeed more so.[5] From the perspective of statesmen themselves, the weightiest political issues are no respecters of the artificial boundaries between academic disciplines. They are connected in complex ways, their relationships governed by a particular logic that is more than the sum of their parts. The grammar that gives these issues their articulation, and the logic that links them—such is statecraft in its comprehensive and proper sense.

Carl von Clausewitz, the great theoretician of the art of war, once observed that war and politics have the same logic but a different grammar.[6] The point is not self-evident, but whatever qualification it might need for our own age, it is helpful in coming to grips with the concept of statecraft. Like strategy in war, statecraft is an art of coping with an adversarial environment in which actions generate reactions in unpredictable ways and chance and uncertainty rule. Like strategy, too, statecraft is also an art of relating means to ends. If, in Clausewitz's formulation, strategy is the art of using battles to achieve the objectives of the war, statecraft is the art of using wars and other instruments available to political leaders to attain national goals.

Statecraft must be concerned both with the goals a nation pursues and with the ways and means necessary to achieve them. The exercise of leadership may amount to articulating a "vision," but statecraft properly understood is also about something more—and something arguably more difficult: the ways visions are implemented. Effective statecraft requires an understanding of the various instruments actually or potentially available to statesmen and an ability to use them in coordinated fashion in differing circumstances to achieve the objectives of state policy.[7]

If statecraft today is largely a forgotten art, much of the responsibility for this lies with contemporary social science. Over a century or more, a vast literature has grown up that claims to seek comprehensive political knowledge using methods derived more or less loosely from modern natural science. It is not to our purpose to rehearse the various inadequacies of this literature. A great deal can be learned from it that is useful for the practice of statecraft. The problem is that political science (a term I shall use expansively of the political or policy-relevant components of all of the social sciences), with its scientific or universalistic pretensions, in effect ignores the perspective of practicing statesmen and slights their concerns. In the eyes of most political scientists, the cognitive status of statecraft differs little from the cognitive status of witchcraft. Political science is preoccupied with the identification of law-like regularities in social and political behavior rather than the dynamics of particular political situations—the kind of knowledge that is of most practical use to politicians. It tends to pay insufficient attention to the various instruments of statecraft, the problems statesmen face in utilizing them effectively, and the strategies available for their use. It discounts the value of "mere" experience and common sense, the stuff of ordinary political judgment. And it tends to focus on impersonal "systems" or "forces" as the key explanatory factors in politics rather than individual leaders.[8]

Woodrow Wilson was one of the founders of American political science; his own outlook on politics had been decisively shaped by the speeches and writings of the great eighteenth-century British parliamentarian Edmund Burke. Abraham Lincoln learned his politics from the Bible and the plays of Shakespeare. When Napoleon invaded Egypt in 1798, the Bible and the Koran were among a few "political" books he took along (Machiavelli's *Prince* was another). The American founding fathers sought inspiration for their "new science of politics" in political philosophers such as Locke and Montesquieu. Machiavelli turned to the Roman historian Titus Livy. In general, history was in older times the principal medium of political education. Classic works such as Tacitus's histories of early imperial Rome, Gibbon's *Decline and Fall of the Roman Empire*, Hume's *History of England*, Grote's *History of Greece*, and Henry Adams's *History of the United States During the Administrations of Jefferson and Madison*—most of them written with an explicit pedagogical intention—taught the secrets of despotism and the principles of republican government to the politically active elites of the modern West over many generations.

One of the fundamental developments in political life in the West over the last century or so has been the displacement of these older sources of political knowledge by political science. In education, the general culture, and even the councils of state, expertise in politics has gradually come to be identified with political science as studied in our universities. This kind of expertise alone is now considered authoritative: it is certified in various ways by professional organizations and journals, extensively underwritten by wealthy foundations, and recognized by the government itself in the form of official commissions, funded studies, and other public roles.

What is more, as political science has become more authoritative, it has also changed its character. Though still concerned with the pursuit of pure scientific truth, it has developed a corporate character and set of interests.[9] And it has become increasingly engaged in day-to-day struggles over public policy. Some years ago, it might have been said that political science simply neglected issues of statecraft in its concern for the timeless and the universal. Today, political scientists are eager to engage current issues and make their mark in the political arena. The result has been to reduce even more severely the scope for judgment and action by politicians. Faced with the challenge posed by political science, political leaders seem to have essentially two options. One is to defer entirely to political science expertise. The other is to ignore this expertise, in the name either of a purely tactical or pragmatic politics or of a charismatic "vision" that rejects ordinary politics altogether.

The critical question is whether or to what extent political science has succeeded in providing an objective, generally agreed, comprehensive, and coherent approach to political phenomena and the issues of contemporary politics. Even in the heyday of the discipline, few would have been hardy enough to affirm this. Today, it is widely acknowledged that political science is in fundamental disarray—scarcely closer to formulating a comprehensive theory of politics than it ever was, fragmented into warring (or non-communicating) schools, and of doubtful relevance to the actual practice of politics in contemporary democracies. Partly in reaction to this situation, the discipline has moved since the 1970s to deal more directly and extensively with issues of contemporary public policy. Unfortunately, this "policy turn" has been unable to escape the technocratic and positivistic spirit that arguably continues to pervade the discipline as a whole.[10] Regrettably, too, a predictable side effect of the greater engagement of political science in policy issues has been to polarize and politicize scholarly disagreements. Apart from the dangers of corruption of the academic enterprise inherent in this development, it further complicates the life of politicians. When political scientists behave more like lawyers arguing a brief than objective analysts, politicians are inevitably thrust into the role of judges; yet they generally lack the intellectual preparation or the patience to grapple with the jargon and intramural disputes of the academy.

The problematic relationship between politicians and scientific knowledge of course extends beyond political science. Given the complexity of economic life and its political importance in all contemporary states, politicians cannot afford to be wholly ignorant of modern economics. Nor can they always avoid direct engagement in highly abstruse scientific-technical matters when these involve large outlays of public funds or become politically sensitive. Even when the experts in these various fields are in agreement among themselves (and there is certainly a larger area of general consensus among economists and practitioners of the hard sciences than among political scientists), it is rarely easy to translate their technical knowledge into language that is comprehensible to politicians, let alone to their constituents. In any event, politicians must regularly make decisions about these matters that demand an independent exercise of political judgment.

What is missing in the contemporary understanding of political knowledge is an appreciation not merely of the scope of its subject matter, but also of its peculiar character or mode. The mode of knowing that is at the core of statecraft in its traditional sense is political judgment, or to use another old-fashioned term, *prudence*. At its simplest, this notion implies that there is a kind of intellectual discernment or cognition that is specially suited to political decision-making. It implies that politicians, because of their greater experience of political matters, develop an intellectual ability that enables them to make sound political decisions — sounder than the decisions that are apt to be made by those lacking such experience, whatever their raw intellectual capabilities or store of relevant knowledge might be.[11]

The classic articulation of the notion of prudence appears in the thought of Aristotle. In his two great works, the *Politics* and the *Nicomachean Ethics*, Aristotle in effect founded the discipline of political science in what may be called its pre-scientific form. Aristotle's term for the discipline of political science (*politikê*) can equally be rendered "political expertise" or "statecraft": there is no sharp distinction for him between the theory of politics and its practice. According to Aristotle, prudence or practical wisdom (as the term *phronêsis* is sometimes translated) is the mode of knowing proper to political science. Prudence differs fundamentally from scientific or theoretical knowledge. It is the faculty we use in applying general principles to particular circumstances that require decision and action. It thus requires both general knowledge of a certain kind and an understanding of circumstances that can only come from experience; an important implication of this is that prudence tends to be found mostly in mature and experienced people, not the young. Part of the general knowledge prudence requires is knowledge of the principles of morality. Prudence in this sense is then a kind of virtue. In its most common form, prudence is a virtue that comes into play in the decisions we make about our own lives. In a special sense, however, it is the virtue of political leaders.[12]

What kinds of general political knowledge do politicians need? Aristotle never fully addresses this question, but he provides several important clues. The first comes in his observation that there are five matters generally at the center of public deliberation or discussion: "revenues and expenditures, war and peace, defense of the territory, imports and exports, and legislation"—or, in more contemporary terminology, finance, foreign policy, defense, trade, and constitutional law.[13] With its perhaps surprising emphasis on the economic dimension of statecraft, this list could not readily be improved upon today. It is worth noting that Aristotle goes on to stress the importance of learning about other states as well as one's own, including lessons that might be gleaned from their domestic politics. He also mentions the value of historical knowledge, particularly as it relates to decisions to go to war—presumably because politicians are likely to have less direct experience of these relatively rare situations.

Clues may also be found in Aristotle's more theoretical remarks concerning what politics is about. In its original meaning, *politics* is simply the affairs of the "city" or city-state (*polis*, the Greek equivalent of our "state"). As Aristotle argues at the beginning of his *Politics*, the city is a kind of community or association. Like other communities or associations, it aims at some good common to its members; but what is distinctive about the city is that it is the ultimate community and aims at an ultimate good, one that embraces all of the lesser goods of the lesser communities (the family, for example). This ultimate good, Aristotle tells us at the beginning of the *Nicomachean Ethics*, is well-being or happiness.[14]

Several implications flow from this. Because the common good pursued by political leaders is comprehensive, it requires them to grasp in some way all of the lesser goods that contribute to it. Aristotle draws an analogy between the politician and the "master builder" (*architektôn*)—in effect, a general contractor. General contractors do not have to have detailed knowledge of all the crafts that are needed to build a house. What they must know, rather, is how to coordinate and integrate the activities of the specialized craftsmen who work for them. And, equally important, they must be capable of judging the final products of these craftsmen, in terms both of their intrinsic excellence and of their contribution to the success of the overall enterprise. The good politician, Aristotle tells us, is someone capable of "architectonic and practical thinking." He "uses" arts or kinds of expertise such as generalship and rhetoric but subordinates them to the overall good it is his own job to pursue. The knowledge of the "user" may well be intrinsically inferior to the knowledge of the maker or doer, but from a practical standpoint, it is superior: the ultimate test of a house is not the quality of its materials or workmanship but how well it suits the needs of the people who are going to live there.[15]

A second and equally fundamental point has to do with Aristotle's identification of "happiness" as the ultimate good, and therefore in some sense the primary preoccupation of political science. At first sight, this seems odd and hard to justify. Americans have long been comfortable with the more restrictive formulation of the objectives of politics—"life, liberty, and the pursuit of happiness"—offered in the Declaration of Independence. This formulation implies that politicians have no business trying to achieve or even define a substantive vision of happiness, but rather should concern themselves only with providing the means necessary for the pursuit of private visions of happiness. It suggests that the primary preoccupation of politics is or should be with things that are instrumental if not simply material. Aristotle, by contrast, insists that politics is also and more fundamentally about things "just and noble." Happiness, so far from being mere subjective satisfaction or pleasure, turns out to be an "activity of the soul in accordance with virtue."[16] Politicians—or at any rate genuine politicians—must therefore give special attention to virtue, since this is what makes citizens good and law-abiding.[17] Furthermore, since happiness is a condition of the soul more than the body, politicians must have some knowledge of the workings of the human soul—of psychology.[18]

All of this sounds alien to contemporary ways of thinking. Is it so in fact? It would not be difficult to make the case that current American thought and practice is closer to Aristotle here than to the classical liberalism reflected in the Declaration of Independence. Consider, to cite an instructive recent example, the emerging national consensus that traditional welfare programs have not only failed to alleviate poverty but have themselves contributed to a range of social pathologies in the urban underclass. This consensus is based on a new appreciation of the importance of family stability and a culture of individual responsibility for the economic and personal success of the poor—which is to say, of the moral and psychological factors that condition social behavior. Fostering these qualities is seen accordingly as a legitimate function of government, if not a political imperative. Even in the contemporary era, statecraft is inevitably a form of "soulcraft."[19]

A related feature of Aristotelian political science is its acknowledged imprecision. "Problems of what is noble and just, which politics examines, present so much variety and irregularity that some people believe they exist only by convention and not by nature. The problem of the good, too," he continues, foreshadowing an important Machiavellian point, "presents a similar kind of irregularity, because in many cases good things bring harmful results." Accordingly, we must not expect the same consistency in politics that we do, say, in mathematics. A properly educated or cultivated person is one who "searches for that degree of precision in each kind of study which the nature of the subject at hand admits; it is obviously just as foolish to accept arguments of probability from a mathematician as to demand strict demonstrations from an orator." This is another reason, it may be added, why political knowledge rests so squarely on experience. Young people cannot be competent politicians because of their lack of experience, though they may well be competent mathematicians. "Each man can judge competently the things he knows," Aristotle continues. "A good judge in each particular field is one who has been trained in it, and a good judge in general, a man who is generally cultivated."[20] This implies that the true education of politicians derives less from any specialized training in political science than from a general or liberal education and wide experience of the world.

Do politicians then not need any kind of specialized training in state-craft? Again, Aristotle does not openly address this crucial question but indicates his view clearly enough. Of the five areas of political delibera-tion he mentions, Aristotle has virtually nothing to say of trade, finance, defense, or foreign policy. His *Politics* is instead dedicated entirely to the last of these—"legislation" or, more accurately, that aspect of legislation which concerns the fundamental political arrangements of a state, or what Aristotle calls the "regime." Why this limitation? Perhaps Aristotle felt the economic and security dimensions of statecraft to be too variable and dependent on external circumstances to lend themselves to useful general analysis. Legislation—better stated, the art of regime manage-ment—is more within the control of political leaders. At the same time, it is at once more intellectually challenging and more problematic. It is the area of political knowledge that most attracts the attention of non-pol-iticians, because it involves fundamental questions of justice and power and necessarily generates political controversy. It tempts intellectuals of various descriptions to propose speculative schemes of reform that are often superficially appealing yet lack basic political sense. Politicians themselves, Aristotle lets us understand, are not entirely immune to the charm of such schemes.[21] Perhaps the most important task of political science is to provide politicians the conceptual armament to resist them. Political science so understood is the ally of prudence.[22]

At the same time, it is critical to recognize that Aristotle's ethical treatises too are an integral part of political science as he conceives it.

Knowledge of "just and noble" things is also of direct relevance for legislation, as well as for the application of law in the courtroom. Indeed, much of the theoretical account of the virtues in the *Nicomachean Ethics* can be understood as providing essential intellectual scaffolding for forensic (courtroom) argument and judicial decision—functions that in Aristotle's time were not sharply distinguished from political judgment. This area too, Aristotle implies, cannot be mastered or mastered adequately through ordinary experience but requires an intellectually disciplined inquiry.

A fully adequate presentation of Aristotle's approach to political science and its implications for the practice of statecraft is impossible here. But a larger point must be made. Under the impact of the doctrines of modern liberalism and their remote source, the thought of Machiavelli, the guiding concerns of Aristotelian political science ceased to be central to the study of statecraft. On the one hand, regime management was discovered to be superseded by the invention of the constitution—a "machine that would go of itself" or that did not require the supervision of wise statesmen or the active exercise of political leadership.[23] On the other hand, ethical inquiry was held to be inessential to a statecraft centered on the satisfaction of men's instrumental and material needs. Indeed, "soulcraft" was found to be fundamentally destructive of statecraft, both on account of the idealistic distortions it introduces in the education of princes and through the opening it affords religious elites and institutions to vie with them for secular power.

It would be a mistake, however, to draw too sharp a contrast between Aristotle and Machiavelli on these fundamental issues. Both offer valuable insights into the nature of statecraft that have in no way been made obsolete by the march of history. Taking our cue from Aristotle, we begin this inquiry into the requirements of contemporary statecraft with a discussion of the character of states and regimes, and what it is that politicians should know about them. This in turn will lead us to elaborate the idea of regime management. Instructed here especially by Machiavelli, we focus on the relationship between political leaders and elites.

IV

ON STATES

That leadership is a single art, a skill readily transferable from one organizational setting to another, seems widely assumed today. Successful business executives routinely move between different sorts of enterprises and, increasingly, between different parts of the globe. In the United States, wealthy businessmen seem to grow ever bolder in asserting a claim to high political office in spite of their lack of prior political experience; and the public generally tolerates such candidacies, if not actually embracing them (as with billionaire Ross Perot's presidential bid in 1992 or Michael Bloomberg's election a decade later as mayor of New York City—or of course Donald Trump's electoral triumph in 2016). There is no doubt much to be said for preserving avenues of access for non-politicians to political office in contemporary democracies. The problem is that such people are prone to gross error in coping with an unfamiliar environment and, if thrust into positions of great responsibility, can cause leadership disasters.

"The first, the supreme, the most far-reaching act of judgment that the statesman and commander have to make is to establish . . . the kind of war on which they are embarking; neither mistaking it for, nor trying to turn it into, something that is alien to its nature."[1] This observation of Clausewitz's is a golden maxim of statecraft. Even more important for politicians (and leaders generally), however, is a proper understanding of the kind of entity they are leading. For politicians, this is the indispensable foundation of political knowledge and prudential decision. There are two distinct though related issues that need to be addressed here. The first is the nature of the state and the question whether a single model is adequate to describe the state (or at any rate its contemporary incarnation). The second is the nature of the internal organization of the state—the form of government or regime—and its many actual or possible varieties. These are obviously large issues. We confine ourselves to stating certain ground truths that have demonstrable relevance to leadership performance.

The fact that all states today enjoy juridical equality under the banner of the United Nations has accustomed us to the idea that states are fundamentally alike. All states today have flags, official languages, recognized borders, and an identifiable locus of sovereign authority; most, whatever their form of government, have a central administrative apparatus of ministries with similar titles and functions. The model that seems to fit contemporary states is the "nation-state," whose rise is usually associated with the Peace of Westphalia (1648) and the international system it inaugurated. Yet all of this is in some respects seriously misleading. There are enormous differences between contemporary states.

To begin with the obvious, states of near-continental scale and vast populations such as the United States, Russia, or China coexist today not only with traditional states of lesser size but with a proliferating assortment of smaller political entities that in many cases are states only by courtesy. Secondly, the differences between economically and technologically advanced states and states that lag in these areas are equally dramatic. Although the term *superpower* is less fashionable now than it was during the Cold War, there is certainly a case to be made for assigning the United States a category of its own (the French have invented a name for it—"hyperpower"). At any rate, the United States represents a combination of military, cultural, economic, and technological power that gives it unrivaled superiority and corresponding responsibilities in the contemporary world. There can be little question that American statecraft is more complex and demanding in its scope and geographical reach than that of any other state.

At the opposite extreme are the small states that have become more numerous since the end of World War II as a result of the process of decolonization and the collapse of the Soviet Union and the Yugoslav Federation. A few of these states (notably Singapore and Israel) have managed to achieve the prosperity and political stability of a modern nation-state. Most of them, however, lack self-sufficiency at even a basic level and are incapable of ensuring their own security. Some—the micro-states of the Caribbean or the South Pacific—are extremely vulnerable to the power not merely of other states but of private organizations such as corporations and drug cartels, and their politics are susceptible to sudden revolutions as well as manipulations from without. At the same time, they hold open at least the possibility of a qualitatively different sort of social existence than that available in larger states, one arguably more intimate and humanly satisfying.[2]

Another variant of the contemporary state should also be singled out. This is a state with weak or merely nominal central administration, reflecting low social cohesion, persisting tribal or clan rivalries, political incompetence, and pervasive corruption. Such states are particularly in evidence in sub-Saharan Africa, but they may also be found in the Caucasus, Central Asia, and even Europe (Albania). At the extreme are the "failed states" such as Somalia, Libya, Syria, or the Congo, where persistent civil war has effectively destroyed central authority and outside forces are required to maintain even a semblance of order. For all practical purposes, Somalia today is not one state but three—at best (depending on the success of current efforts to reimpose a government on the warlords of the southern part of the country)—while Syria and the Congo are little more than a name.

It is customary to trace these pathologies to the legacy of Western colonialism and to assume that the nation-state on the Western model is the key element in any strategy for overcoming them. A good case can be made, however, that the experience of state-building in Africa and elsewhere in the developing world—before as well as after colonization—has been fundamentally different from the paradigmatic European experience. Great distances, inhospitable terrain, and sparse populations throughout these areas pose unique challenges to the projection of state power and create political dynamics of their own.[3] Political leaders and elites in these countries are sometimes surprisingly blind to such realities. Although often fashionably anti-Western, they are generally Western-educated and tend to think in the categories of contemporary political science even if they reject Western-style liberal democracy as the solution to their local political ills.

More important in the scheme of things, however, and at the same time much less well understood, are two other political formations that differ yet more sharply from the traditional nation-state. One is "empire."[4] The overseas empires of the European powers are of course a thing of the past. One of the striking failures of political imagination in recent decades, though, was the very general blindness to the imperial character of the former Soviet Union. Western politicians and analysts greatly underestimated the strength of the national fault lines that eventually led to the breakup of the USSR in the early 1990s.[5] More surprising is that this misassessment seems to have been shared by Mikhail Gorbachev and other reforming elements of the Soviet leadership and contributed directly to the disastrous course they set. Nothing better illustrates the practical importance of an accurate understanding by political leaders of the basics of their own system.

The Soviet implosion might be thought to remove the imperial model once and for all from the horizon of contemporary statecraft. Nothing seems more certain on the world scene today than the obsolescence of empire as a political option, given the perceived illegitimacy under contemporary international norms of military or political expansion at the expense of other sovereign states. Yet there are two ways empires can come into being. One is through territorial expansion; the other is through what one might call a state's internal political devolution.[6] Yugoslavia prior to its breakup is probably the best recent example of empire creation in the latter sense; another is Mobutu's Zaire. In the Yugoslav case, a nation-state with a federal structure designed to recognize and safeguard the rights of a number of historically distinct ethno-national communities gradually degenerated into an instrument of Serbian domination of the rest of the country. At the core of the process of devolution is the emergence of a clearly dominant "center" exercising control over a clearly subordinate "periphery," and a corresponding decline in the legitimacy of the central government and in national identity and cohesion. Counterintuitive as it may seem, imperial states are thus weaker than normal nation-states in crucial respects. Understanding the nature of this weakness is the key to successful imperial governance.[7]

Imperial devolution may not be avoidable, as was probably true in the Yugoslav case in spite of the active abetting of Serbian nationalism by Slobodan Milosevic and others in the old Yugoslav communist leadership. At the same time, the Yugoslav solution—bloody breakup of the nation into its constituent parts—is not necessarily desirable as an alternative to it. From this perspective, imperial states cannot be considered simply illegitimate or imperial statecraft something entirely beyond the pale of contemporary respectability. On the other hand, there seems little reason to choose to pursue this option. This is why it has been baffling to watch recent British governments toy with political devolution in Scotland and Wales, in the absence of any compelling or even intelligible argument for it. This apparently *bien-pensant* effort to right historical wrongs seems likely to have no other result than to strengthen previously vestigial regional identities and cause grievances to be manufactured against the central government. At the end of this road could well lie an unpleasant transformation of the political consciousness of the nation if not the structure of the British state itself.[8]

The other alternative to the traditional nation-state is "confederation" on the model of the European Union (EU). Regional groupings of states more or less formally linked as a single entity may someday come into their own as a political option (they have played an important role at earlier times in world history),[9] but for now the EU stands essentially by itself in this category. It is impossible to discuss statecraft in the nations of contemporary Europe without taking account of the impact of the EU, but much about the EU, the direction it is taking, and its eventual fate remains unclear. What is perhaps most striking about the EU as a political entity is the eerie absence of leadership, or at any rate of overt leadership, in its higher reaches. The EU today is essentially a vast regulatory bureaucracy formally answerable to an array of multinational committees with very uncertain relationships and lines of command—but for this reason enjoying much informal autonomy. The argument is sometimes made or insinuated that the EU is a covert instrument of French, German, or Franco-German hegemonic ambitions in Europe. It seems more likely that appearances are closer to the reality—that the EU is a lumbering, headless machine that is close to being beyond the control or even the full comprehension of the national leadership of its member states.[10]

It is often said today that the traditional nation-state is obsolescent.

The rise of the European Union seems to reflect both a decisive weakening of traditional national loyalties and a conviction throughout the European political class that only a continental-scale European entity can compete effectively in the global economy. Other transnational organizations—the United Nations and its various agencies in the first instance, but also the burgeoning international NGO (nongovernmental organization) sector—are also competing vigorously to attract the loyalties and supplant critical functions of the nation-state. And let us not forget the Muslim world. The recent emergence of transnational Islamic terrorism as a security threat is only one manifestation of a deeper process at work there, the growth of a pan-Islamic politico-religious identity at the expense of national loyalties. Increasingly, fundamentalist Muslims are looking for a political alternative to the weak, fragmented, and secular-minded states of the current Islamic world community (*umma*)—whether a formally revived caliphate or some sort of bloc of revolutionary Islamist states that could more effectively oppose the might of the West.

At the same time, the worldwide explosion of information technology and the globalization of economic activity has made it plausible to speculate that the most advanced nations are currently in the process of transforming themselves into "virtual states"—entities whose power is measured by their human and financial capital and technological prowess rather than the traditional yardsticks of territory, manpower, material resources, industrial production, and armed might.[11] States in this sense would seem to lack essential political and psychological features of states in the traditional sense. It is not clear that they could sustain themselves against raw threats to their security. They offer little to rally the loyalties of their citizens and are unlikely to be able to resist effectively pressures for political devolution or for regional economic collaboration at a level that blurs established political boundaries. It is not difficult to imagine them being captured under certain circumstances by powerful transnational corporations.

To explore further the implications of so-called globalization and related phenomena for contemporary statecraft would take us too far into the realm of science fiction.[12] The trends just discussed are real enough; what political leaders should think or do about them, though, is far from clear. Moreover, there remains a large question as to their staying power. Changed international circumstances such as we have recently witnessed—an immediate security threat, economic hardships, immigration pressures—might well lead to a dramatic slowing down or even reversal of some of them (consider the impact on European elites of the coming of World War I). There is surely little reason to anticipate the disappearance of states as such anytime soon. Above all, the jury of popular opinion remains very much out on the question of the future of the pan-European project.

V

ON REGIMES

"All states, all dominions that have held and do hold empire over men have been and are either republics or principalities." Thus Machiavelli.[1] Appropriately retranslated, this distinction seems broadly pertinent today: our world is divided between what most people would call "democracies" and what they might call "dictatorships" or (less harshly) government by "strong men"—between regimes where the people rule and regimes where they are ruled by a single man.

In fact, of course, the situation is more complicated. In the first place, while all democracies are republics, not all republics are democracies. The republics Machiavelli speaks of were mostly aristocratic republics, whereas democracies today are, formally if not actually, popular regimes. In consequence, democracies today enjoy a legitimacy not enjoyed by the frequently oppressive and faction-ridden republics of late medieval and Renaissance Italy.[2] Moreover, contemporary democracies are constitutional regimes. Not only do they lay claim to representing the people as a whole rather than any particular group or class, but they are committed to upholding a general legal framework that safeguards the rights of all. Hence the term *liberal democracy*, commonly used to distinguish today's democracies from those of premodern times.[3]

In the second place, it is hardly adequate to characterize the alternative to liberal democracy as one-man rule. Our world has certainly had its share of Renaissance-style princes (Saddam Hussein of Iraq, to name one), but many of today's "strong men" rule within a constitutional framework and accept limitations of various kinds on their personal power. Some of them assert a claim to rule only for a transitional period of military rule leading to the reestablishment of full constitutional government—though such professions are of course not always genuine. It is important furthermore not to be misled in cases where individuals wielding formal authority in non-democratic regimes are in reality mere figureheads—spokesmen or representatives of an elite group. This is frequently the case in military regimes, where power is lodged in a junta of senior officers one of whom serves as head of the government (Argentina in the 1980s, for example). It is sometimes true in Communist states, where a persistent tradition of "collective leadership" has been able to defeat countervailing tendencies toward one-man rule on the model of Stalin or Mao (consider the differences in this respect between Vietnam or China on the one hand and North Korea on the other). Finally, it is generally true of traditional monarchies. The Saudi monarchy and the sheikdoms of the Persian Gulf are in reality family enterprises, with the ruler in effect a broker of the family's interests and ambitions and answerable to it for his actions.

Third, it has been evident for some time—though the fact is not widely recognized—that democracy today cannot simply be equated with liberal democracy.[4] The clearest case is the Islamic Republic of Iran. Few would have predicted that the seizure of power in Tehran nearly four decades ago by the Ayatollah Khomeini could have led to anything other than clerical tyranny on a medieval scale. Yet the fact of the matter is that Iran's clerical rulers have created a regime that has the trappings and at least some of the reality of parliamentary democracy: elections are genuine and reform elements are permitted access to office, but clerical conservatives control important levers of power and are able to shape social and cultural activity in ways that would be unthinkable in the liberal West. To the extent that democracy has a future in the Middle East, it may well take a similar form. But perhaps of greater ultimate importance is the case of self-consciously illiberal Singapore, a constitutional democracy that adheres more closely than Iran to the classical pattern of Western parliamentary government. The Singaporeans have claimed that their system, which looks to community-oriented "Asian values" rather than what it views as the radical individualism of the contemporary West for its ideological underpinnings, can serve as a model of democratic development for East Asia as a whole if not beyond.[5]

For additional useful perspective on contemporary politics, one could do worse than turn to Aristotle's seminal discussion of the nature and varieties of "regime" (*politeia*), challenging as it does some of the unspoken assumptions that govern the way most of us today think about such issues. What exactly is a regime? Aristotle defines it as "an arrangement in cities connected with the offices, establishing the manner in which they have been distributed, what the authoritative element of the regime is, and what the end of the partnership is in each case."[6] There are two distinct aspects to this definition. The regime is, first, a set of fundamental rules or laws regulating the most important offices or functions of the government of a state—establishing which they are, what matters they deal with, which persons may hold them, and how these are selected, and above all, designating the body that has final or sovereign authority over all the rest. This may be described as the institutional or procedural side of the regime. Equally important, however, is the second aspect of the definition, that relating to the "end" the state or society (for Aristotle does not distinguish them) pursues. Implicit in this remark is Aristotle's view that the ruling or authoritative element in every regime stands for something beyond itself—for a principle or set of principles reflecting a particular substantive vision of "happiness" for the community as a whole. Let us call this the substantive aspect of the regime. It is to the city, Aristotle might say, as soul is to body or form to matter. In more modern language, it is a nation's ideals or fundamental values, informing and giving life to the whole and shaping its distinctive political culture.[7]

Aristotle indicates that every regime is constructed around an "authoritative element"—an identifiable person or group that is ultimately in charge. This he calls the "governing body," the political leadership or political class. Desirable as it might be in some sense to have laws rule instead of men, we are told, this is not a practical option. "For laws should be enacted—and all are in fact enacted—with a view to the regimes, and not regimes with a view to the laws."[8] The realities of power and the limitations of law itself make it inevitable that some people rule others. And be it noted that democracy is no less a regime in this respect than any other. In a democracy, the common people or the majority are the governing body, and they dominate the regime as surely as does any monarch. Democracy no more than any other regime can substitute the rule of law for the authority of this body. Indeed, for reasons touched on earlier, Aristotle thought the standing of law to be significantly more precarious in democracies than in other regimes.[9] Whether or to what extent this analysis of democracy remains applicable to the constitutional democracies of our day is a question we will return to later.

In thinking about the varieties of regime on the world scene today, Aristotle remains an indispensable point of departure. His classic typology of six basic regime forms is in some ways hard to improve upon. Regimes, he tells us, are run by one, few, or many; and they are run either for the common good of the city or the private benefit of the ruling element. Tyranny, oligarchy, and "democracy" are the bad or deviant versions of personal, elite, and popular rule; the good versions are kingship, aristocracy, and "polity." We need not be put off by the consignment of "democracy" to the wrong side of this ledger, since Aristotle makes plain his sympathy for popular rule when it transcends mere class interests. Tellingly, the Greek term he assigns or invents for this type of regime (it is the same as the word for *regime* itself) is the only one that does not immediately identify an "authoritative element."[10]

This scheme is exposed to the objection that the distinction between good and bad regimes is arbitrary and subjective and the numerical criterion superficial at best. It is, however, far from Aristotle's last word. He makes it clear at once that numbers are not really the decisive factor in determining a regime's character. An oligarchy is a regime dominated by the wealthy few, but wealth, not the fewness of the ruling element, is what gives this regime its distinguishing features; it is the "end" the rulers pursue and hence what most particularly shapes its spirit or culture. A democracy is a regime dominated by the many, who also happen to be poor and lacking in education. What makes it truly distinctive, though, is its embrace of the ideals of freedom and equality. Similarly, aristocracy is not merely rule of the few in the common interest but rule of the few who are well-bred, educated, and habituated to public service; its distinctive feature is its embrace of the ideals of honor and gentlemanly virtue. And polity is a form of popular rule built around a relatively prosperous, well-armed, and public-spirited class of small farmers—a far cry from the resentful urban proletariat Aristotle thinks of as the natural support for "democracy." Finally, one-man rule takes very different forms according to whether it is the legitimate and long-established rule of a hereditary monarch or the rule of a tyrant who is oppressive at least in part because of his very lack of legitimacy. In each of these cases, the positive or negative valuation of the regime rests on basic structural factors, not arbitrary judgment.[11]

It would be a mistake to infer from all this that Aristotle identifies regimes largely with their socioeconomic base. In some ways, Aristotle's approach is reminiscent of Marxism, with its claim that state institutions and ideologies are little more than a "superstructure" reflecting the domination of society by a particular class. Yet there are crucial differences. Aristotle places much more emphasis, in the first place, on ideology—or to remain closer to his own language, on the various claims to political justice that are advanced by the contending parties in the city. Democrats and oligarchs have differing conceptions of justice, each with a logic of its own that necessarily transcends the narrow material interests of these groups. By the same token, there is a powerful argument to be made for kingly rule, highlighting the limitations of republican governance and the rule of law.[12] In the second place, Aristotle is more open than Marx to the idea that political institutions have a certain life of their own—and therefore offer significant opportunities for statecraft.[13]

This brings us to a further key aspect of Aristotle's analysis. Democracies and oligarchies can themselves be narrow or broad, partisan or reasonably tolerant, arbitrary and oppressive or law-abiding; and they can differ significantly according to the particular social or economic interests that predominate in them. Among oligarchies, for example, Aristotle identifies a variant he calls "rule of the powerful" (*dynasteia*)— essentially, government by a committee of the heads of a few powerful families or clans with little regard for settled law. Similarly, monarchies can range from the very limited to the virtually absolute. In short, there are many more actual or possible varieties of regime than the six offered in Aristotle's initial schema. Nor is that all. Regimes can reflect all sorts of degrees not only of domination but also of cooperation between the various classes or elements making up the city. By contrast with Marx, Aristotle holds that the competition for power by diverse socioeconomic groups does not necessarily lead to a "zero-sum" result ratifying final victory for one of them. It can also result in a political accommodation that gives some satisfaction to all parties concerned.

The latter outcome is what Aristotle has in mind when he speaks in several passages of the *Politics* of the "mixed regime."[14] Typically, the mixed regime represents an accommodation between the two most powerful elements in the cities of his day, the people and the wealthy few, giving both a share in offices and honors and creating an institutional structure that ensures their participation. In a variant of this arrangement, a "middling element" helps bridge the partisan divide between rich and poor and lends the regime stability—a striking anticipation of the role of the commercial middle class (the "bourgeoisie") in the rise of modern constitutional democracy. But the mixed regime can also take the form of what Aristotle refers to as "aristocracy" in a weak sense of the term, where the traditional elite assumes a leadership role and virtue is publicly honored, yet power is shared with the wealthy and the people. The most prominent historical example of such a regime discussed in the *Politics* is the Phoenician city of Carthage, the future rival of Rome. It also well describes Rome itself. The popularization of the idea of Rome as mixed regime, by a Greek historian (Polybius) very probably influenced by Aristotle, had a significant impact on the theory and practice of republican government over many centuries. It reappears in Machiavelli's account of Rome in his *Discourses on Livy*. And it forms the background of the thought of the American founders, who copied the mixed institutions of the Roman republic even as they rejected any formal political role for an aristocratic leadership class.[15]

What relevance does all of this have for the present, if any?

Aristotle's regime analysis is obviously not directly transferable to the contemporary world, but it is helpful in sensitizing us to various aspects of political behavior that tend to be obscured by the impersonal and legalistic façade of the modern state. We tend to equate a regime with a "constitution," that is, a formal written document that has the status of a fundamental law. Yet constitutions never tell the whole story about how a state is run—and sometimes the story they tell is intentionally misleading. The "people's democracies" of the old Soviet bloc looked on paper not too different from the liberal democracies of the West, with elaborate formal institutions and procedures, protections for individual rights, and the like. In fact, of course, such constitutions were propaganda exercises, not reliable guides to the underlying structure of power in these countries. On the other hand, at least they gave some formal acknowledgment to the special role played by the Communist Party. In some states today, written constitutions provide almost no clue to the way institutions operate or the identity of the individuals or groups who actually hold power.

Moreover, particularly in the developed West, we tend to take for granted the permanence and immobility of the regimes under which we live. As Aristotle himself shows at length, however, regimes change over time, sometimes in spectacular collapse (as in the Soviet case) but more often through an accumulation of minor developments that are barely noticed or insufficiently understood at the time they occur (he gives the example of fluctuations in the value of money that have the effect of eroding the political strength of the dominant class).[16] Statesmen must be conscious of the vulnerabilities of the regimes they lead. They must take a long and profound view of the requirements of political stability in their states or of the need for fundamental regime change, and take action accordingly—and not only in areas where the stakes for the regime are obvious (such as amendments to written constitutions). Their dealings with elites, leaders, factions, and institutions, their approach to day-to-day policy decisions, must all be shaped by an awareness of the potential impact of their policies and actions on the underpinnings of the regime.

Aristotle's political science, we have suggested, is intended to be practically useful rather than scientifically exact. In an important passage at the beginning of Book IV of the *Politics*, Aristotle tells us that those who had previously discussed regimes had made a characteristic error: concentrating on the regime that is simply best yet difficult to attain, they failed to provide a useful analysis of the range of regimes available to states. An adequate study of regimes must indeed look at the simply best regime, but, Aristotle insists, it must also consider the following: the regime that is best for a particular city given its overall circumstances; regimes that are acceptable for a particular city under a varying set of assumptions about what it can achieve given its overall circumstances; and the regime that is best or most suitable for most cities.

This approach combines elements of the ideal and the practicable in a way that is highly instructive. Until recently, the question of the abstractly best form of government had been off the table of serious political discussion. It had generally been considered a philosophical issue beyond the ken of political science and of little interest to practicing politicians. With the formation of a number of new states following the breakup of the Soviet Union and Yugoslavia and the emergence of new democratic regimes there as well as in parts of the third world, this situation palpably changed. As Aristotle himself indicates,[17] the opportunity to found new states and regimes is the primary impetus for thinking systematically about the best form of government and justifies its inclusion in a practical science of politics. In the contemporary world, these sudden opportunities have revived interest in fundamental constitutional issues such as the advantages and disadvantages of presidential and parliamentary systems,[18] voting procedures and the role of parties, and federalism. The problem is that these issues are too often addressed piecemeal and in an overly technical fashion. As Aristotle reminds us, regime analysis in the proper sense is not just about political mechanics; it is also about the soul of a nation.

This brings us to a final point. Aristotle assumes that the abstractly best regime is one that holds its citizens to such a high standard that it is unlikely to be realized except under the best imaginable conditions. This means that political scientists charged with the task of constitutional engineering need to be prepared to lower their sights to take account of the impediments to realizing the ideal likely to be present in a given state as well as to consider alternative regimes that might be more suitable. It was not so long ago that political scientists and practitioners alike saw liberal democracy in much the same way Aristotle understood the abstractly best regime—as a demanding ideal that could not be expected to take root everywhere. Today, we are much more inclined to see liberal democracy as a practical model for most if not all nations on the world scene, one that can be exported with only minor adjustments to societies that have had no experience of it.[19] There can be no question but that democracy has made greater progress in many parts of the world than one might have predicted only a few decades ago, and that in certain places (such as southern Europe) it seems to have put down permanent roots. When such developments are taken into account, there may well be sufficient justification for treating liberal democracy today not as an ideal but as the regime Aristotle would describe as "most fitting for all cities."

On the other hand, this approach is not without its risks. It raises expectations both at home and abroad of a quick transition to democracy and increases pressure on political leaders to produce it, when this may simply not be possible—and indeed, if attempted, may have dramatically unwelcome consequences for the stability of the country and for the prospects for democracy there over the longer term.[20] The real problem, though, lies deeper. This is that the democratic ideal itself tends to be reinterpreted—"defined down"—so that it becomes easier to attain or to claim to have attained.

That a certain defining down of liberal democracy has occurred in recent years is apparent. For many in the West today, to pronounce a nation democratic it is enough to know only that it holds reasonably free and reasonably frequent elections. It is true that current methodologies for assessing degrees of progress in democracy are capable of much more sophisticated assessments.[21] But the fact remains that, as a matter of public policy, it is convenient for many reasons for states and their leaders to set the bar of democratic performance as low as possible. Politically, it is becoming increasingly difficult to sustain the argument that democracy demands effort and sacrifice from citizens or that it has unique social, educational, or cultural preconditions. Contrary to Aristotelian regime analysis, democracy tends to be treated simply as a collection of institutions and procedures rather than a substantive ideal. One of the most profound challenges contemporary statesmen face is understanding the dangers this development poses to the future of democratic governance.

VI

Elites and
How to Manage Them

We have suggested that knowledge of the character of regimes is an essential component of the political knowledge leaders require. But regimes cannot be understood properly without paying due attention to the elites that so largely control and define them. This is an uncomfortable thought for many today. The reality of elite power in contemporary democracies tends to be either denied or denounced, raising as it does a fundamental question about the legitimacy of democratic governance; rarely is it analyzed dispassionately. If one looks closely at contemporary democracies, a compelling case could be made—to borrow again the language of Aristotelian political science—that they are "mixed" rather than simply popular regimes, given the extent to which political decision-making is influenced if not actually monopolized by elites.[1] At all events, the relationship between leaders and elites generally is plainly a central issue for the study of statecraft. The basic case for this proposition has already been stated; let us elaborate it further.

One of the remarkable features of contemporary politics in America is the extent to which cultural issues in a broad sense have displaced social class or status as sources of personal identity and political conflict. Attitudes toward race, ethnicity, and gender, toward pornography and drugs, toward prayer in the schools or the burning of the flag, are now more reliable touchstones of political commitment than social origins or personal wealth. Traditional class lines have at the same time become increasingly blurred in our ever more fluid and mobile society. With the exception of an urban underclass that has little political weight, it is not at all implausible to assert that in the United States (and in other advanced societies) today, class no longer matters. Elitism is routinely derided, yet our elites remain strangely invisible. Could it be that the contemporary West has actually achieved the ideal of the classless society so long championed (but in practice grotesquely betrayed) by its former Soviet adversary?

In a broad sense, there can be little doubt that the "social question," as it came to be called in the nineteenth century, has been drained of much of its political salience by the dynamism of the modern economy and the diffusion of its benefits to ever-widening social strata under the benevolent guidance of the liberal welfare state. In the United States, the "equality of condition" which Alexis de Tocqueville noted in his classic *Democracy in America* (1835–40) as a fundamental characteristic of American society is still with us; and American political culture remains as robustly egalitarian as it was then, if not indeed more so. Tocqueville's expectation or hope that lawyers might eventually constitute an elite that could serve as a needed counterweight to the popular will has not materialized—at least not in the sense he intended. And Tocqueville's fear that the barons of industry would succeed in forming a new aristocracy within American society, while nearer to the mark, has in the end proven groundless. The great fortunes made in America over the last century and more have built many universities and museums but few centers of corporate power or enduring political dynasties; and the social influence they once radiated is today virtually extinct.[2]

Still, social and economic differentiation remains an inescapable fact of contemporary life, invisible only to the extent that a certain democratic prudishness inhibits open discussion of it.[3] In the United States, many argue that disparities in income and social stratification have increased markedly in recent years; others decry the dominance of key cultural institutions by an elite that is increasingly remote from the concerns and values of the mass of the population. According to a widely shared view, a new elite has displaced the old (largely Anglo-Saxon and Protestant) "establishment," one recruited on the basis of merit rather than shared social characteristics and engaged in the handling of information and ideas more than in the traditional wealth-producing professions.[4]

The emergence—actual or in prospect—of such an elite is often applauded as a final resolution of the social tensions necessarily created by the persistence of class differences within a democratic polity. A purely meritocratic elite of the sort just described seems to offer the functional benefits of older elites without their well-known liabilities—above all, without permanence and the invidious social and cultural distinctions to which it inevitably gives rise. But is a purely meritocratic elite really possible, given the well-known frailties of human nature? Is an idea-based elite any less vulnerable to corruption and social sclerosis than elites of the more traditional variety? The highly ideocratic Soviet system, after all, encouraged the formation of a privileged class (the so-called *nomenklatura*) that had acquired at the end many of the trappings of a hereditary order.[5] Are the advanced societies of the contemporary West necessarily immune to such developments?

Yet even the desirability of a meritocratic elite is by no means self-evident. That raw intelligence will increasingly determine social and economic success in technologically advanced countries, as some have argued,[6] may well be true. But the exclusive use of intelligence-related criteria to distribute social benefits is problematic in a number of ways. Highly intelligent people may be socially dysfunctional. Others may compensate for a deficit of intelligence by self-discipline and effort—moral qualities that would seem to have a better claim to be socially rewarded than simple natural endowment yet are harder to measure. The extreme social and geographic mobility implied in the increasingly global meritocracy of today inevitably weakens valuable family and community ties, not to mention national loyalties. But perhaps most importantly, the ethos of meritocracy tends to promote a radical individualism that erodes traditions of morality and public service and threatens to destroy the solidarity of democratic society.[7]

Are elites actually necessary? This is a question not often raised even in our pervasively egalitarian culture but one worth pondering. There seem to be two sorts of answers to it: elites are needed in order to rule (or in more acceptably democratic language, to provide political leadership); or they are needed in order to satisfy a fundamental human impulse. In the United States today, many support term limits on state and national legislators that would make it difficult or impossible to sustain professional political careers and hence a permanent political class. But opponents of term limits have a strong counterargument: handing power to a constantly changing cast of inexperienced and ill-informed citizen-legislators would only increase the influence of non-elected policy experts both in and outside of government. It is hard to get around the need, if not for political rule, at any rate for political leadership. Is it possible to have political leadership without political elites? The lessons of history, some of it very recent,[8] suggest that political leadership so understood is a recipe for tyranny.

Less often addressed, yet equally interesting, is the second aspect of this issue. It is taken for granted in most quarters today that liberal democracy, with the economy of abundance it seems uniquely able to sustain, satisfies basic human needs, at least to the extent that they can be satisfied by political means. Liberty, security, prosperity, recognition of the dignity and the equal rights of all—this is the promise, and not far from the reality, of the advanced democracies of our age. Yet what of the human need for distinction?

That ambition in democratic ages is in some ways more febrile and obsessive than under the old aristocratic order is an argument advanced by Tocqueville and seconded by many.[9] When no one knows their place, everything is up for grabs; not family lineage or social standing but individual achievement becomes the measure of success in life—but a measure that is fragile and fatally relative to the achievements of others. It is comforting to imagine that the impulse to succeed in democratic society can be satisfied entirely within the private sphere. Business, sports, the entertainment industry, the intellectual world—all offer avenues for achieving personal distinction wholly apart from politics. But one can hardly leave the matter there. Certainly for some (consider the case of Donald Trump), the security of wealth or general notoriety is certain to prove far less satisfying than the recognition accorded to noteworthy achievement or influence in the public arena. And for a few, satisfaction will only be found in politics itself, or to state it more pointedly, in ruling others. Even in a society of perfect abundance, it would be unreasonable to expect (to adapt Marx's formula) a withering away of elites. Status, prestige, recognition, and honor are motivations unlikely to be expunged from the human spirit, however much they may be driven underground by the culture of egalitarianism. They will continue to generate and sustain a political elite in democracies as in any other regime today.[10]

If elites are necessary, are they necessarily malign? This is simply taken for granted in many quarters today; it is pervasive in American popular culture as well as in fashionable modes of academic thought throughout the West.[11] In the United States, this reflects the persisting influence of progressive liberalism, with its emphasis on the corrupting impact of the barons of commerce and industry (the "special interests") on the American political system. Ultimately, though, it reflects deeper currents in the history of modern political thought. The notion that those in superior positions in any society are necessarily interested only in preserving and enjoying their own power and not at all in benefiting the society as a whole can be most readily identified with the teachings of Karl Marx. In fact, the figure who first advanced this fundamental argument was Machiavelli. As he tells us in *The Prince*, in every city the people and the great constitute two diverse "humors," arising from the fact that "the people desire neither to be commanded nor oppressed by the great, and the great desire to command and oppress the people."[12]

Machiavelli implicitly denies the crucial distinction Aristotle draws between regimes where the few rule in their own interest and those where they rule in the common interest. Elites, it seems, are all alike in the decisive respect. Yet is this really the case?

In the United States, there can be little question that the progressive critique of modern capitalism has become increasingly detached from the reality of American business in an age of pervasive government regulation, media scrutiny, consumer litigiousness, and ideologically driven sensitivity or compassion, though individual capitalists of course remain capable of spectacular misbehavior. The broader point is that elites vary enormously over time and across nations and cultures. The Nazi SS was an elite of an entirely different sort than the British peerage, which in turn has little in common with the American entrepreneurial elite or the liberal meritocracy. Elites are decisively shaped by education and by the wider culture of the societies to which they belong. These influences can and often do run counter to their narrow class interests and lead to behavior that is to varying degrees in tension with those interests. Elites frequently engage in conflict with the general population over resources or prerogatives. Yet the history of mankind is—to repeat what was said earlier—not simply the history of class struggle; it is also a history of bargaining, accommodation, and cooperation among classes. Elites may oppress; they may also demonstrate farsighted leadership, engage in heroic self-sacrifice, and provide competent and honest administration of the public business.

The image of elites in the contemporary mind is distorted by other misconceptions as well. One is that elites in every society are of a piece—culturally and socially homogeneous and united by a shared set of material interests, not to say actively conspiratorial in protecting their own privileged position.[13] This may be true in some times and places, but it is far from the situation in the highly differentiated societies of the advanced democracies today. In the United States particularly, there are nationally important elites in many social sectors, linked only weakly if at all with one another. What is more, some of them are in competition, or tend for other reasons to be hostile to one another and to engage in political struggle. This brings us to a second misconception—that what constitutes an elite is inherited privilege or formal status rather than earned distinction, or to state it more pointedly, that there are no elites on the left. Our meritocratic elite tends to be invisible to itself. Leaders of labor unions or minority groups are not thought of as elites; neither are TV news anchors. In fact, of course, such persons frequently wield more raw political power in the nation than do most corporate executives, not to speak of religious leaders, military officers, or college presidents.

If political elites are inevitable, indispensable, menacing, yet also malleable, the key issue becomes how to manage them effectively. Broadly speaking, there are two sorts of solutions to the problem of elite domination in any society. Either elites are checked or constrained by institutional means, or they are molded by education. Popular election and the rule of law are obvious examples of the first; but many political systems—not least that of the United States—also rely on a variety of other constitutional mechanisms to check, balance, or diffuse elite power. Some laws have a direct and potentially critical impact on the shape, composition, and behavior of an elite class—for example, those affecting land ownership and inheritance.

The path of institutional constraints is the one recommended by Machiavelli. Let us return to the passage just quoted concerning the humors of the people and the great. The people and the great in every society seem irreconcilably at odds. Enter the would-be prince, who looks to come to power with the help of one of these factions rather than through violence. Which does he choose? The conventional answer in Machiavelli's day would have been the great—the aristocratic elite that supported the sovereigns of early modern Europe by fighting their wars, collecting their taxes, and maintaining the public order. Machiavelli's answer, which deserves to be quoted at length, is different:

> He who comes to the principality with the aid of the great maintains himself with more difficulty than one who becomes prince with the aid of the people, because the former finds himself prince with many around him who appear to be his equals, and because of this he can neither command them nor manage them to suit himself. But he who arrives in the principality with popular support finds himself alone there, and around him has either no one or very few who are not ready to obey. Besides this, one cannot satisfy the great with decency and without injury to others, but one can satisfy the people; for the end of the people is more decent than that of the great, since the great want to oppress and the people want not to be oppressed. Furthermore, a prince can never secure himself against a hostile people, as they are too many; against the great, he can secure himself, as they are few.[14]

But this is not to say that the prince cannot make use of the great.

> Either they conduct themselves so that in their proceedings they are obligated in everything to your fortune, or not. Those who are obligated, and are not rapacious, must be honored and loved; those who are not obligated have to be examined in two modes. Either they do this out of pusillanimity and a natural defect of spirit; then you must make use especially of those who are of good counsel, because in prosperity they bring you honor and in adversity you do not have to fear them; but, when by art and for an ambitious cause, they are not obligated, it is a sign that they are thinking more for themselves than for you; and the prince must be on guard against them, and fear them as if they were open enemies, because in adversity they will always help ruin him.[15]

Machiavelli's fundamental point is that elites can be managed effectively only by princes who do not have to depend upon them for their political survival. Elites, he argues, are generically more dangerous to the well-being of political leaders than are the people at large. Hence the strategy of leaders must be to curry favor with the people, while employing elites for the tasks of governance in ways that minimize the threat they pose to the basis of princely power. Machiavelli's novel argument has an oddly familiar ring—for good reason. It is nothing other than the original form of the idea of executive power in modern constitutional democracies.

Let us return to the issue of elite education. This can take many forms. Education may be state-sponsored or private; martial, religious, or literary, or some combination of these; practical, ideological, or intricately formalistic. In Confucian China, in spite or because of the weakness of law and political institutions, a remarkable system of literary and moral education employing competitive examinations played the key role in the recruitment and control of a vast gentry class over many centuries. A state-sponsored regimen of education and training geared to the inculcation of the martial virtues was the defining feature of social and political life in classical Sparta. The public schools and elite universities of modern Britain may be said to have combined elements of both of these systems.[16] In the United States today, the idea of "liberal education" continues to reflect, if in an increasingly attenuated way, the tradition of genteel education deriving from the Renaissance and ultimately from Greek and Roman antiquity.[17]

Partly because of the continuing influence of our own political tradition, which in its defining incarnation (in the *Federalist Papers*) contains one of the most important modern statements of the institutional approach to regime management, Americans have difficulty taking entirely seriously the question of the role of elite education in the larger political order. Yet as signs multiply today of the erosion of traditional standards of behavior in the elite professions of business, law, science, and education, to say nothing of the public sector, it is becoming harder to ignore the impact of contemporary cultural pathologies on the American political system. The term limits movement is only one manifestation of what may be described as a crisis of confidence on the part of the American public or large segments of it in the character of its elites. This crisis no doubt reflects to some extent the role of the media or the deconstruction of authority generally that is so apparent throughout American popular culture. But a case can also be made that the virtual disappearance of moral, religious, and civic education at all levels, not to mention the ongoing postmodernist subversion of the teaching of the humanities and social sciences in our universities, bears significant responsibility for this state of affairs.

VII

MODERN FOUNDERS

All states past or present, Machiavelli tells us at the beginning of *The Prince*, are either republics or principalities; and principalities are either hereditary, "new," or some combination of these. In spite of its obvious limitations, this scheme of classification points to a central and distinctive feature of Machiavelli's political science. Princes who are newly established in their state face fundamental political challenges. Success in maintaining their position therefore requires a more active exercise of political skill than is the case for those who come to power through an accident of birth in a stable hereditary monarchy—or, for that matter, through regular electoral processes in a democracy. In ordinary political settings, a politician's success is as much a function of luck as of anything else. In extraordinary circumstances, however, princes or potential princes can survive and prosper only if they possess the appropriate qualities of mind and personality—the comprehensive political excellence Machiavelli calls "virtue" (*virtù*).[1] These sorts of circumstances provide the critical arena and the true test of statecraft.

Extraordinary circumstances in the sense indicated are those accompanying changes in ruling families or regimes, or the birth, expansion, or collapse of states. These circumstances offer ambitious politicians great opportunities but also pose severe dangers. At such times, authority is weak or under challenge, political loyalties are up for grabs, and violence becomes an ever-present possibility. To quote Machiavelli again on this key point, "It should be considered that nothing is more difficult to handle, more doubtful of success, nor more dangerous to manage, than to put oneself at the head of introducing new orders. For the introducer has all those who benefit from the old order as enemies, and he has luke-warm defenders in all those who might benefit from the new orders." It requires significant political skill for a prince to annex new territories to an existing state. It requires political skill and personal courage of a high order to displace an existing dynasty or to overthrow an entire regime. A greater and more difficult achievement, however, is the establishment of a wholly new state. Machiavelli offers the semi-legendary examples of Theseus's creation of ancient Athens from a collection of independent villages and the founding of the Persian Empire at the hands of Cyrus the Great. Greater still is the establishment not merely of a new state or regime but of a new political dispensation, that is, a distinctive creed or national culture. The classic case is Moses's founding of the Israelite nation.[2]

For Machiavelli, then, the act of "founding" is the pinnacle of state-craft. It is the ultimate expression of princely *virtù* as well as the surest route to political glory, and it constitutes a model that should guide the actions of all who aspire to political power. At first sight, this analysis seems to have little relevance to the present, an age where kings are decorative figures and politicians no longer thirst for glory in dubious political and military enterprises. Yet it is not hard to recognize in Ma-chiavelli's virtuous—or better, virtuoso—prince the distant forerunner of the "transformative" leader sketched by James MacGregor Burns. The idea that "change" is the touchstone of democratic leadership, bloodless though it may be, concedes Machiavelli's fundamental point.

Machiavelli was the first thinker to reflect on politics from what may be called a revolutionary perspective. This is not intended as a criticism of him; on the contrary, Machiavelli's approach is valuable and enduring precisely because it calls attention to aspects of statecraft that tend to be neglected or poorly understood. We are unaccustomed to associating terms such as statesman or statecraft with street-fighting leftist revolu-tionaries or the leaders of military coups. Yet many of the greatest polit-ical figures of the last several centuries have in fact been revolutionaries in one sense or another, or have been skillful at creating and exploiting revolutionary situations. Simon Bolivar and Napoleon Bonaparte, military adventurers on a continental scale, gave a decisive impetus to the diffusion of republican government in the modern world. Lenin and Mao Zedong were extraordinary revolutionary leaders who founded not merely new regimes but a new political dispensation. Mussolini and Hitler attempted to do the same.

But it is well to keep in mind that revolutionary transformations have also been carried out by statesmen of more traditionalist or conservative bent, and often with greater ultimate success. The outstanding example, of course, is the American founding. The American project was revolutionary not only in its challenge to British imperial authority, but more fundamentally, in its embrace of the novel principles of democratic republicanism, federalism, and constitutional government—the principles of a "new political science," as Alexander Hamilton called it, suited to a new age.[3] Yet the founding fathers were far from revolutionary ideologues. They sought to appeal to ideas of self-government deeply embedded in the Anglo-American experiences, and they believed that change could be managed through reasoned deliberation and the development of consensus rather than through force and terror.[4]

Less appreciated today but nonetheless of major historical impact are the great conservative revolutionaries of recent times. Otto von Bismarck in Germany, Count Camillo Cavour and King Vittorio Emanuele of Savoy in Italy, and the Meiji reformers in Japan wrought large changes in their respective countries in the course of a few decades in the mid-nineteenth century and remade the geostrategic map of Europe and indeed the world.[5] At the end of World War I, Mustafa Kemal (who would become known to history as Atatürk, "father of the Turks") single-handedly rallied his defeated nation against the continuing encroachments of the Allied powers, overthrew in short order the imperial and religious institutions that had supported Ottoman rule for five centuries, and founded a secular and modernizing Turkish Republic on the Western model. During this same period, Haile Selassie succeeded to the throne of Ethiopia and set out to transform an essentially feudal order into a recognizably modern state, beginning (in good Machiavellian fashion) by systematically destroying the political and military power of the hereditary nobility.[6]

What is the primary requirement in a founding prince? Machiavelli puts it this way: "The principal foundations that all states have, new ones as well as old or mixed, are good laws and good arms. And because there cannot be good laws where there are not good arms, and where there are good arms there must be good laws, I shall leave out the reasoning on laws and shall speak of arms."[7] If or to the extent that the founder is a prophet, Machiavelli avers, one has to remember that only "armed prophets" succeed, whereas the unarmed ones fail. Yet founders always face a problem: where to get the arms they need? And they are always tempted to commit a capital mistake—to rely on "the arms of others" rather than their own, since military forces you don't control are notoriously fickle, unreliable, and ineffective. The chief preoccupation of the founder-prince, therefore, has to be the military art. "Thus, a prince should have no other object, nor any other thought, nor take anything else as his art but the art of war and its orders and discipline; for that is the only art which is of concern to one who commands. And it is of such virtue that not only does it maintain those who have been born princes but many times it enables men of private fortune to rise to that rank; and on the contrary, one sees that when princes have thought more of amenities than of arms, they have lost their states."[8]

The classic portrait of the founder-prince along these lines is the now-forgotten masterpiece of Greek literature, Xenophon's *Education of Cyrus*, the apparent source of Machiavelli's interest in this figure. Cyrus vastly expanded the power of his native Persia using as his instrument an army he was able to build—and in the process make loyal to himself—while ostensibly in the service of his uncle, the king of neighboring Media. This is a tale (in Xenophon's hands, both inspirational and cautionary) of leadership writ large. Its great theme is how human beings can be ruled by others in some sense against their natural inclination. Cyrus is undeniably a charismatic figure, but more importantly, his example shows how men can be recruited, motivated, and used by a leader through a calculated combination of rewards and punishments, or more precisely, how they can be motivated to fight and die for that leader's greater glory.[9]

Comfortable in our bourgeois democracies—where war is abhorred and military leaders are rarely anything more than bureaucrats in uniform, where we are taught as children that force never solves anything and as young people can easily avoid military service—we are no longer in touch with these elemental realities. In much of the world even today, however, the story is different. Regimes are more fragile; military leaders and organizations, more feared and respected. Atatürk, a career officer in the Ottoman army and a war hero, is only the first of many generals in the twentieth century—not to mention colonels, majors, or in two noteworthy African cases, a flight lieutenant and a sergeant—to take power in their countries through extralegal means. It is well to remember that even the American founding was far from a bloodless affair and to ponder the wisdom of Washington's strategy of preserving the Revolutionary army at all costs as a vital symbol of the national will. Contrary to a common view of the matter, modern revolutions are rarely brought on by spontaneous uprisings of oppressed classes or peoples, or even by the ideological agitation of well-organized political parties (the Leninist model). Rather, they succeed when governments lose effective control of the army and the police. Nothing better illustrates this fundamental truth than the Bolshevik seizure of power in Russia in October 1917.[10]

Contemporary statesmen who neglect Machiavelli's advice do so at their peril. For a recent example of feckless reliance on the "arms of others," consider Eduard Shevardnadze. This humane and admirable man, who as the last foreign minister of the Soviet Union played a critical role in ensuring its peaceful demise, assumed the presidency of newly independent Georgia in 1992 in an effort to rescue his homeland from gross misrule and to stem growing separatist tendencies, particularly in the ethnically distinct Abkhazia region. With moral and material help from elements of the Russian military, the rebels there soon routed the ragtag Georgian forces and their paramilitary auxiliaries, led by Shevardnadze's two key supporters, Tengis Khitovani and Jaba Ioseliani—the latter a man who had spent almost two decades in a Soviet jail for armed robbery. Shevardnadze then turned to the Russians. He managed to secure their help as "peacekeepers" in Abkhazia, a deal which gained him little but for which he paid a steep price that included new Russian bases in Georgia and other concessions. Reliance on such dubious and self-serving allies only damaged Shevardnadze's prestige and further weakened his hold on the country.[11]

Humane and admirable men, it goes without saying, are greatly to be desired as statesmen in most countries at most times. In extraordinary times, as Machiavelli plausibly teaches, they can become a liability. Reluctance to use or to prepare to use force when circumstances call for it, or personally to associate oneself with such activities, is a common tendency in such men.[12] It needs to be consciously resisted if vital national purposes are to be served and power is not to be forfeited to unscrupulous thugs. Machiavelli would have it that unscrupulous thugs can themselves prove to be outstanding founders,[13] but it is not necessary to go to the end of that road with him. If ordinary princes are prey to character flaws that can have highly damaging political consequences, this is all the more true for rulers of this sort. (Consider the case of a more famous Georgian, Joseph Stalin.)

Yet skill and resolution in the use of force hardly exhaust the *virtù* of the founder-prince. Machiavelli himself admits as much when he invokes the "prophet" as a model for founders, thereby begging the question of the source of the enduring strength of armies and the regimes they support. Machiavelli's irreverent comment concerning the priority of arms over laws is a half-truth at best. Moses's promulgation of the Decalogue was central to the creation of a Jewish national identity, and (as we learn from Machiavelli's *Discourses*) the real founder of Rome was not so much Romulus as his successor Numa Pompilius, who also gave to his people a divinely sanctioned code of laws.[14] Nor can Machiavelli have failed to note the great exception to his maxim that unarmed prophets never succeed. In *The Prince* itself, his satirical portrait of the "ecclesiastic principality" and its clerical rulers—"these alone have states, and do not defend them; they have subjects, and do not govern them; and the states, though undefended, are not taken from them; the subjects, though ungoverned, do not care, and they neither think of becoming estranged from such princes nor can they"[15]—nevertheless tacitly acknowledges the political strength that states can derive from religion and the extent to which such regimes are exempt from the normal calculus of military power.

Indeed, part of what makes Machiavelli a revolutionary thinker in the modern sense of the term is precisely his grasp of the power of belief or opinion as an instrument of statecraft. This emerges most clearly later on in *The Prince* in a chapter entitled "How Faith Should be Kept by Princes," where Machiavelli takes advantage of the ambiguity of the Italian word *fede* ("trustworthiness" as well as [religious] "faith") to carry on a barely disguised discussion of how religion is to be used to support princely government. Machiavelli now tells us that princes engage in two kinds of "fighting"—one with "laws," the other with force; that the successful prince must combine the qualities of the lion and the fox; and that the prince who has known how to play the fox has generally come out better, so long as he is a "great simulator and dissimulator" who is able to deceive others about his true nature.

> A prince should thus take great care that . . . to see him and hear him, he should appear all mercy, all faith, all honesty, all humanity, all religion. And nothing is more necessary to appear to have than this last quality. Men in general judge more by their eyes than by their hands, because seeing is given to everyone, touching to few. Everyone sees how you appear, few touch what you are; and these few dare not oppose the opinion of many, who have the majesty of the state to defend them.[16]

Machiavelli's curious remark that princes "fight" using "laws" can only be understood in this larger context. Religions are fighting creeds, organizations that seek to build spiritual (and sometimes earthly) empires through the promulgation of God's law and a promise of salvation through obedience to it. Christianity, which invented the term *propaganda*, represents for Machiavelli a new model of statecraft, one recognizable in recent times in the ideological warfare of Communism and Fascism as well as the religious warfare of contemporary radical Islam. Machiavelli would have no difficulty in accounting for the overthrow of the shah of Iran in 1979 by a Shiite cleric whose only weapons were smuggled cassette recordings of his sermons. The shah's formidable army and secret police could in the end do nothing against the tide of popular discontent the Ayatollah Khomeini had set in motion.

Revolutionary or political warfare in the sense we are describing is of special importance in a founding situation. This is because it helps the aspiring prince overcome what is perhaps the central problem facing him: the hostility of powerful elites who benefit from their privileged position in the old regime. Political warfare offers, first, a way to separate elites from the general population, turning the latter into a more or less active strategic ally. Second, it can also serve to divide and demoralize elites themselves. The Jesuits were pioneers in the techniques of elite penetration and recruitment; the Communists proved masters of it in our own day.[17]

As the Georgian case shows, the founding of new states and regimes is not a phenomenon of merely historical interest. Just as the breakup of the overseas European empires earlier in the twentieth century led to the creation of dozens of new nations in the less developed world, so the breakup of the Soviet Union and its East European empire has opened up vast opportunities for enterprising founder-princes. The new republics carved out of the former Soviet space have little or no experience of nationhood and face daunting challenges to their basic security and identity. Accordingly, the tasks that confronted the first generation of leaders in these countries are bound to be more formidable than those required of more routinely situated statesmen. Founder-princes (and such are needed even and precisely in newly minted republics, to repeat Machiavelli's key point) must take a more self-conscious, comprehensive, and longer view. At the same time, they must remain exquisitely sensitive to the political stresses and strains in the fragile edifice they are attempting to construct and must be prepared to act promptly and vigorously to shore it up if it begins to collapse.

Nationalism and modernization are too often conceived today, particularly by political scientists, as impersonal forces that carry politicians with them willy-nilly. This greatly underestimates the extent to which national feeling can be manipulated if not simply manufactured by political leaders to suit a revolutionary agenda (consider the history of post-Communist Yugoslavia, which saw a deliberate and relentless stoking of such feeling by leaders to advance their political agendas[18]). More importantly, it fails to give due weight to the role of deliberate political action in the process of modernization. Bismarck's success in creating (and Hitler's in exploiting) a pan-Germanic national identity and loyalty emerges clearly only against the backdrop of the extreme political, religious, and cultural fragmentation of the German-speaking world over many centuries. The cases of Germany and Japan—and more recent ones such as Singapore or South Korea—illustrate the extent to which modernization understood as a process of economic development can be imposed rapidly and from the top by enlightened statesmen, rather than in the unplanned and incremental style of the classic earlier modernizers Britain and America. Finally, the case of Turkey in particular (Ethiopia and Singapore are others) strikingly underscores the potential importance of culture as a tool of statecraft in the hands of modernizing leaders or in the founding or refounding of states generally. Atatürk's campaigns to abolish the fez (the traditional Ottoman hat) and introduce the Latin alphabet, quaint as they may appear to us, were highly effective (and also risky) moves in his larger project to create a new Turkish man. They are an important point of reference for the leaders of Muslim countries today faced with the formidable ideological challenge of radical Islam.

These cases are especially instructive because they are largely off the radar screen of politicians (and political scientists) today. Yet they show that statecraft can have a role in modernization that is at once more effective and more benign than the totalitarian projects of the last century. The Communist attempt to create a new Soviet man through a combination of brute force and utopian social engineering failed predictably and deservedly. In part, it is simply that the founding visions of Atatürk and other conservative modernizers were more compatible with ordinary human limits and aspirations. In part too, however, they remained respectful, as the totalitarians were not, of the supreme importance of the rule of law in the construction of a genuinely modern state.

This brings us back to Machiavelli. The soundness of Machiavelli's analysis of foundings ultimately rests on his depreciation of the rule of law. The asserted priority of arms over laws reflects, as we have seen, the need for a single will to command in times of revolutionary upheaval. But more than that, it reflects the inadequacy of laws and the need for princes—or the equivalent of princes—in all states at all times. This argument frontally challenges the theoretical outlook of all today who profess attachment to constitutional democracy. But is it so remote from contemporary practice? Leadership in the advanced democracies seems increasingly to mean executive leadership. What exactly is the chief executive's place in contemporary constitutional democracy? The answer reveals a surprising persistence of the great Florentine in our own political universe.

VIII

EXECUTIVE POWER AND CONSTITUTIONAL GOVERNMENT

Let us grant Machiavelli's case: strong leadership is essential at the founding of states and regimes, whether they are principalities or constitutional democracies. But why must it follow that strong leadership should be institutionalized in democracies in the form of a powerful chief executive? Prior to the eighteenth century, after all, republics favored divided or weak executive officers—Rome's two consuls, for example, or the Venetian doge. Both for the making and executing of policy, they looked primarily to a single collective body, a senate or council, representing the prominent families of the state. Jealous of their prerogatives, these notables feared—generally with good reason—that undue concentration of power in the hands of one of their number would pose a fundamental threat. And constitutional democracy in England and America itself developed out of a struggle between national parliaments and autocratic monarchs, a struggle protracted over several centuries but one whose final outcome seemed never in doubt. Today, however, princes under other names once again vie for power with theoretically sovereign popular bodies. And as often as not, they appear to enjoy the upper hand. How to explain all this?

The modern political executive has to be understood in the broader context in which he operates. This context consists of a particular institutional setting and the wider cultural outlook that lends it fundamental legitimacy. The institutional setting is of course the familiar one of constitutional democracy. Here law not man is king, and government consists of partly autonomous and competing institutions—representative assemblies, courts, bureaucracies—that greatly limit the field of action of those who most visibly "rule." But even more important is the political culture—the often unspoken set of beliefs and attitudes—that underpins these institutional mechanics. That all men are created equal and endowed with fundamental rights; that government or the state exists or ought to exist primarily to secure those rights; that government is therefore the servant not the master of the people; that government cannot be trusted to act accordingly unless it is controlled by the people's elected representatives—such are the political axioms that shape the expectations of peoples and the ambitions of politicians today, certainly in the developed West, but even in many parts of the world that do not yet enjoy stable constitutional democracy.

The institutions and culture of contemporary democracy did not simply evolve; they emerged from a particular system of thought. This system of thought—let us call it liberal constitutionalism—found its most influential exponent in the English philosopher and publicist John Locke. Locke's best known work, the *Second Treatise on Government*, was first published shortly after the Glorious Revolution of 1688, which brought an end to the Stuart dynasty and checked once and for all the absolutist pretensions of English monarchs. Locke's formulation of the principles of limited government was fundamental in shaping the development of constitutionalist thought and practice in the century following—its critical formative period. His influence was felt not only in England itself but in the American colonies and even—thanks to Charles Secondat, Baron de Montesquieu, the second great expounder of liberal constitutionalism—in absolutist France. When the American founders spoke of a "new political science" guiding their own endeavors, they were thinking principally of Locke and Montesquieu.[1]

Liberal constitutionalism is not the same as the ideology (if there is one) of contemporary constitutional democracy. It is a theory not of democracy as such but of limited government. Its central concern is not empowering the people but limiting the ability of governments of whatever sort—democratic ones included—to dominate society. There is, in fact, a tension within contemporary liberal democracy between its liberal or constitutionalist component and its democratic component. If democracy in its purest sense is the untrammeled exercise of the sovereign will of the people, constitutions stand in its way. They create institutional obstacles that delay and complicate the exercise of the majority's will and protect the rights of unpopular minorities and individuals.[2]

Central to this new political science is the idea that the basic powers of government should be separated and placed in the hands of different persons, thus creating a system of "checks and balances" that acts to safeguard the people's liberties. In Montesquieu, we find for the first time the familiar distinction between executive, legislative, and judicial functions. Locke regarded the judicial power as part of the executive but recognized an additional power he calls the "federative," which deals with what we would today describe as foreign policy or national security. In practice, though, the executive and federative powers are almost always wielded by the same person or persons; thus the fundamental distinction is between executive and legislative power, the two properly political functions of government.[3]

Why should these two functions be separated? English constitutionalist writers prior to Locke had a simple answer to this question. The executive—that is, the royal—power had to be recognized as wholly subordinate to the sovereign power of Parliament in order to prevent its arbitrary exercise, while Parliament itself should not be in the potentially corrupting position of applying laws it has made. Both steps are essential if the rule of law is to become a reality. When Locke turns to this issue in the *Second Treatise*, the answer seems at first the same, at least with regard to the fundamental principle of parliamentary supremacy. As his argument proceeds, however, Locke paints a more nuanced picture, one much more favorable to the traditional prerogatives of the English monarchy.[4]

The "federative" power, Locke explains, is "much less capable to be directed by antecedent, standing, positive laws than the executive, and so must necessarily be left to the prudence and wisdom of those whose hands it is in to be managed for the public good." This suggests that executive power proper is purely instrumental or under the direction of the laws or the legislature. But Locke soon speaks of the need for "prudence," "discretion," and "choice" in those in executive positions, regardless of whether they happen to be dealing with domestic or foreign affairs, and he even allows the executive a share in the legislative power—a veto, like that enjoyed by English kings. Part of the reason for this, it appears, is to arm the executive with sufficient authority to convene and dismiss Parliament and even to regulate membership in it when its representative character becomes compromised as a result of "corruption or decay."[5]

But even this is not the full story. Since "in some governments the lawmaking power is not always in being, and is usually too numerous and so too slow for the dispatch requisite to execution, and because also it is impossible to foresee, and so by laws to provide for, all accidents and necessities that may concern the public, or to make such laws as will do no harm if they are executed with an inflexible rigor on all occasions and upon all persons that may come in their way, therefore there is a latitude left to the executive power to do many things of choice which the laws do not prescribe." This power Locke calls "prerogative"—the power to act "according to discretion for the public good, without the prescription of the law and sometimes even against it." In case we are tempted to give too Machiavellian a gloss to all this, Locke is careful to emphasize the executive's option of pardoning those under threat of the law's "inflexible rigor."[6] Nevertheless, it is disconcerting to hear him speak approvingly in this context of those "godlike princes" for whom the people's safety is the highest law. What standard permits the people to distinguish between good or necessary and abusive exercises of prerogative? Locke candidly admits there can be none: the people themselves must decide in any particular case whether their interests have been served by their leader's actions; if they decide otherwise, however, their only recourse is to "appeal to heaven"—to take up arms.[7]

Locke's argument is at one level a clever compromise between Whig and Tory views of the English monarchy—a fact which helps account for its extraordinary influence. At another level, though, it can be read as a compromise between emerging constitutionalist thought and Machiavelli, one designed to defuse the challenge of Machiavellianism precisely by borrowing its fundamental insight into the indispensable functional role of "princes" in every regime. Whether Locke really pulls this off is another question. The fundamental problem is that prerogative remains a potentially disruptive or subversive element of executive power, one that is exercised only against and not within the constitutional framework. That the English model did not survive the eighteenth century is, from this perspective, not altogether surprising.[8]

More successful, and more interesting for our purposes, is the American model. The presidential office that emerged from the debates of 1787 as a linchpin of the American Constitution was novel in many respects. The United States itself posed a novel challenge: traditionally, republics were thought to be sustainable only in small territories, but the new nation was the largest republic since Rome. Moreover, given its federal or quasi-federal character, the central government had only limited powers. Given also the widespread hostility to monarchy in a population—steeped in any event in Whig or constitutionalist political ideas—that had just wrested its freedom from the British Crown in a long war, one might have anticipated that any chief executive office created under the new regime would be granted very limited if not simply symbolic powers.

In fact, of course, what the founders created was a uniquely powerful republican executive. The office they designed was intended to impart energy, unity, and force to the machinery of government—qualities notoriously missing in the makeshift confederacy of the Revolutionary period (and in many of the governments of the states). It was directly elected by the people, and like Locke's executive, armed with a veto that provided it institutional protection against the legislative branch and a checking role in the process of legislation. Also like Locke's executive, it was given command of the nation's armed forces and a special role in the conduct of foreign policy generally.

There was surprisingly little discussion of the presidency during the Constitutional Convention. (Strikingly, the delegates seemed to have assumed until very late in the day that the president would be elected by Congress.) The founders' thinking on this critical subject therefore has to be sought primarily in *The Federalist*, the authoritative analysis and defense of the Constitution by "Publius" (Alexander Hamilton, James Madison, and John Jay), originally published as a series of newspaper articles during the ratification debates.[9] Particularly illuminating is the series of papers (nos. 67–77) by Alexander Hamilton on the executive power. But it is useful to begin with some account of Madison's famous discussion (in no. 10) of "faction" as the characteristic disease of republican government and how the proposed Constitution would help to control it.[10]

By permitting men to give vent to their opinions, pursue their particular interests, and form associations with others of similar outlook, the very liberty of republican societies encourages the growth of parties or factions. As Madison uses the term, *faction* is not simply what we would today call an "interest group" but rather "a number of citizens, whether amounting to a majority or minority of the whole, who are united and actuated by some common impulse of passion, or of interest, adverse to the rights of other citizens, or to the permanent and aggregate interests of the community." Faction so understood is deeply rooted in human nature. Not only divergent material interests, but "a zeal for different opinions concerning religion, concerning government, and many other points, as well of speculation as of practice; an attachment to different leaders, ambitiously contending for preeminence and power; or to persons of other descriptions, whose fortunes have been interesting to the human passions, have, in turn, divided mankind into parties, inflamed them with mutual animosity, and rendered them much more disposed to vex and oppress each other, than to co-operate for their common good." Note also that a faction is not necessarily a disaffected minority. The majority itself can behave factiously if it invades the liberties of others or acts in ways fundamentally destructive of the larger community. Because it seems to be sanctioned by the very principle of democracy, majority faction is the most dangerous and the greatest challenge for theorists of republican governance.

The most common and durable source of factions, Madison tells us, has been "the various and unequal distribution of property." Majority faction in this context is simply another name for classical democracies like Athens, where the poor threaten to oppress the wealthy few. But Madison's view of the nature of socioeconomic conflict should not be confused with a Marxist-style vision of class struggle. In the first place, as is clear from the passage just cited, human "passions" play a role in the development of parties that is plainly independent of material "interests"; and leaders—Madison is no doubt thinking particularly of the classical demagogues—play a key role in mobilizing those passions.[11] Secondly, Madison emphasizes differences not only in degrees but also in kinds of property. Just as the poor do not necessarily combine factiously just because they are poor, neither do the rich, for they are internally divided according to whether their wealth comes from land, trade, manufacturing, banking, and the like. Nevertheless, at least in modern times, clashing economic interests remain front and center on the political stage. As Madison strikingly puts it, "The regulation of these various and interfering interests forms the principal task of modern legislation, and involves the spirit of party and faction in the necessary and ordinary operations of government."

It might be imagined that what is needed most of all in a modern republic is a strong and capable executive who could arbitrate among these competing forces. Yet, Madison continues, "It is vain to say, that enlightened statesmen will be able to adjust these clashing interests, and render them all subservient to the public good. Enlightened statesmen will not always be at the helm." The national leadership cannot be expected to have the wisdom necessary to aggregate complex economic preferences and ought not have the political authority to impose its views. The answer has to lie elsewhere.

The fundamental remedy to the problem of minority faction is a republican political order—one where the people at large are in control of the key levers of government. But what is the remedy to the problem of majority faction? It flows from two of the key features of the American constitutional system. The first is representation. The effect of this device—one of the capital discoveries of the "new political science"—is "to refine and enlarge the public views, by passing them through the medium of a chosen body of citizens, whose wisdom may best discern the true interest of their country, and whose patriotism and love of justice, will be least likely to sacrifice it to temporary or partial considerations." The second is the extent and diversity of the nation itself. "Extend the sphere, and you take in a greater variety of parties and interests; you make it less probable that a majority of the whole will have a common motive to invade the rights of other citizens; or, if such a common motive exists, it will be more difficult for all who feel it to discover their own strength, and to act in unison with each other." In a large republic like the United States, "the influence of factious leaders may kindle a flame within their particular states, but will be unable to spread a general conflagration." People and elites alike are divided against themselves in a system of what might be called societal checks and balances that dilutes the force of class conflict and helps sustain a system of balanced national institutions. There is, then, Madison claims, a "republican remedy for the diseases most incident to republican government."

Yet none of this should be taken simply as an argument against the need for leadership in republics. The clash of economic interests in an extended republic does not automatically lead to a harmonious result. There is no "hidden hand" guaranteeing the equitable outcome of economic behavior, because human passions regularly interfere with the free play of the market. This is why Madison says that "protection of different and unequal faculties of acquiring property" is "the first object of government," and why he can speak of the "regulation" of "these various and interfering interests" as the principal task of "modern legislation." Economic statecraft is a central aspect of modern republican government. The only question is to what degree such statecraft has an executive component.

Madison is often taxed as an undemocratic elitist because of his claim that elected representatives in a republic are likely to have a greater share of wisdom, patriotism, and love of justice than the people they serve. In fact, however, this claim is immediately qualified: "On the other hand, the effect may be inverted. Men of factious tempers, of local prejudices, or of sinister designs, may by intrigue, by corruption, or by other means, first obtain the suffrages, and then betray the interests of the people." This danger is mitigated in a large republic, where "it will be more difficult for unworthy candidates to practice with success the vicious arts, by which elections are too often carried"; it is by no means eliminated. But there is a further question, one concerning not so much the wisdom of representative bodies as their competence to conduct the public business. As we shall see, Publius is emphatic in calling attention to the limitations of collective governance and the importance of efficiency in "administration." The general point that should be made here is that Publius's expectations concerning the role of elites in democratic politics are far from utopian. As we have learned from Machiavelli, however, to the extent that leadership cannot be reliably provided by elites, a place needs to be found for the princely executive.

Alexander Hamilton's brief treatise on the presidency in *The Federalist* remains a key document of American constitutionalism and an indispensable beginning point for thinking about executive leadership in contemporary democracies.[12] Hamilton begins with a discussion of the mode of election of the president. The Electoral College mechanism ensures both that the president is elected by the people independently of Congress and that elections are mediated by a body of preeminent citizens that is both capable of discerning merit in candidates and, because of its temporary nature, little inclined to "cabal, intrigue, and corruption." This process favors the selection of the most qualified candidates. "It will not be too strong to say that there will be a constant probability of seeing the station filled by characters pre-eminent for ability and virtue." Significantly, the immediate conclusion Hamilton draws from this probability of worthy presidents is its contribution to the administration of the country. For "the true test of good government is, its aptitude and tendency to produce a good administration."[13]

Yet Hamilton's case for a strong executive does not rest primarily on the argument from administrative competence. Rather, the key requirement in the design of the presidency, and indeed in the design of the new nation as a whole, is what Publius calls "energy." In a democratic republic, it is more important that the chief executive show vigor and initiative in pursuing the challenges of his office than that he be outstandingly prudent or virtuous. (Consider the Trump presidency from this perspective.) As Madison had said, it cannot be expected that "enlightened statesmen will always be at the helm" in a democracy. It can be assumed, however, that ambitious and capable men will seek and gain high office. But is this not in effect to invite a seizure of power by the potential prince in Machiavelli's faction-ridden republic? Publius's response is that because of the separated nature of the powers of government under a constitutional regime, "ambition will counteract ambition," so that public liberty will in the end be preserved.[14]

Executive energy presupposes two things above all. The first is unity; the second, duration. A divided executive is a weak and potentially fractious one. Only when a single person is in charge can the government perform executive tasks with "decision, activity, secrecy, and dispatch," in Hamilton's telling formulation. Moreover, dividing the executive power among several persons "tends to conceal faults, and destroy responsibility." There can be no real accountability for executive behavior when the public cannot tell which of their leaders ought to be blamed for misguided policies or who should have the credit for wise ones. The truth of this insight should be obvious to anyone who follows the maneuverings of American senators or congressmen today as they try to take or evade credit for particular legislative measures.[15]

As for duration, one of the great limitations of republican government in the past was its tendency to impose short terms of office (one year being very common) and to limit or prohibit reelection. Under such circumstances, magistrates had difficulty accomplishing anything of note and had few incentives to try. In the original Constitution, presidents were of course limited to four-year terms, but they could be reelected indefinitely. (Partly under the influence of the precedent established by George Washington, no president before Franklin Roosevelt even sought to serve more than two terms; after FDR's death, the Twenty-second Amendment formalized the two-term limit.) Hamilton makes the obvious points that long tenure in office helps to form experienced leaders and provide stability and continuity to government policy, particularly in times of national emergency.[16] More intriguingly, he also argues that this provision is vital not only for attracting persons of the highest quality to seek the presidency in the first place but for giving them incentives for good performance. "Even the love of fame, the ruling passion of the noblest minds, which would prompt a man to plan and undertake extensive and arduous enterprises for the public benefit, requiring considerable time to mature and perfect them, if he could flatter himself with the prospect of being allowed to finish what he had begun, would, on the contrary, deter him from the undertaking, when he foresaw that he must quit the scene before he could accomplish the work."[17]

What is remarkable here, in the first place, is Hamilton's assumption not only that ambitious men should be tolerated in democratic politics but that their participation ought to be actively encouraged. But even more striking is the apparent reason for this—a democracy's need for leaders with the ability to see farther than others and the tenacity to "plan and undertake extensive and arduous enterprises for the public benefit" over a period of many years.[18]

Why this need? Although Publius does not answer this question explicitly, there seem to be two sorts of answers. The first has to do with the president's role in foreign affairs. From a contemporary perspective, the president's preeminence in the conduct of foreign policy is usually presumed to be a reflection of his ability to function well in sudden crises or contingencies. Much more emphasis is given by Publius to the question of the making of treaties. Hamilton himself admits that this power is neither legislative nor executive in the ordinary sense of these terms. He also argues that the importance of the function, and the operation of treaties as laws, suggests the need for some participation in them by the legislative branch; and he admits further that it would be dangerous (because of his exposure to bribery) to give the president sole responsibility for it. But the president is to be given a role nonetheless. The reason seems to be that "accurate and comprehensive knowledge of foreign politics; a steady and systematic adherence to the same views; a nice and uniform sensibility to national character; decision, *secrecy*, and dispatch" (emphasis in original) are more likely to be found in a president and his assistants than in any "variable and numerous" collective body. This remark, though explicitly made with reference to the House of Representatives, inescapably applies to the Senate as well, in spite of the formal role granted the latter in treaty-making and the confirmation of ambassadors. Commentators have too often been misled into thinking that the foreign policy responsibilities assigned the president and the Senate under the Constitution are coequal. In fact, there seems little doubt that Hamilton and the founders generally tended to view foreign policy—on the model of Locke's "federative" power—as a distinct and preeminently executive function.[19]

The second answer to the question raised above has to do with the president's domestic role or roles. Taking into account Madison's argument concerning the extent and diversity of the United States as well as the fact that the president (with his vice president) is the only official elected by all of the people, a good case can be made that the president is likely to be uniquely positioned beyond faction or sectional interest and with a perspective on developments throughout the nation that is more comprehensive than that of federal legislators, not to mention state officials. Some such view seems implicit in the constitutional requirement that the president from time to time make available to Congress "information of the state of the Union." Moreover, as the chief administrator and enforcer of the nation's laws, the president is likely to be more sensitive to failure in the system of justice and to developing threats to the political and constitutional order. Again, the presidential role in these areas is sometimes narrowly conceived as a domestic emergency function (which is not to say that this was not a significant concern of the founders—Shay's Rebellion was a fresh memory). But something larger is at issue.

As suggested earlier, Publius did not conceive of the extended republic as a self-regulating system. Government, and in particular a federal government, is necessary in order to "regulate" the diversity of private interests and thereby to manage if not forestall the emergence of faction. Properly understood, that task is one that requires, in Madison's words, "taking into view indirect and remote considerations." In particular, it requires sensitivity to economic developments and their long-term impact on the relation among the various classes, interests, and sectional groupings of the nation. But it also requires a certain sensitivity to issues of ideology and culture. Presidents are uniquely advantaged in this regard. They are well situated to take the broader and the longer view, and they are uniquely able to exercise a leadership that automatically enjoys a measure of national legitimacy. They can initiate legislation or legislative projects to address what they see as regime-threatening economic concerns, as did Jackson in the bank controversy of the 1830s or FDR in response to the Great Depression a century later. They can use the presidency as a "bully pulpit" to shape an intellectual and political climate favorable to needed reforms, as did both Roosevelts and Ronald Reagan. Presidents can even with propriety stand against the popular will in cases where it threatens "the permanent and aggregate interests of the community." In short, to put the matter in the language of statecraft, they can exercise a form of leadership that seeks to manage national elites and popular passions in the interests of ensuring the long-term health and safety of the regime.[20]

Some will object that such a conception of the American presidency leaves far behind the limited presidency provided for in the Constitution of 1787. No one can argue that it is the conception held by all of the founders or every president. Nevertheless, it reflects the fundamental logic of the constitutional presidency. Lincoln fastened on the "necessary and proper" clause of the Constitution's grant of presidential powers to justify his recourse to extraordinary measures during the Civil War; but Hamilton had already said that "the circumstances that endanger the safety of nations are infinite; and for this reason, no constitutional shackles can wisely be imposed on the power to which the care of it is committed."[21] Hamilton's long tenure as secretary of the Treasury and close adviser to Washington demonstrates the centrality of economic statecraft in the early Republic. Woodrow Wilson was the first president to make systematic use of the Constitution's license or requirement that the president make suggestions bearing on legislation to the Congress; but the qualified veto, if nothing else, shows that the Constitution intended the president to have a significant role in the legislative process.

None of this is to suggest that there has not been considerable controversy over the role of the presidency in the American constitutional order. At various times, the presidency has been seen both as a dangerously weak institution and as a threat to republican liberty. Lincoln's suspension of habeas corpus (allowing the Union to imprison thousands of Confederate sympathizers without formal charges), FDR's court-packing scheme, and Nixon's claims to executive privilege (to cite the most obvious examples) have been roundly denounced as gross constitutional usurpations. Presidents have been criticized since the early days of the Republic for ignoring congressional prerogatives in committing the nation to war. The presidents of the late nineteenth century, on the other hand, are still routinely castigated for excessive subservience to Congress and to the lords of industrial capitalism. Controversies continue to simmer today over the extent of presidential prerogatives, particularly in the areas of war powers, covert action, and executive privilege, reflecting the larger ideological split within the political class over the proper uses of American power in the contemporary world.[22]

It can be argued that a broad consensus nevertheless exists in the United States concerning the character of the presidential office. Americans expect their presidents to be leaders of the nation in peace as in war. Accordingly, where controversies arise, presidents are generally given the benefit of the doubt. On the other hand, no one believes that American presidents should enjoy "prerogative" in Locke's sense, that is, a license to ignore or defy the law in the interests of serving the broader public good. The presidency, in the ambition and energy it invites and indeed requires, bears more than a passing resemblance to its Machiavellian original. But the founders showed how it was possible for republics to live with a powerful prince within the confines of the law and under a stable constitutional order.

That the presidency can be criticized both for strength and weakness suggests that there is a kind of indeterminateness or ambiguity to the office. Given the widespread hostility to monarchy at the time of the founding, it is not at all surprising that the drafters of the Constitution were reluctant to spell out (or even privately debate) the exact parameters of the presidency, or even to explain what they understood by executive power in general. Rather, they seem to have been content to establish an office strong enough to defend itself against two coequal branches, and armed with authority sufficient to allow it to assume or assert its leadership role should circumstances require. This is not necessarily a bad thing. Indeed, the flexibility it provides can be seen as part of the genius of the American Constitution.

The practice of modern political leaders, and particularly American presidents, it has been suggested, reflects a kind of "doctrine" of executive power that can only be properly understood against its Machiavellian backdrop.[23] The core of this doctrine is precisely "the ambivalence of executive power." The American presidency, the model for the modern constitutional executive, is neither a strong nor a weak institution but a deliberate combination of the two, each reinforcing the other. Paradoxically, the presidency can be strong precisely because it is weak. Because of its formal subordination to the people and the legislative power, it is seen fundamentally as an instrument of others or as not fully responsible for its actions and therefore can disarm to a degree the resentments of those adversely affected by them. At the same time, its strength enables its weakness.

If the modern prince is a peculiar compound of weakness and strength, though, how stable is that compound? Or to put it another way, how successful has modern constitutionalism proven in practice in maintaining the dynamic equilibrium prescribed by its own theory? Has separation of powers, checks and balances, and the rest of the machinery of modern constitutionalism actually worked?

This is a complicated question and one that cannot be addressed solely within the framework of formal political institutions. Among other things, it demands that some attention be paid to the phenomenon of parties. Prior to the eighteenth century, parties were generally considered an endemic disease of republican politics; this view is reflected in Madison's treatment of "faction" in *Federalist* no. 10. That parties can be a normal, respectable, and indeed valuable component of the politics of free societies is a proposition that had to be established by political argument. The original version of such an argument can be found in Machiavelli, but the most influential case for party government is the one articulated by the great English parliamentarian Edmund Burke.[24] For our purposes, the key point concerns the relationship between parties and politicians. For Burke, the great advantage of parties is that they discipline and constrain those who contend for political office. They force ambitious politicians, in other words, to tie themselves to a party program that is tolerably representative of the views and interests of important segments of society, thereby reducing their ability to engage in cynical political maneuvering designed solely to advance their own careers. Understood in this way, parties provide a sort of extra-constitutional check on the executive or would-be executive. (Again, the Trump presidency provides an instructive illustration.) At the same time, however, they also threaten to undermine a state's institutional checks and balances by creating a powerful instrument of executive domination of the legislature.

When Walter Bagehot analyzed the English regime of the 1860s, he was struck by the gulf between the prevailing theory of separated powers and the reality of "fusion" of powers in the emerging system of cabinet government anchored in the House of Commons.[25] In this system, the authority of a prime minister commanding a majority in Parliament was in theory unlimited, subject only to informal rules of consensus within his own cabinet and to the sanction of votes of confidence in the House. At the end of the nineteenth century, this model of democratic constitutionalism had come to be widely admired. Indeed, it was the model looked to by American reformers, above all Woodrow Wilson, who had become dissatisfied with the immobilism of the American system and, in particular, its apparent inability to sustain vigorous presidential leadership.[26] It is far from clear, however, that parliamentary systems are generically superior to the American model as reliable providers of leadership. The leadership performance of the British cabinet in World War I left a great deal to be desired, for example. Winston Churchill, in his account of the origins of World War II and also in his *Marlborough*, which deals with the formative period of party politics in England at the beginning of the eighteenth century, places surprising emphasis on the pernicious effects of parliamentary and party governance on the waging of war and the conduct of foreign policy by British leaders.[27]

There have, however, been fundamental changes in the nature of party politics in Europe, America, and elsewhere in the world in recent years. Generally speaking, parties have lost much of their ideological and organizational cohesion. Instead of providing salutary discipline for aspiring politicians, they have proven increasingly vulnerable to capture and manipulation by charismatic figures of (often) very uncertain political identity—when they are not actually created by such people out of whole cloth. At the same time, with the rise of a modern administrative state, executives have developed a base of power undreamed of by the framers of liberal constitutionalist doctrine. Both of these developments have in turn tended to diminish the power and importance of legislatures.

What is the result? A case can be made that the distinction of functions and separated powers of modern constitutionalist theory no longer describe the realities of contemporary governance. With the (partial) exception of the United States, the legislative function seems increasingly to fall under the domain of the executive. (In the United States, it is not a great exaggeration to say that the executive and judicial branches together have come to play a central if not dominating role in the legislative process, while the Congress seems to exercise its checking function largely by meddling in administrative details that are more properly the responsibility of the executive branch.) This development may vindicate Machiavelli's fundamental argument concerning the indispensability of princely rule in a republic. But it does so at the expense of the liberal constitutionalist solution to Machiavelli's challenge—and perhaps of the very idea of republican government.[28]

IX

DEMOCRACY WITHOUT LEADERS

I s it possible to cope effectively with the complexities of policy-making in the advanced democracies today in the absence of strong executive leadership, not to say of a unified and energetic government? Are there viable alternatives in the contemporary world to the American model, with its crypto-monarchic temptations?

Switzerland is surely an interesting case. It is closer than any nation in the contemporary era to a regime of direct democracy, where fundamental policy decisions are routinely made through popular referenda and executive power is sharply circumscribed. The country is governed at the national level by a Federal Council of seven members chosen by its parliament every four years in accordance with a complex formula designed to preserve a balance between political parties, the major cantons, and the country's three major ethno-linguistic groups. These serve simultaneously as ministers of executive departments and take annual turns acting as "president" of the Swiss Confederation. The Swiss like to boast that they are unable to name this virtually symbolic chief executive at any given time. Some have argued that the current global revolution in information technology holds the potential for transforming contemporary politics through re-creating the conditions of direct democracy as it existed in ancient Athens, a development that could well make the Swiss model of greater interest to others. For the present, however, Switzerland's unique confederal arrangements, reflecting its ancient traditions of communal liberty and identity, seem more an interesting anachronism than a signpost on the way to the politics of the future.

Japan offers another example—baffling in many ways, but highly instructive—of a successful advanced democracy that seems culturally allergic to strong individual leadership. The most striking fact about the history of Japan since time immemorial is the extreme weakness of the ostensibly all-powerful leader—and the reverse side of that coin, the reluctance of the real wielders of power to rule in their own name. The emperor of Japan was for many centuries a figurehead, with real power held by a kind of military governor, the shogun. (In one period, the shogun himself was reduced to being a front man for one of his own advisers.) Today, of course, as throughout the era of the supposed "restoration" of imperial rule following the collapse of the Tokugawa Shogunate in 1867, the emperor is equally powerless.[1]

Who, then, actually governs contemporary Japan? Given its parliamentary system ostensibly based on the Westminster model, the prime minister seems the logical candidate; but the Japanese prime minister almost certainly has less influence in his own country than the head of any other Western government. Is it then the political party or parties supporting him? Yet the Liberal Democratic Party (LDP), which has been in power almost continuously since the early 1950s, has long been split into a number of competing factions; and in any event, most legislation is prepared within the bureaucracy rather than by the Diet (the Japanese parliament). The bureaucrats? The bureaucracy is a fragmented arena of competing fiefdoms. Corporate interests? Yet former officials hold key positions in many Japanese corporations, and the government's informal dominance of the private sector has been variously praised or decried as the key determinant of Japan's economic behavior.

That Japan does not operate on the same principles as the democracies of the liberal West has long been understood by careful observers. In recent years, the question of Japanese exceptionalism has been burdened with much political freight and caused sharp disagreements among political scientists and other observers, as explanations were sought first for the Japanese economic boom of the 1980s, then for the prolonged stagnation of the 1990s and beyond. What can be called the official view in the West (and in Japan itself) is that Japan is essentially a normal liberal democracy with a market economy that functions in ways similar if not identical to Western models. A so-called revisionist view holds to the contrary that Japan represents a distinct model of political economy with a unique political system designed to serve it.[2]

The revisionist school has offered two sorts of accounts of the Japanese political system. The first may be called the "Japan, Inc." model. This holds that behind the apparent disorder of Japanese politics is a well-oiled system of elite governance that is firmly anchored in the state bureaucracy. The Ministry of International Trade and Investment (MITI), the strategic organizer, on this view, of Japan's enormously successful export-led growth of the postwar period, and the Ministry of Finance (MOF), with its control of the national budget as well as the economy more generally, are at the heart of this system. Staffed by the cream of the Japanese educational system, these agencies have exercised extraordinary influence and played an informal but potent coordinating role throughout the bureaucracy itself, in the strategic sectors of the economy, and in the political world. The politicians who fill ministerial positions in the government generally exercise little control over these or other agencies, while legislators tend to be highly dependent on the bureaucracy for substantive policy expertise. At the same time, the strategic placement of retired officials in top positions in the private sector (a practice referred to as the "descent from heaven") and their frequent recruitment into the ranks of the ruling party provide influence on a national scale that is without parallel in other democracies today.[3]

The second model, which might be called "the truncated pyramid," acknowledges the central role played by the bureaucracy, but it also insists that politicians and the private sector are not simply its tools; rather, no one is ultimately in charge. This model invokes the burden of Japanese history, in particular, the effective absence of a Japanese state during the shogunate period, the failure of the Meiji founders of modern Japan fully to remedy this situation, and the rudderless course taken by the government during the decade and more of rising military influence prior to World War II. It holds that the major centers of power in the Japanese system today are semiautonomous and that effective central coordination is lacking. Accordingly, the system can only function through an elaborate process of consensus that seems to make leadership in any recognizable sense difficult if not impossible. It functions nevertheless and, in its own odd, quasi-organic way, provides a degree of social control and strategic direction that is unique among the advanced democracies.[4]

Virtually all observers agree that Japanese political culture puts a very high premium on consensus, conformity, and the avoidance of confrontation. Leadership itself therefore tends to be seen as part of a process of consensus formation. Hence, for example, the phenomenon of Japanese organizational behavior known as *gekokujo*, literally, "rule of senior by junior officials."[5] Caution is warranted in such matters, however. Japan is too often seen in the West in gross caricature as a place of meek conformity and blind attachment to communal values. In fact, a case can be made that Japanese consensus-seeking behavior reflects something quite different: the continuing influence of the samurai tradition of medieval Japan, with its fierce individualism and concern for personal honor. The elaborate rituals, the deference to one's seniors, the concern for maintaining "face" that is so central to Japanese life—all of these are perhaps best understood as mechanisms for controlling powerful individualistic impulses.[6] It was not so long ago that sessions of the Diet regularly featured brawling among its members, and the jockeying for political position among the ambitious faction leaders of the LDP is as intense and ruthless as anywhere. Indeed, factionalism is rife not only in the ruling political party in Japan but within most large organizations.[7]

In the second place, there is also much evidence that Japanese culture is not immutable. Political choice and changing historical circumstance can clearly affect Japanese political mores in significant ways. To cite only one example, senior officials in the Japanese cabinet and bureaucracy—and to some degree prime ministers as well—have tended to become more assertive in recent years in response to growing pressures for intra- and cross-departmental coordination. Moreover, there has been something of a reaction in Japan itself against the pretensions of the bureaucracy, and the MOF in particular has seen its power and prestige significantly diminished.

The Japanese people have also demonstrated much dissatisfaction not only with the ruling party and its recent standard-bearers but with the incapacity of the political class generally to deal with Japan's current economic woes and the sclerotic nature of the system as a whole. The election of the highly unconventional Junichiro Koizumi as prime minister in 2001 was a clear expression of these attitudes. To understand the prospects for leadership under Koizumi or his successors, however, it is necessary to take a brief look at the evolution of the Japanese political system since 1970 or so.

An observer of the Japan of 1970 would not have been far wrong in describing the Japanese regime as rule by the mandarins of the bureaucracy in the name of constitutional democracy. Ironically, Japan after 1945 was actually less pluralistic in key respects than prewar ("authoritarian") Japan, thanks to the efforts of the American occupiers to break the political power of the armed forces and the big corporations in order to extirpate Japanese militarism; the primary if unintended beneficiary of these measures was the state bureaucracy. The Liberal Democratic Party was an extension of the regime whose primary purpose was to keep the Communists and Socialists from power and provide a façade of democratic accountability. The regime's success in engineering Japan's great postwar economic boom, however, stifled potential opposition to this arrangement and cemented a national constituency (primarily among farmers and the small business sector) for the LDP that has ensured its dominance of Parliament ever since.

Enter Kakuei Tanaka, without question the most remarkable political figure of postwar Japan. A highly intelligent and ambitious man of modest social origins who (like the current American president) had made a fortune in the construction business before entering politics, Tanaka worked his way into the senior ranks of the LDP and the government, eventually taking over the critical Ministry of Finance and later MITI. In 1972, after an intra-party coup against his former mentor and LDP faction leader Eisaku Sato, Tanaka became prime minister. Then, in a scenario reminiscent of Machiavelli's *Prince*, Tanaka set out to transform Japanese politics by taming the power of the bureaucratic elite and remaking the LDP into a vehicle for the exercise of his personal leadership. Tanaka's populist style reflected a larger vision that sought to put Japan's new wealth to work for the people—notably, in a grandiose scheme for redeveloping the nation's infrastructure, which he promoted under his own name. At the same time, money was the mechanism Tanaka used to extend his control of the LDP. Taking another leaf out of *The Prince*,[8] he began to channel large amounts of cash obtained from kickbacks and bribes from companies doing business with the government into constituency services for favored LDP candidates. In this way, he was able to create a faction qualitatively different in size and political strength from all others—Tanaka's *gudan* ("army corps"), as it came to be called. Like Machiavelli's new prince, Tanaka was determined to rely only on his own arms.

Tanaka's premiership demonstrated decisive leadership in a number of areas (notably, foreign relations, where Tanaka moved forcefully to recognize the People's Republic of China), and it reestablished the slipping popularity of the Liberal Democratic Party with Japanese voters. Tanaka showed a willingness and ability to impose himself on the state bureaucracy that was novel in Japanese politics. This ability reflected partly Tanaka's own high intelligence and his mastery of the bureaucracy in the course of his own rise to power; but it also owed much to his rewriting of the rules governing Japan's "money politics." Scandal surrounding LDP finances was hardly new in the 1970s, but Tanaka's reckless and virtually public extortions were not sustainable. Forced to resign in the face of newspaper exposés in the fall of 1974, Tanaka was later indicted and arrested when the notorious Lockheed bribery scandal broke in the United States in 1976. In spite of being subject to a series of trials and appeals, however, Tanaka was by no means finished as a political force. Although he had actually resigned from the LDP, Tanaka continued to build his faction, and he used his very considerable influence behind the scenes, in a reversion to the ancient pattern, to crown prime ministers and manipulate intra-party politics.[9]

Yasuhiro Nakasone headed a small LDP faction and could never have reached the premiership on the strength of it alone. His alliance with the Tanaka *gudan*, rather than his own leadership style or program, explains both how he became prime minister and the relatively independent role he succeeded in creating for himself. Much of the reason for Nakasone's elevation had to do with foreign affairs, and in particular the felt need to repair relations with the United States, damaged under the stewardship of the particularly inept Zenko Suzuki. Nakasone, who had headed the Self-Defense Agency and was eager to strengthen Japan's international role and standing, quickly developed an unprecedented personal relationship with President Reagan and stepped up cooperation with the United States against the Soviet threat in the Pacific; at the same time, he sought to evoke Japanese nationalism and patriotism in more overt ways than any of his predecessors. All of this generated a certain amount of controversy, but Nakasone nonetheless remained extraordinarily popular at home, in spite—or because—of the fact that his leadership style more nearly resembled the straightforward and aggressive manner of American politicians than anything in the experience of ordinary Japanese.

Nakasone lasted for five years as prime minister, an unprecedented run. Normally, Japanese prime ministers do not serve more than two years, and much of their time is devoted to preparing their party for the (very frequent) elections the system requires and fending off challenges to their leadership from other LDP factions. Nakasone was a determined activist, and his tenure in office and virtually assured political support enabled him to undertake a variety of reforms and policy initiatives. He fully understood the problem posed by the bureaucracy and took measures to curb it, first by appointing unusually strong cabinet ministers, but also by strengthening his personal staff, creating a new Management and Coordination Agency headed by a highly capable official with close ties to Tanaka, and establishing advisory boards made up of top businessmen, academics, and retired bureaucrats to provide him with independent policy advice. Nakasone likened these changes, with pardonable if revealing exaggeration, to the reforms following the Meiji Restoration: they point to his ambition (privately confided in 1985) to be a president-type prime minister along the lines of Reagan or Thatcher.[10]

In spite of its promise, however, the Nakasone era produced little of lasting note. A major Nakasone initiative to reform the Japanese educational system encountered stiff bureaucratic resistance and was fruitless. While it is fair to say that Tanaka had effected a significant and permanent shift of power from the bureaucracy to the LDP, the effect of this shift was not necessarily to strengthen the prime minister. Members of Parliament with expertise in certain areas (so-called *zoku*—"policy tribes") had become a more important part of the decision-making process, but they tended to collude with bureaucrats and interested parties in the private sector to block serious reform. Tanaka's incapacitating stroke in 1985 effectively ended the Nakasone era, while the political system as a whole reverted to the model he had originally created. Real power was in the hands of the LDP magnates who inherited the Tanaka machine—Noboru Takeshita, Shin Kanemaru, and Ichiro Ozawa; a series of virtually ceremonial prime ministers came and went at their pleasure. Eventually, money scandals brought down all three of these

LDP power brokers, thoroughly discrediting the party and opening the way to the temporary triumph of an opposition coalition in the elections of 1993.[11]

Since that time, and in the context of an increasingly stalled and dysfunctional economic system, public and political support for fundamental reforms has steadily grown. In 1993, in a striking apostasy from the machine politics he himself had effectively practiced, Ichiro Ozawa launched a campaign to streamline the electoral system and make the bureaucracy more politically responsive, among other things by creating new senior positions to be filled by political appointees in the American manner.[12] The new mood in the country has clearly contributed to a greater political space for prime ministerial leadership, never wholly absent in any case.[13] Subsequent prime ministers have all sung the tune of reform. The basic competence of the bureaucracy has come into question, and the MOF in particular has seen its vast powers significantly curbed. At the end of the day, however, little finally seems to have changed in these years in the relationship between the bureaucracy, the LDP, private-sector interests, and the political leadership. In spite of its deep unpopularity, no competent alternative to the LDP and no substitute for its traditional money politics have yet emerged.[14]

The weakness of Japanese leadership certainly has more than a little to do with structural political factors—the electoral system, the factionalized character of the LDP, and legal as well as customary limits on prime ministerial authority over the bureaucracy. In this regard, it bears a family resemblance to certain European parliamentary regimes, notably that of Italy.[15] Cultural factors too clearly play a role. Britain and Japan have similar parliamentary-type political systems. But there is a world of difference, for example, between the way parliamentary question time is carried on in the two countries, reflecting deep differences in education and in the role of discussion and debate in their respective political cultures. British prime ministers, their skills honed in constant parliamentary exchanges, tend to be extraordinarily articulate; Japanese prime ministers (with rare exceptions like Nakasone and Koizumi) quite the opposite. Indeed, what is prized in politicians in Japan is not only not clarity of expression; it is the practiced ability to obfuscate unpleasant truths. Politicians in the West are certainly not strangers to the art of the spin. But political communication in Japan amounts to a kind of "management of reality" that has no real equivalent in the other advanced democracies.[16] This works directly against the effective exercise of political leadership.

At what is arguably a more fundamental level, however, Japan's leadership deficit reflects the dominant position in Japanese society of a highly homogeneous and cohesive meritocratic elite.[17] This elite, the functional successor of the long-extinct samurai class of medieval Japan, retains much of the psychology though not the outward trappings of a premodern aristocracy, with the strong sense of honor and face that is typical of such societies. Traditional aristocracies exhibit a fundamental paradox. They are sensitive and deferential to distinctions of rank; yet in another sense they are fiercely egalitarian.[18] This appears to be the truest explanation of the Japanese leadership allergy. The failure of contemporary political science to appreciate any of this reflects its congenital neglect of history and, more specifically, its insensitivity to the aristocratic dimension of traditional societies.[19]

Clearly, Japan offers little in the way of a model of contemporary leadership except in a negative sense. None of this is meant to suggest, however, that the Japanese are forever mired in a system that is manifestly dysfunctional in the contemporary world. What we have witnessed over the last five decades in Japan, under the impact of Tanaka's Machiavelli-style challenge to traditional elite governance, is very probably a period of transition in the direction of a society and style of leadership that is more conventionally Western. Unfortunately, Tanaka managed only to corrupt the old order, not to institute the new.

X

AUTOCRATIC DEMOCRACY

In his famous history of the Peloponnesian War, Thucydides says of Athens in the age of Pericles that it was a democracy in name only, in actuality rule by a single man. Even a democracy as jealous as Athens was of the prerogatives of its own leaders could, it seems, permit one of them to gain a position of authority in the state comparable to that of traditional monarchs.[1] Today, leaders in democracies generally enjoy institutional powers much superior to Pericles's (who was only one of a board of ten generals elected annually), and the resources they can call upon, both formal (an immense state apparatus) and informal (party financial and other support), are greater still. It is hardly surprising, then, if contemporary democracies should succumb from time to time to what might be called the autocratic temptation.

In fact, the general trend in democracies today seems to be in the direction, if anything, of a further strengthening of the executive element, especially at the expense of legislatures. This trend appears most obviously in the growing appeal of directly elected chief executives, whether in hybrid presidentialist regimes like France or in more traditional parliamentary systems (Israel is a notable example). It is also evident in the growth of administrative staffs and bureaucratic coordinating mechanisms answerable to the chief executive personally. Finally, it is a feature of many of the newly emerging democracies of the developing world or the former Soviet bloc. Is this trend a good thing or not? Does it provide needed "energy" to the overall political system, as *The Federalist* predicted? Or does it suffocate and enervate other governing elements, like the French monarchy of the ancien régime?

It is not clear that any useful general answer can be given to this question, since it depends on a host of factors that vary radically in time and place—not least, the character and personality of the leader. Nevertheless, it is worth examining at some length two advanced contemporary democracies that have a marked autocratic flavor: France and Singapore. Do these countries provide in any sense a model of executive leadership that has advantages compared with typical parliamentary systems or with American constitutionalism?

The creation of the Fifth Republic is a milestone in modern French history. The Third and Fourth Republics, the regimes that governed France from the fall of Napoleon III in 1870 until 1958, were dominated by Parliament and parties. Charles de Gaulle, who rallied the nation when it was defeated and occupied by the Germans in 1940 and saw it through to ultimate victory in World War II, became convinced that revitalizing French political life after the war required a major reform of its constitutional arrangements so as to provide greater governmental stability, continuity, and direction. De Gaulle's reform program, first laid out in a speech shortly after he left office in 1946, had little immediate impact. An opportunity came, however, during the protracted political crisis stemming from the Algerian revolution of the 1950s. The constitution of the Fifth Republic, endorsed in a popular referendum in 1958, was the price for de Gaulle's return to power in order to avert a looming coup d'état or civil war. Its most important feature was an office of the presidency with real powers—including, notably, sweeping powers to deal with national emergencies, the right to dismiss Parliament, and the right to call for a referendum. This was to be overlaid on the traditional French parliamentary system and charged with the overall mission of maintaining the unity of the nation from a vantage point above everyday partisan politics. Following a constitutional amendment in 1962, the president has been directly elected by the people. De Gaulle himself held the presidency throughout its formative first decade and shaped the new regime in ways that have proven surprisingly permanent given the eclipse of Gaullism as a political movement. Indeed, de Gaulle is a striking example of the lasting impact a founding leader can have not only on the institutions of a regime but on its defining spirit or culture.[2]

Much commentary on the political system of the Fifth Republic has centered on the question of the relationship between president and prime minister, particularly when these offices are held by individuals of different parties (a situation referred to as "cohabitation"). At first sight, a divided executive of this sort, each enjoying an independent popular mandate and with no clearly defined sphere of authority, seems a recipe for the kind of weakness foreseen and feared by the American founders. Especially during periods of cohabitation, high-level French decision-making has certainly given evidence of confusion. Yet the fundamental reality of the current system is the overweening power of the presidency. Well before de Gaulle left office, the monarchic tendencies of his regime were becoming apparent.[3] Far from dissipating, however, they have only become more pronounced, even—or perhaps one should say particularly—during the long reign (1981–95) of socialist François Mitterrand.

In a penetrating (and entertaining) critique of the governance of France in the Mitterrand era, the onetime socialist Jean-François Revel attempts to unravel the paradox at the heart of French politics—the "ineffectuality" of the all-powerful presidential office. "The presidency of the Republic," he claims, "is today what is responsible for France not being governed. The presidency does not work, and prevents all the rest from working."[4] How is this possible?

The key points in Revel's indictment are as follows. First, the Parliament has lost any real role in initiating legislation or in choosing or dismissing governments. These are functions performed in the Élysée Palace—by the president and his advisers.[5] Nor is the president answerable to Parliament or indeed to the people, except when he himself stands for office, since he never feels it necessary to resign after a lost referendum or a poor showing in local or European elections. The president responds only to "the media and the street." Second, the prime minister, far from being a powerful competitor to the president, has come to play a peculiar and deliberately ambiguous role: though enjoying little real power, he is left with enough apparent authority to be useful to the president by serving as a kind of lightning rod or safety fuse, melting conveniently when the president takes political heat. Third, the president is increasingly involved in managing every facet of French life. There is still a widely shared perception that the president tends to restrict his policy role to a so-called reserved domain of foreign and security matters, leaving most issues of domestic and economic policy to the prime minister and his cabinet. The truth is, however, that while the president is particularly jealous of his prerogatives in the security arena, he has never hesitated to intervene in other policy matters of interest to him. And in fact, his role both in the budget process and in the appointment of officials of all kinds has grown significantly, as has his involvement in sensitive domestic policy areas such as culture, public works, and the national media. Under the constitution of the Fifth Republic, the president's appointment power is also virtually absolute throughout the judicial system.

How has all of this affected the actual functioning of the French political system? Instead of enhancing its performance, the result is very nearly the opposite. Sheltered from criticism and challenge, the president tends to lose touch with the country and its problems and lacks incentives to address them seriously. The method of governing is a mixture of placid authoritarianism and, in moments of social unrest, sudden and ill-considered demagoguery. Media opportunities tend to take the place of actual deeds. Hence Mitterrand's poor record in undertaking major projects of reform in spite of controlling the necessary levers of power and a favorable time horizon in which to see them through.

What is more, the personalized power radiating from the office of the presidency is profoundly corrupting. Mitterrand's (admittedly extravagant) tendency to give preferment to cronies, loyalists, party hacks, and other personally favored individuals further undermined the efficient operation of government and created a pervasive courtier mentality. The resulting carnival of self-promotion and self-enrichment was corrupting in the ordinary sense of the term; but it also encouraged more subtle and insidious expressions of corruption, feeding on tendencies already present in French political culture to blur the line between state and private interests.[6] Finally, and in some ways most serious of all, concentration of power in the hands of the president stifled initiative and competence throughout the government. "This is the explanation of the paradox of a strong and stable executive who, however, is unable to govern well. By his excessive weight, the president prevents his ministers from doing it, and however great his own intelligence may be, it's not sufficient to allow him to do it by himself. But he doesn't see that the whole problem stems from him, and so attributing setbacks to the ineptitude of the ministers, he reduces them more and more to inaction, concentrating all the time in his own hands powers he is less and less capable of exercising." The presidency acts like an "incapacitating gas" that paralyzes all around it—including political rivals in the president's own party and even in the opposition, who are consumed with the game of preserving their own standing as future candidates for the only office in the land that can truly reward ambition.[7]

If the French political system as a whole has a certain air of unseriousness about it, part of the reason plainly lies in the powerful role played in French governing institutions by a select and highly trained administrative elite.[8] In this respect, France resembles no other country in the contemporary world so much as Japan, in spite of the radical differences in their respective leadership practices. In some ways closer, however, is the parallel with Singapore, a country which has nurtured an elite class "open to talents" while gaining notoriety for the strong leadership style of its founder and cicerone, Lee Kuan Yew. Yet these nations are far from alike, and the contrast between them holds some interesting lessons.

Singapore has a poor reputation in some quarters today, especially in the United States. Though widely admired for the phenomenal economic success it has enjoyed since its creation in 1959, Singapore tends to be seen as obsessively puritanical, harshly punitive in its approach to law enforcement, and politically authoritarian if not simply antidemocratic. Singapore is the only country in the world that has outlawed chewing gum and enforces the death penalty for drug trafficking. Its government has a history of using legal measures to harass political opponents and discourage negative coverage of the country in the foreign press. Moreover, Singapore is the only non-Communist country to have attempted to mount a serious ideological challenge to the global hegemony of Western (and particularly American) liberalism. Its championing of so-called "Asian values" as an alternative to what it regards as the excessively individualistic and rights-oriented outlook of Anglo-American political thought has generated predictable irritation in academic and government circles in the West, while being warmly welcomed in the People's Republic of China.

Most of what Singapore is today it owes to one man. A brilliant Cambridge-educated lawyer, Lee Kuan Yew built a socialist-oriented political movement that successfully navigated the tricky shoals of communal and class politics in what was then an impoverished outpost of the British Empire, smoothed the transition to an unlikely independence, and then served as Singapore's prime minister for some three decades. In that capacity, he was the architect of the new nation's constitutional system and governing institutions, and developed the sophisticated economic strategy that was directly responsible for Singapore's rapid entry into the first world.[9] Lee's early struggles with the local Communists were a decisive influence in shaping his political outlook—and his political style.[10] He kept Singapore firmly if informally aligned with the United States and Britain throughout the Cold War. At the same time, he remained convinced that the country's ethnic fragility, its continuing vulnerability to the appeal of Communism (particularly among the dominant Chinese community), and the political inexperience of its elites required a more interventionist and paternalistic approach to governance than that prevailing in the liberal West.

This is not the place to assess the overall performance of the government of Singapore under the Lee regime or to adjudicate the various disputes between the regime and its critics. What is necessary to insist on, however, is the seriousness of Singapore's commitment to constitutional democracy. Lee Kuan Yew's education in the law and his early exposure to the values and procedures of parliamentary democracy in the English mode helped form a political culture that is profoundly attached to the rule of law and singularly immune to the cronyism and corruption that is endemic in most of present-day Southeast Asia.[11] And in spite of the fact that his People's Action Party (PAP) has enjoyed virtually absolute control of the Singaporean parliament since the late 1960s, Lee and his political heirs (notably, former prime minister Goh Chok Tong) have gone to considerable lengths to enhance the representative character of this body and preserve its role as a forum of real political debate and decision.[12] They have also undertaken major constitutional reforms designed to limit the power of future governments. These reforms, centering on the creation of an "elected presidency" with certain carefully defined powers, are without parallel in other Western-style democracies today and deserve more attention and respect than they seem to have received outside of Singapore itself.

Under the Westminster model it inherited from the British, Singapore had a largely ceremonial presidency, the incumbents being selected on a rotating basis with a view to their ethnic identity. The idea of an elected president with real powers was originally floated by Lee Kuan Yew in 1984, formally proposed to Parliament as a constitutional amendment in 1990 (the year of Lee's retirement as prime minister), and approved after considerable debate in 1991. Though some suspected that the new office was intended simply as a vehicle for Lee himself, it soon became clear that the government did not at all intend to move in the direction of a presidentialist regime on the French model. The new presidency was designed to perform a reactive or checking function on the government, not to compete with it as an independent source of decision-making authority.[13]

Two purposes above all motivated the constitutional change. The first was to block misuse of the nation's wealth by a future government. "In many countries," according to an official White Paper accompanying the proposed amendment,

> irresponsible governments have mismanaged their nation's finances and economically ruined their countries. This is done to win votes by providing handouts and heavy subsidies which naturally make those governments very popular. Singapore has so far been fortunate to have a responsible government, but with over US $30 billion in the national reserves, the temptation for a future irresponsible government will be very great. Indeed, in times of economic strife and flagging support, an irresponsible government will find this temptation irresistible. Hard-earned money will be spent on short-term vote buying and on popular measures.

The second purpose was to uphold the integrity of the public-service sector of the country and fight tendencies in the government to foster nepotism and corruption.

The new Singaporean presidency has a number of unique features. Candidates do not run as representatives of a political party and must resign any party membership in order to qualify. In addition, they have to satisfy a Presidential Elections Committee that they are persons of "integrity, good character and reputation"; and they must have no less than three years' experience in senior positions in the government or private sector involving the management of financial affairs. The president's powers are considerable, but they are limited almost exclusively to financial and budgetary issues and personnel appointments, and to the use of the veto; quite unlike the Machiavellian-Lockeian executive, he has no emergency powers and is explicitly denied any role in decision-making on defense or security matters. The fundamental responsibility of the prime minister in Parliament for the formulation and execution of government policy is preserved.

It is, then, seriously misleading to view the Singapore experiment through the optic of contemporary France. As indispensable as Lee Kuan Yew was to the emergence of modern Singapore, the regime he created betrays few traces of the monarchism of the Fifth Republic. His own political style was unpretentious, egalitarian, and collegial. Yet Lee was also an unapologetic elitist. Indeed, what is perhaps most distinctive about the current regime in Singapore is the extent to which it is dominated by a cohesive, disciplined, and highly competent political-administrative elite.

Lee himself says that "the single decisive factor that made for Singapore's development was the ability of its ministers and the high quality of the civil servants who supported them." As he makes clear, his own contribution here was fundamental. As Lee and other leaders of the first generation since independence approached retirement, he became increasingly preoccupied with recruiting a younger cadre of professionals into politics and government service. But Lee had come to realize much earlier that a special effort would be needed to identify, recruit, and develop the political talent his party and the country as a whole required. What Lee in effect did was to create his own executive development program. "I systematically scanned the top echelons of all sectors in Singapore—the professions, commerce, manufacturing, and trade unions—to look for men and women in their thirties and forties whom we could persuade to stand as our candidates." Character was as much or more of a concern than raw ability. Psychological tests were given potential PAP MPs to provide insight into their character, intelligence, personal backgrounds, and values. Lee was particularly taken with the recruitment approach of the Shell Corporation, which considered executive promise a function of three qualities—"power of analysis, imagination, and sense of reality"; this approach was adopted for the civil service of Singapore in 1983.[14]

What lessons can be gleaned from these cases for the practice of statecraft today? Probably the most striking is how much difference a single great leader can make in shaping a regime and, through it, the character of a nation. Charles de Gaulle set out in deliberate fashion to correct the ills of republican France by recovering aspects of the traditional monarchy of the ancien régime and, in the process, to heal once and for all the psychological wound inflicted on the French nation by the Revolution of 1789 and its aftermath. Lee Kuan Yew created a nation where none existed or could have been predicted. A second and related lesson concerns the ability of such statesmen to create and shape a competent and public-spirited political-administrative elite.

A final lesson, however, is that the autocratic temptation is difficult to resist, even—indeed, particularly—for leaders of the stature of de Gaulle and Lee. It is easy enough to understand why. Both men were far from ordinary politicians; and their greatness threw into relief the littleness of the political competition. Aristotle observes that in a situation where the virtue and political capacity of a single individual is so great that it is no longer commensurable with that of others, there are only two choices: to exile such a person, or "for everyone to obey [him] gladly, so that persons of this sort will be permanent kings in their cities."[15] The key difference between de Gaulle and Lee, however, is that the latter undertook a sustained effort to create the institutions that would enable him to withdraw gracefully from power while preserving his larger political legacy of nation-building and constitutional construction. In France, deep cultural memories of the divine right of kings ("God" was Mitterrand's affectionate nickname) seem to stand in the way of such a salutary development. All of these are lessons to be taken to heart by the various princes engaged today in the founding or building of democratic regimes in places lacking solid traditions of liberal constitutionalism.

XI

WHAT GOALS
LEADERS PURSUE

S tatecraft, like strategy, is about the relationship of means and ends. Most political leaders are preoccupied most of the time with questions of means and trouble themselves little over questions of ends. This is hardly surprising. Statesmen tend to be practical people. They tend to focus on matters that urgently demand their attention and that respond to their actions. They see little point in worrying about ultimate issues, partly because such issues seem too remote, partly because they are too difficult to do anything about. However, lack of clarity about goals can sometimes have unfortunate practical consequences. It is therefore worth thinking about them more carefully than is usually done.

As Machiavelli teaches, all states need good arms and good laws. Everywhere and always, statesmen have to worry about two things above all: protecting the nation against domestic criminal activity and foreign threats, and ensuring at least a modicum of justice and social peace. "Security" and "order" are convenient shorthand expressions to designate these ends or goals of statecraft.

That statesmen do and should concern themselves with the economic well-being of their societies would also be very generally agreed. Just how far this concern should extend, though, is controversial. While most people and politicians today would no doubt identify "prosperity" as one of the fundamental goals of national policy, such an understanding is by no means universal. The Spartans and the Romans considered material prosperity—"luxury," they would have called it—inimical to the spirit of martial virtue and republican government and actively sought to limit it.[1] On a common interpretation, modern liberalism is virtually defined by government's commitment to respecting the free play of market forces, and therefore to a policy of non-intervention in the domestic economy. While all states throughout history have performed key economic functions, particularly coinage of money and regulation of foreign trade, and have been very interested in taxing productive economic activity for their own purposes, they have generally not taken responsibility for the health of the economy overall. For the most part, government intervention in economic life in earlier times was limited to ensuring a stable food supply and providing emergency assistance in times of famine or other natural disasters.

The idea that government is competent to manage the economy to produce prosperity and its attendant social and political benefits is most directly associated with the socialist tradition of modern times. Yet as is apparent from a document of high liberalism such as *The Federalist*, as has been seen, even the liberal tradition admits that government has a role in "regulating" clashing groups or factions in the name of a public good that is in substantial part defined by the advancement of private economic interests. Today, in spite of the intellectual discrediting of socialism that has resulted from the collapse of the Soviet system and the demonstrated successes of market-oriented economic policies, it is fair to say that there is a consensus throughout the political class in the Western democracies that what might be called the management of prosperity is an inescapable imperative of contemporary statecraft. Even though many recognize the limited nature of the impact politicians can generally have on economic performance, they are resigned to the inevitable calling to account of politicians on this score by democratic electorates. The problem is that politicians too often find it difficult to resist taking credit for good economic news, thus reinforcing this dynamic—and setting themselves up for political failure down the road.

However this may be, prosperity, like security and order, may justly be considered a core goal of statecraft in the sense that it corresponds to basic human needs and is a major preoccupation of most societies at all times. Yet it would be a mistake to suppose that these three goals necessarily dominate the calculations of leaders and determine their key decisions. Culture, historical experience, domestic politics, and the imagination of leaders themselves, together or in combination, not infrequently create an overlay of additional goals or (perhaps better) "missions" that states pursue. These sometimes support core goals, or at least tend to be rationalized in terms of them (especially security); they may also run directly counter to them. Such missions may reflect the historical aspirations of a particular nation or ruling elite; they may also reflect a nation's sense of its calling to promote a particular transnational cause.

Let us call the first of these kinds of mission "national," the second "transnational." The distinction may be illustrated in the American context by the contrast between "Manifest Destiny"—the idea behind the continental expansion of the United States during the nineteenth century—and Woodrow Wilson's claim to "make the world safe for democracy." It is the difference between Wilhelmine Germany's effort to claim for the nation its "place in the sun" as a great power and Hitler's apocalyptic vision of Germany as leader of a racially purified Europe ruling the planet. Communism in the Soviet Union, France's "civilizing mission" in its former African empire, Britain's global naval war against the slave trade in the nineteenth century, America's war on terrorism at the beginning of the twenty-first—all may serve as examples of transnational missions pursued by great powers in recent times. Prominent earlier examples are the Orthodox-inspired vision of Moscow as the "third Rome" or the championing of the Catholic cause in Europe by Philip II of Spain.

Accustomed as we are to thinking of Nazism and Communism simply as ideological tools of state policy, it is important to remember the very real tensions between these movements and the strategic interests of Germany and Soviet Russia respectively. The Nazi obsession with racial purification, by alienating potential allies (particularly the disaffected Ukrainians) among the subject peoples of the Soviet empire, contributed in a major way to Germany's defeat on the Eastern Front in World War II. The early infatuation of the Soviet leadership with world revolution led to a disastrous war with Poland in the early 1920s; and even in more recent times, in spite of the waning of genuine ideological commitment at home, the Soviets were led into dangerous international waters (Cuba in the 1960s, Ethiopia and Afghanistan in the late 1970s) by a felt need to show the Communist flag in support of revolutionary-minded clients in spite of costs and consequences. Philip II's heroic exertions on behalf of the Catholic Church served little purpose other than fatally weakening the foundations of Spanish imperial power.[2]

One way to approach this subject is to think more specifically about the place in statecraft of the intangible factor of national prestige or honor. At first sight, this subject seems as antiquated as the feudal knight or absolute monarch of European history. And yet, considerations of honor explain as well as or better than anything else, for example, the decision by Japanese leaders to attack the United States in December 1941, thus launching a war they knew they were unlikely to win. Similar considerations seem to figure prominently in Germany's naval rivalry with Britain prior to World War I, in Soviet Russia's development of a blue-water navy and commitments in Africa in the 1970s, and in China's unwillingness to tolerate the independence of Taiwan today.

It might be objected that these examples prove nothing about contemporary democracies, which conduct their affairs in a more utilitarian spirit. Yet consider the contrast between France and Britain at the outset of World War II. The sudden collapse of France in May 1940 when invaded by a German army actually weaker by many objective measures than its own left a stain on the national honor, which de Gaulle used effectively to rally a resistance movement and which helps explain much of his prickly behavior during and after the war toward his British and American benefactors.[3] Churchill's decision on becoming prime minister to fight on after the fall of France—against the inclinations of many senior politicians—reflected less a confident calculation of military realities than a sense that a political accommodation with the Germans would irretrievably undermine the nation's morale and perhaps its basic identity. Better, as he once put it, to "go down with all flags flying."

Contemporary political science, in spite of its vaunted value neutrality, has a very pronounced bias when it comes to assessing the goals of states and statesmen. It tends to endorse the pursuit of tangible goals like security and order and to recoil from the intangible goals that underlie national and transnational missions or factors such as honor. Indeed, there is a striking absence of systematic analysis of this latter dimension of statecraft. The reason for this is plain: tangible goals seem reasonable and moderate, both in absolute terms and to the historical actors involved, while the intangible ones too often overreach and threaten other nations, leading to international conflict and war. As the examples of Britain and France in 1940 indicate, however, it is by no means as simple as that. Honor is not merely the personal vanity of a ruling monarch or an aristocratic class. It is intimately bound up with national character and national identity. As such, it is not something that can or should be lightly sacrificed to other goals, no matter how "rational" they may be according to ordinary political calculation.[4]

We have so far discussed intangible goals in mostly traditional terms. Today, however, one could argue that statecraft is in the process of re-defining itself with reference to a new set of national and transnational missions. These involve global concerns such as democratization, human rights and humanitarianism, disarmament, the global environment, terrorism, and outer space, and presuppose cooperation rather than competition between sovereign nations. It is probably fair to say that these concerns exert an appeal to statesmen (at any rate, statesmen of the advanced democracies) that is in inverse proportion to the size and importance of their countries. This is not to say that democratization and human rights, for example, do not carry genuine weight with American statesmen; it is only to suggest that they rarely outweigh in practice more traditional strategic goals such as security or prosperity. Still, there can be no question but that these sorts of concerns loom larger on the world scene than ever before and may eventually succeed in transforming the character of contemporary statecraft in ways that are presently difficult to predict or even imagine.

This being said, it should be added at once that there is some histori-cal precedent for cooperative forms of statecraft in pursuit of a common transnational mission. The crusades of the Middle Ages (still very much alive, as we have seen recently, in the political imagination of the Islamic world) united otherwise warring Christian sovereigns in a common enterprise against the Muslim lords of the Holy Land. During the nine-teenth century, the Holy Alliance united the conservative monarchies of Prussia, Austria, and Russia in opposition to the threat of social and national revolution. The nineteenth century also saw the evolution of a system of diplomacy in Europe that prefigured the formal directorate of great powers created within the United Nations organization after World War II to act as surrogate global policemen. Figures like Churchill looked to the Anglo-American alliance of the twentieth century as the core of a transnational system that would preserve and enlarge the heritage of Christianity and liberal constitutionalism. De Gaulle had similar hopes in the postwar period for the European democracies. The reality behind all of these systems and visions is, as should perhaps go without saying, subject to question. Yet they nevertheless reflected powerful aspirations.[5]

This issue takes practical form today, of course, most prominently in the United Nations. The UN, let it not be forgotten, provides a unique arena for ambitious and capable politicians from lesser states to make their mark on world history. Since the end of the Cold War, the UN has gained greatly in stature and in the scope of the functions it is able to perform, and it has profited from a noticeable erosion in the rigid understanding of state sovereignty that had prevailed in the West since the seventeenth century. The UN secretary general is a figure of global importance who exercises leadership in significant ways independently of the countries whose interests he is supposed to serve, including the great powers represented in the Security Council. There is little reason to anticipate a greatly enhanced role for the UN in global governance anytime in the foreseeable future, particularly given its disappointing performance in a variety of peacekeeping or nation-building missions in recent years. But it would also be a mistake to underestimate the moral authority the organization enjoys, and an extraordinary secretary general just might be able to effect truly transformational changes in the way it functions.

Transnational impulses are clearly alive and well in Europe, as we have already seen. The problem seems to be that the transnational calling of "Europe" lacks both clarity and fundamental appeal. Europeans are hardly galvanized by an external threat, or even by a compelling set of values or a vision of domestic governance. To the extent that (mere) prosperity is the overriding rationale for a continental European confederation or crypto-state, the entire enterprise will remain subject to challenge by states that feel economically disadvantaged by the new arrangements (consider most recently Greece) or that find the loss of their autonomy too steep a price to pay for mere increments of material gain. It is also noteworthy that Europe has not produced any leaders that can remotely be considered to have a pan-European identity or appeal.

To attempt to discuss global transnational missions such as democratization, human rights, or environmental protection would take us too far afield. Suffice it to say that these missions remain both inherently controversial and insufficiently compelling in terms of national interests to force themselves to the top of the agenda of most contemporary statesmen. In the United States, some have signed on to a neo-imperial notion of America's role in the world, one that combines old-fashioned imperial policing in the British manner with the systematic promotion of liberal democracy abroad. This notion has gained in plausibility with the sudden emergence of transnational terrorism as a critical security threat to the United States itself and the main source of resistance to the global hegemony of Western liberalism. It seems certain, however, that ultimate success in the war against terrorism, while undoubtedly requiring American leadership, will depend decisively on international cooperation, especially in areas of largely sovereign prerogative such as law enforcement and cultural policy. What forms this cooperation takes, and how lasting they prove to be, remain to be seen. It is conceivable that they will permanently alter the way all nations today think about their security problems.

XII

WHAT TOOLS LEADERS
HAVE AVAILABLE

Statecraft, to say it again, has to do with ends and means and the relationship between them. Today, it is sometimes asserted that the fundamental challenge of leadership, whether in business or politics, consists in identifying and articulating ends—in crafting a "vision" that can inspire an organization or a nation. Yet the most difficult and demanding aspect of statecraft actually lies in the realm of means, and leadership is needed here even more. Particularly in the context of the highly developed modern state, there is a certain tendency to imagine that the tools available to politicians are well defined and ready to hand, requiring only to be set in motion at their nod. This is far from the case. Leaders face daunting problems in wielding the instruments of statecraft. Not least among them are the political and legal constraints affecting the exercise of executive power in a constitutional democracy. But leaders must also be able to manage effectively the various elites who act as the custodians and operators of these instruments.

There are two sorts of obstacles to the effective employment of the tools of statecraft. The most obvious is the institution or array of institutions leaders have to rely on to implement their goals. These institutions—the court system, for example, or the military—have their own histories and ways of doing things and often prove highly resistant to outside authority. Less obvious but equally problematic is the conceptual world in which these institutions exist. This world is an amalgam of the local culture of the institution itself, intellectual influences in the society at large (or beyond), and not least, the wider culture of the regime. A national military, to use the example just cited, is apt to behave very differently if it is a land or a sea power, if its officers are technically oriented or traditional warriors, and if its civilian masters are elected leaders or autocrats of doubtful legitimacy. Leaders need to have at least a working understanding of such differences. Absent that, not only may the instrument in question prove unresponsive to their wishes; it may turn into an active threat to their own position or political standing.

To cope with this dynamic and often complex conceptual world requires an active and sympathetic exercise of political imagination, as well as a style of leadership that is at once deferential and probing, open to different perspectives yet firmly in command. What is at issue is not intellectual mastery of each element of statecraft. It is rather (to recall Aristotle's understanding of political expertise) an ability to "use" each such element intelligently and prudently or, in other words, to adapt or adjust the means at hand to the ends the leader has in view.

As indicated earlier, study of the tools of statecraft has been relatively neglected by contemporary political science. What is particularly lacking, however, are accounts of the tools of statecraft from the perspective of the requirements of leaders themselves. Probably the most considerable exception to this generalization is the study of civil-military relations. There are good reasons for paying particular attention to civil-military relations as an aspect of statecraft, given the regime-threatening potential of military forces. But the potential for serious political damage is real enough in other areas as well. Only when leaders possess a clear awareness of the problematic aspects of the tools of statecraft will they be able to employ them effectively to achieve national goals.

Machiavelli was a practitioner not only of the military art but also of diplomacy and administration during the period of his service to the Florentine republic, and he was undoubtedly reasonably familiar with most if not all of the other policy instruments that statesmen make use of today. From this point of view, one is entitled to speak of the transhistorical structure of the discipline of statecraft. At the same time, it is important to be sensitive to cultural and national variations in the practice of statecraft. In different times and places, the instruments of statecraft may be differently valued or governed by different operational codes. Differences in the structure of regimes and the composition of ruling elites also produce certain biases in the choice and employment of the tools of statecraft. The strategist Sun Tzu's maxim that victory goes to those who know the enemy and know themselves is in this perspective a profound and enduring truth. Leaders who project their own style of statecraft on foreign adversaries do so at their peril.[1]

The chapters to follow will look briefly and very selectively at the principal instruments of statecraft today, with particular reference to the advanced democracies. In each case, an attempt will be made to understand the ways in which political leaders tend to view and to use these instruments, the difficulties they confront in doing so effectively, and the errors they typically commit along the way. Particular attention will be paid to the various *corps d'élite* that operate the tools of statecraft while bending them to purposes that are not necessarily the purposes of the prince.

XIII

ADMINISTRATION

Alexander Pope's famous couplet puts the case nicely: "For forms of government let fools contest; / That which is best administered is best." Any true friend of republican government would have to demur; but the case is nevertheless a powerful one.[1] The day-to-day management of the machinery of administration is the single most important thing that governments do most of the time, and whether it is done well or badly directly affects the fortunes of regimes and those who rule them.

We are not accustomed to thinking of our political leaders as administrators. In the business world, the tendency in recent years has been to distinguish sharply between "managers" who are (mere) administrators and "leaders" who supply entrepreneurial energy and vision. Similarly, politicians are expected to concern themselves mainly with making policy, less if at all with implementing it. In the United States, where public administration first became established as a subdiscipline of political science in the late nineteenth century, a sharp distinction between "policy" and "administration" has long been axiomatic.[2] In reality, however, few important administrative decisions are without consequences for policy, and hence political leaders cannot afford to remove themselves entirely from the administrative loop. By the same token, bureaucratic managers cannot be, and should not consider themselves, simply neutral technicians. At least at senior levels, administrators are inextricably involved in "policy" and in a position to exercise genuine leadership. Administrators can have as much claim to the name of statesman as most (mere) politicians.[3]

Democracies have not always been noted for administrative excellence. Indeed, there is an obvious tension between democracy understood as popular self-government and the idea of the administrative state. In ancient Athens, many of the functions carried out today by professional bureaucrats were performed by bodies of citizens elected (or chosen by lot) for relatively brief periods; and officials entrusted with sensitive tasks, especially in the areas of public finance and war, were subject to intensive scrutiny and not infrequently prosecuted for real or imagined misbehavior. Not surprisingly, the result was much administrative inefficiency. The efficient bureaucracies of world history have flourished not in democracies but in autocratic empires. In China, for example, a vast administrative apparatus staffed by a scholar-gentry class served from very early times as a key enabling tool of the Chinese state. In Western Europe, the earliest advances of non-traditional or bureaucratic governance in modern times occurred in states run by absolute if enlightened monarchs like the kings of Prussia.[4]

The relationship between democracy and bureaucracy is a complex one. Modern constitutional democracy seems to require a break with the traditional monopoly of administration by a privileged class of notables, in favor of merit-based recruitment of state officials operating in a framework of settled and impersonal law. Bureaucracy in this sense—Max Weber's "rational-legal" mode of governance—can be seen as one of the great driving factors in the development of modern capitalist democracies and a key (if insufficiently appreciated) cause of their success. It vastly improved the efficiency of large-scale organizations both public and private, rationalizing and routinizing the tasks they perform, subjecting them to fair and impartial rules, and creating specialized forms of expertise that brought scientific knowledge to bear on practice. Building genuinely modern administrative capabilities is one of the most important (and daunting) challenges facing leaders throughout the less developed world today.[5]

At the same time, as Weber also cautioned, bureaucracy poses unique challenges to democratic statesmen—indeed, to political leaders generally. As he once observed, in a comment frequently echoed, "once fully established, bureaucracy is among those social structures which are hardest to destroy." There is an inherent tendency in bureaucracies to maximize their own control of the levers of social power, to obstruct or ignore the popular will, and to evade political superintendence as a result of their near-monopoly of policy expertise. Effective political control of government agencies is made difficult not only by the inevitable failure of leaders to master their (frequently highly technical or esoteric) jargon and expertise but also by the requirements, real or asserted, of government secrecy. At the same time, by vastly increasing the reach of state power, bureaucracy also has a tendency to insulate governments and leaders from the people: because bureaucracy greatly improves governments' control of society, modern revolutions take the form of coups d'état rather than popular uprisings. Finally, Weber was depressed by his vision of a future in which bureaucracy would sap individual initiative and the vitality of political life, leading ultimately, as he famously put it, to the extinction of every human possibility except "specialists without spirit or vision and voluptuaries without heart."[6]

These anticipations of the challenge posed by bureaucracy to contemporary statecraft were shared by the great nineteenth-century student of the American democratic experiment Alexis de Tocqueville. For Tocqueville, there is a close if hidden link between the progression of the democratic idea in modern times and the growth of the centralized administrative state. Egalitarian social conditions help sustain free political institutions, yet they can also contribute to an undue strengthening of the power of the state as well as a psychology of dependence on the state that in the end seriously threatens political liberty. As Tocqueville strikingly puts it, the administrative state is apt to become a power absolute and apart, "thoughtful of detail, orderly, provident, and gentle. . . . It does not break men's will, but softens, bends, and guides it; it seldom enjoins, but often inhibits, action; it does not destroy anything, but prevents much being born; it is not at all tyrannical, but it hinders, restrains, enervates, stifles, and stultifies so much that in the end each nation is no more than a flock of timid and hardworking animals with the government as its shepherd."[7]

No doubt the worst fears of Weber and Tocqueville have not been borne out. The apparatus of the contemporary welfare state (as recent history in the United States demonstrates) is far from simply unresponsive to public opinion or reforming political leadership. On the other hand, it is hard to deny that they identified a problem. Bureaucracy is a great power in contemporary societies, one that often pursues its own agendas and is controlled only with difficulty and effort.[8]

Nor is bureaucracy a problem just for democracies. As Weber noted, there is a sense in which absolute rulers are even more vulnerable to bureaucratic manipulation than democratic leaders, given the closed nature of the system in which they function.[9] The disarray and infighting of the German bureaucracy under the Nazi regime is a cautionary tale of the limitations of even the most absolute personal power. Part of this story, of course, is that autocratic leaders often feel a need to play off various government agencies against one another in order to maximize their freedom of action and protect themselves from overthrow.

The problem of bureaucracy is inseparable from the problem of elite power. Bureaucracy tends to be studied by political scientists from the vantage point of techniques of administration, but bureaucracy is also about the exercise of political and societal power. Weberian assumptions about the nature of "rational-legal" governance should not be allowed to obscure the realities of elite recruitment and preferment or the ways in which bureaucratic institutions serve to support or undermine regimes. In Germany itself, and indeed in most European countries (and Japan), domination of the state bureaucracy by the aristocracy well into the last century explains much about their political evolution.[10] In many parts of the less developed world today, the bureaucracy—particularly the military—is the primary vehicle for the development of a national elite and the main repository of an elite consciousness. But this means that management of the bureaucracy by political leaders is not or not merely an administrative matter. Rather, it is an essential aspect of managing or maintaining regimes.

The United States is unusual among developed countries in the relative political weakness of its bureaucracy. This is partly a function of the greater degree of administrative control exerted over the bureaucracy by the legislative branch of the federal government, partly of the modest prestige associated with government work and the tenuous links of the bureaucracy (particularly the military) with elites of the wider society. Nevertheless, it would be a mistake to underestimate the power of the American bureaucracy or the challenges it poses to American statecraft.

It is worth noting to begin with that the separated powers of the U.S. political system provide a unique space for bureaucratic maneuver between the president and the Congress: the idea that the president controls the executive branch in the way its chief executive controls a corporation is a complete fallacy. Particularly interesting in this regard is the position of the military services. In spite of their unquestioning loyalty to the president in his role as commander in chief, military leaders have long felt free to lobby Congress for monies and programs not endorsed by their civilian superiors. In the second place, the American bureaucracy is, at least by the standard of developed nations, highly permeable and open to co-optation and mobilization by private interests of all kinds. Agencies frequently look for intellectual leadership to universities or public-policy think tanks more than to the government itself; and they use and are used by individual companies, corporate sectors, professional associations, public interest lobbying organizations, and other groups in ways that greatly reinforce their clout. The uniquely American system of political executives inserted in substantial numbers at high levels throughout the executive branch certainly helps counteract these tendencies toward autonomous behavior. By itself, however, it is far from sufficient to guarantee presidential control of the bureaucracy.[11]

American presidents have often complained about the incompetence or unresponsiveness of the bureaucracy.[12] Rarely, however, have they lent their full energies to the task of implementing national policy or to institutional reforms that would improve the administrative capabilities of the federal government. With some reason, presidents tend to regard administrative issues as a waste of their time. Tinkering with the machinery of government is always difficult, arousing as it does many sleeping dogs, and the results are never guaranteed and rarely visible. In the twentieth century, only four or five presidents can be said to have shown more than a casual interest in administration. Theodore Roosevelt laid the foundation for the contemporary American regulatory state as part of his campaign to reduce the political influence of private economic interests; he also brought the American military establishment into the modern era. For Franklin Delano Roosevelt, organizational innovation was a vital tool of transformational leadership in dealing with the crises of the Great Depression and World War II.[13] Dwight Eisenhower brought lessons learned from the helm of military command during that war to the White

House, creating the first real presidential staff system. Finally, Richard Nixon experimented (not always happily) with radical organizational change in order to enhance presidential control of what he regarded as a recalcitrant and politically hostile bureaucracy.[14]

Eisenhower made the fundamental point: "Organization cannot make a genius out of an incompetent; even less can it, of itself, make the decisions which are required to trigger the necessary action. On the other hand, disorganization can scarcely fail to result in inefficiency and can easily lead to disaster. Organization makes more efficient the gathering and analysis of facts, and the arranging of the findings of experts in logical fashion. Therefore organization helps the responsible individual make the necessary decision, and helps assure that it is satisfactorily carried out."[15] How did Eisenhower try to make organization work for him? Though it is too often forgotten, he was the first to create a White House chief of staff, a cabinet secretariat, a congressional liaison function, and a press office. He was also the first president to realize fully the potential of the National Security Council. The Congress in 1947, and the Truman administration in the intervening years, created the National Security Council (made up of the senior officials responsible for foreign and defense policy) and set it in motion, although it was not until the outbreak of the Korean War in 1950 that Truman began to see it as a valuable tool of presidential decision-making rather than as a device of the Congress to limit his own prerogatives. But Eisenhower really created the National Security Council "system" as we know it today. It was Eisenhower who first designated an Assistant to the President for National Security Affairs as overall director of a structure of interagency decision-making under presidential authority, as well as head of an advisory staff for managing national security that was answerable to the president alone.[16]

Probably the most important lesson of the Eisenhower presidency, however, is the impossibility of leaving administrative matters to the tender mercies of agencies or staff, no matter how loyal or efficient they may be. The president has a perspective that is above and apart from the bureaucracy; an essential task of effective leadership is to ensure that this perspective is reflected in actual government operations. Eisenhower understood this requirement, and he committed his own time and energy in generous measure to seeing it realized. He met personally with his National Security Council several times a week on average throughout his presidency—much more than any of his successors. Even when the issues on the table were not of great magnitude, he considered it essential to signal his personal interest in them as a way of inspiring his subordinates and developing a clear and solid consensus. The overall process served an important controlling function, yet without the antipathies generated by such an effort in the hands of a less skilled or engaged practitioner (for example, Nixon, who had absorbed some of these lessons as Eisenhower's vice president).[17]

The need for a hands-on approach to presidential management of the bureaucracy is evident in times of crisis and war, and particularly so in an age of nuclear weapons, intercontinental missiles, and instantaneous global communications. It is less evident in more normal times—yet may be just as important. For absent compelling external circumstances, administrative leadership from the top is apt to be crucial in any effort to make changes in bureaucratic organizations or procedures that disturb powerful vested interests. Presidents need to be prepared to expend political capital in such an effort. If they are wise, they will understand that today's stubborn administrative shortcomings can turn into tomorrow's policy disasters and that an investment of this sort is worthwhile. This is one of the lessons of the American government's multiple failures in its domestic security measures prior to the terrorist attacks on New York and Washington in September 2001.[18]

It is customary to think of administrative leadership in terms of the reform of organizational structures and procedures. Just as important, however, is organizational culture. The culture of an organization is difficult to describe with any precision, but those who have worked in bureaucracies (or business corporations) generally understand how real and powerful a phenomenon it is.[19] At the core of an organization's culture is its people. This is especially true of its leadership cadre. How such people are recruited, trained, utilized, promoted, and otherwise rewarded are critical factors in the success or failure of an organization. For a variety of reasons—nepotism and corruption in the first instance, but also ideological motivation—these practices can become severely dysfunctional, requiring high-level intervention to correct them. Leaders of bureaucratic agencies need to be very alert to this dimension of their job. But even national leaders cannot afford to neglect such issues, particularly in the case of sensitive organizations such as the military or security services. At the extreme, a leader may be forced to contemplate wholesale firings (let us not flinch from calling them *purges*) of officials, or even the dissolution of an entire agency. Short of that, leaders may take direct steps to reshape the culture of an agency through changes (let us not flinch from the term *re-education*) in recruitment practices, indoctrination, and training.

It is necessary to dwell at least momentarily on the extreme, because it holds important lessons for our political leaders even in the benign circumstances in which they find themselves most of the time. "For one can say this generally of men: that they are ungrateful, fickle, pretenders and dissemblers, evaders of danger, eager for gain."[20] Machiavelli's observation is no less valid for persons operating within the "rational-legal" framework of the modern administrative state than for those schooled by the treacherous political environment of his own day. His conclusion is that it is better for princes to be feared than loved. This maxim will find little favor with contemporary management experts or political scientists. Unfortunately for them, it has a large element of truth. Leaders who are unwilling to use power available to them when the situation requires it must eventually lose the respect of their subordinates, and therewith their loyalty and obedience. This is not to say that modern leaders can or should act with the ferocity of princes of old: contemporary pieties must be observed, and there are many ways of slipping in the poisoned stiletto.

XIV

LAW

To speak of law as a tool of statecraft may seem odd, not to say sinister. In constitutional democracies, laws are supposed to be made by legislators and applied by judges. Enforcing the laws, to be sure, is a function of the executive, but one that hardly seems to involve great issues of statecraft. In most advanced democracies, and especially in the United States, the independence of the judicial branch from executive interference is an article of political faith. What role do political leaders legitimately have here?

First, and most obviously, political leaders can exercise legislative leadership. Even under the separated powers doctrine of the American Constitution, the president's qualified veto over legislation makes him an integral part of the legislative process, and presidents have frequently taken advantage of this to put forward laws and legislative programs of their own. Such leadership, once largely confined to emergency situations (such as the Civil War or the Depression), has now become routine and indeed a measure of presidential merit. Beyond such policy leadership are other important but frequently neglected roles having to do on the one hand with legal institutions and on the other with law and culture.

As Machiavelli teaches, "good laws" presuppose the existence of princes who establish the state structures that make them possible. Princes, even unsavory ones, create and sustain legal institutions because the domestic order these ensure is a fundamental requirement of statecraft. Most political leaders of course inherit some established legal system. Often they simply take it for granted and invest their energies elsewhere, or else tinker with it opportunistically in response to political pressures. But wise leaders understand that their political standing as a whole is tied closely to their demonstrated capacity for satisfying demands for the swift and fair administration of justice. There are times when leaders initiate fundamental reforms—at the extreme, the promulgation of sweeping new legal codes—as part of larger projects of state founding or consolidation. Typically, such reforms (for example, the codes of Hammurabi, Justinian, or Napoleon) are carried out in vast, ethnically heterogeneous empires where uniform laws are vital not only for administrative reasons but as a political tool for strengthening central authority.

Law is a tool of regime management as well as of state formation. Codes of laws can serve to consolidate the authority not only of the state but also of particular elements within it. In early modern Europe, the growth of law and legal institutions owes much (contrary to the conventional view) to monarchs intent on increasing the strength of the state against the feudal nobility.[1] Laws governing hereditary succession are a key element of regime management in monarchies. In modern democracies, of course, written constitutions have come to be accepted as fundamental law designed to ensure the preservation of a democratic regime as well as appropriate safeguards for individual and minority rights. The body of law growing out of this framework—"constitutional law"—has central importance for the political health if not the very survival of contemporary democratic regimes. As such, it has to be a matter of vital interest to the political leadership of these regimes. But law and legal institutions generally are not something any leader can afford to take for granted.

Leaders can play a role in safeguarding the rule of law in constitutional democracies in several critical respects. The theoretically sovereign legislature can in practice bring law into disrepute by gross incompetence or corruption (consider, for example, the Russian Duma during the Yeltsin years). Recall that Locke had considered the reformation of corrupt or unrepresentative parliaments a key aspect of executive prerogative. In the United States, recruitment of qualified and attractive candidates for legislative office by presidents and their chief aides is a routine party-political function; yet in certain circumstances such activities could well rise to the statecraft level. Singapore is an instructive case in point, as we saw earlier.

But it is in the judicial area that the leader's role is most critical. As just noted, constitutional law, like every other kind of law, tends to be regarded in today's democracies as belonging to the exclusive province of the judicial power. In the United States, the Supreme Court enjoys the right to review acts of Congress and strike down those it regards as unconstitutional—in spite of the fact that the Constitution itself is silent about such a sweeping judicial prerogative, which (unlike the presidential veto) is exercised in a manner that is final and beyond appeal. This American model is by no means followed everywhere, but it has certainly had the effect of legitimizing not only greater judicial independence but a greater role for the courts in political and administrative matters generally than would seem to be countenanced by classical liberal constitutionalism. In the United States, the Supreme Court has become deeply engaged (not to say entangled) in the highly political process of redrawing the lines of congressional districts, while lower courts have taken it on themselves to manage failed school districts and to restructure the largest corporation in the nation, among other things. In Italy, in what has to count as the most extraordinary political revolution since the collapse of the Soviet Union, a group of audacious state prosecutors used the tools of their trade to destroy or discredit virtually the entire leadership of the centrist parties of the old anti-Communist coalition, thereby remaking the face of Italian politics.[2] And throughout the nascent European Union, the courts serve increasingly as a handy cover for administrative and political decision-making safely removed from any democratic control.[3]

The Supreme Court's practice of reviewing the actions of the other branches of government is generally regarded as a characteristic feature of American constitutionalism. It has to be said, however, that it seems very unlikely that the American founders intended the Court to play the role it plays today.[4] After the famous case (*Marbury v. Madison*, in 1803) that is held to have established the principle of judicial review, no act of Congress was voided until the disastrous *Dred Scott* decision of 1857, which helped push the country toward the brink of civil war. The power was used sparingly through the rest of the nineteenth century. In the century following, however, the Court's obdurate resistance to government regulation of the economy led eventually to a serious political crisis, as

Franklin Roosevelt in 1937 attempted to increase the number of justices in order to gain a majority for his legislative reform program.

It is customary to decry FDR's move against the Court as a prime example of the abuse of executive power by an American president. In fact, as the Constitution specifically empowers Congress to fix the number of justices on the Court, his action was not legally or constitutionally improper, or for that matter unprecedented.[5] Politically, though questions can be raised about the way it was handled, it can certainly be defended as an extraordinary act of statecraft in circumstances of national crisis. In the event, though Roosevelt was forced to back off, the Court got the message and began to accommodate presidential requirements.[6]

Roosevelt's crucial mistake in his handling of this "court-packing" scheme was his attempt to present it as part of a package of administrative measures intended to increase the efficiency of the federal courts, rather than as the constitutional and political matter it so plainly was. The result was to make the scheme appear devious and sinister. Politicians have long been reluctant to criticize Supreme Court decisions or to engage in argument with the Court on the constitutional merits of important cases. Even Lincoln was slow to react to the *Dred Scott* decision.[7] Yet there is no reason for presidents or aspiring presidents (or for that matter congressmen) to defer automatically to the judgments of the Court on constitutional issues. In the first place, of course, the Court itself is frequently divided, and for this reason is not always capable of producing consistent or even intelligible lines of cases. Second, though, the kind of reasoning on display in constitutional cases is generally political or prudential more than it is technically legalistic. Even where decisions turn on technicalities, the principles at issue can be discussed in terms accessible to at least the educated public (an instructive recent example is the series of battles in the Florida courts and eventually the Supreme Court over the outcome of the 2000 presidential election). Presidents (and congressional leaders) should avail themselves of the opportunities offered by decisions of the higher courts to educate the people on matters of political importance for the country. If nothing else, the climate of opinion thus created can help shape or reshape the deliberations and decisions of the judiciary of the future.

This brings us to the question of law and culture. Tocqueville observes that there are three factors that maintain a democratic republic in

America: the unique history and configuration of the country; its laws; and its manners, morals, and intellectual outlook in the broadest sense (as he defines the untranslatable French word *moeurs*). In arguing that the last of these—let us call it "political culture"—is actually the most critical, Tocqueville affronts the sensibilities and assumptions of contemporary liberalism.[8] In fact, however, there is much in our own experience to confirm this view. Contemporary criminology, for example, increasingly recognizes the importance of attacking the symptoms of serious criminal activity—public disorder, vandalism, petty crime; and it understands that reliable enforcement of existing laws is more important than having good laws on the books that are regularly ignored. As Aristotle once put it, "Law has no strength apart from habit."[9] Culture is what creates and sustains the habits that centrally condition human behavior and shape, in particular, men's attitude toward law.

All of this is to argue that statesmen should pay attention not merely to the formal structure of law and legal institutions but to the "spirit of the laws"[10]—the broader political and cultural context in which law is embedded. They need to pay attention, for example, to the impact of law or government regulation more generally on the lives of citizens. Laws that are excessively detailed or difficult to understand (tax laws, notably) can impose enormous opportunity costs on the public and foster a dislike and disrespect for law generally. They need to pay attention particularly to how law is interpreted and applied. These issues in turn are inseparable from the character of those responsible for interpreting and applying it. Public-spirited judges and lawyers are an important support for regimes dedicated to the rule of law. By the same token, corrupt judges and venal or cynical lawyers can do considerable damage, eroding the basic legitimacy of democratic institutions and of elite leadership generally. To recall again Aristotle's fundamental observation, law by itself cannot rule. Even in the most advanced constitutional democracies, the rule of law is mediated through the elites that give each regime its distinctive stamp. What is more, lawyers make up perhaps the most politically important elite in these democracies after politicians themselves.

Traditional political science recognized that there is an inherent tension between democracy and the rule of law. Majorities resent limitations imposed by standing laws on the exercise of their sovereign will.[11] Tocqueville was very attentive to the prominent role of lawyers in American society, already visible in the early nineteenth century. He believed lawyers provided a vital counterweight to the potentially tyrannical rule of democratic majorities. Their influence, moreover, was not limited to their practical functions in legislatures or on the bench; it was also apparent in the way law was conceptualized by Americans. Thinking primarily of the common law background of American jurisprudence, Tocqueville held that lawyers were a powerful source of resistance to the tendency of democratic majorities to succumb to the appeal of what he called "general ideas," or what today might be called abstract thinking or ideology.[12] As a young lawyer and an aspiring politician, Abraham Lincoln offered a careful analysis of the tendency of established democracies to encourage an erosion of the rule of law and the rise of dangerous demagogues who would play on the passions of the people to advance their own fortunes. His prescription: genuine leaders who would teach the people reverence for the laws and the constitution as a kind of "political religion."[13]

All of this will no doubt sound strange to the contemporary ear—and for good reason. Developments in American jurisprudence and in the wider culture in the intervening years have greatly altered attitudes toward law among elites, if not the general public. To begin with, the common law has been increasingly eclipsed as a source of legal judgment, and with it a way of thinking that is not embarrassed to understand law as an inherently reasonable enterprise that is in some sense grounded in the nature of things.[14] Instead, our reigning doctrine is a legal positivism that holds that law is nothing other than what legislators or judges pronounce it to be. At the same time, the Constitution has also come to be seen less as the authoritative source of legal interpretation than as a text to be deconstructed and creatively manipulated to suit the policy preferences of judges. The reverence for the Constitution of which Lincoln spoke is indeed still strong among the people, but enlightened opinion has been decisively shaped over the last century by the critique of the founding generation launched by Woodrow Wilson and absorbed in the tradition of progressive liberalism. Under the impact of this critique, it no longer seemed desirable to base constitutional interpretation on the "original intent" of the document and its drafters. Instead, certain very general provisions of the Constitution (notably, the First and Fourteenth Amendments) could be seized upon to provide cover for a jurisprudence that drove the political agenda of the progressive liberals.[15] To the extent that this jurisprudence looked anywhere for its intellectual underpinnings, it was not to the law at all but to contemporary social science.

In the traditional view, as reflected in Tocqueville's understanding of the salutary political role of law and lawyers in democracies, legal judgment is an aspect or expression of prudence. Contemporary jurisprudence, by contrast, has been thoroughly penetrated by the "general ideas" Tocqueville denounced. Special ideological pleading by feminists, civil libertarians, environmentalists, and others has long helped to furnish the contemporary judicial mind. At the same time, judges have actively sought to bring various social science methodologies to bear in crafting their opinions. Postmodern literary theories have even been plumbed for their contribution to questions of legal interpretation.

A further point worth noting in this context is that America has become a notoriously litigious society. Private disputes tend to escalate quickly into court battles. A culture of victimization has taken hold. Real or imagined grievances are deployed in barely disguised schemes of legalized extortion, especially against wealthy and politically vulnerable targets such as the big auto manufacturers or drug or tobacco companies. Indeed, the most important lawyer's organization in the country at present, and perhaps its single most powerful political lobby, is the Trial Lawyers' Association. Trial lawyers have reaped literally billions of dollars in profits from what has been a virtual judicial expropriation of the tobacco industry, and they are now the single largest contributor to America's politicians and political parties. As a result, they have managed to block long overdue efforts to reform tort law in the United States. And because of relaxed rules about advertising their services, trial lawyers are now able to make appeals that in effect encourage the general public to use the law opportunistically to enrich themselves.

The point is not to lament the cultural decline that is so apparent in all this. Rather, it is to note that the various cultural influences at work here have important implications for statecraft. Where law is seen as a tool not of an impartial state but of particular class, economic, or ideological interests, where it is seen as grounded not in a set of objective standards or a settled body of law but in the sovereign will of judges, where judges themselves are and consider themselves full partners with elected officials in substantive policy-making, respect for law must suffer—or, to put it more starkly, the difference between law and arbitrary compulsion becomes increasingly blurred. No regime can welcome such a development.[16]

It goes without saying that the problems outlined here are not susceptible to quick or easy solutions, by political leaders or anyone else. On the other hand, political leaders can clearly have a major impact over time in shaping both the courts as an institution and the wider judicial culture. This happens above all through the process of judicial appointment. In the United States, the nomination of judges for the higher federal courts and for the Supreme Court itself is a presidential prerogative, while the Senate is required to confirm them. It is no secret that this process has become increasingly politicized in recent years, while the courts have become more and more internally divided along ideological lines. While some believe that paper professional qualifications and personal probity should be the only criteria for selecting judges, increasing attention is now being paid both by the Senate and the White House to candidates' judicial philosophies. There is every reason to welcome public debate over judicial appointments within the Congress and in the media. Unfortunately, character assassination seems to be the preferred weapon of some of the players in this game. All the more reason to hope for energetic and principled presidential leadership in the selection and public defense of an administration's nominees.[17]

XV

EDUCATION AND CULTURE

Opinion polls in the United States show that education is regularly seen by the general public as a political issue of the highest priority, and politicians—particularly state legislators and governors, but also congressmen and presidents—routinely pay at least lip service to its importance. The reason, of course, is that the quality of public education has immediate and visible effects on people's lives and on their futures. In our egalitarian and diverse society, it is a key avenue of cultural assimilation and social mobility. It is all the more remarkable, then, that contemporary political science seems to pay so little attention to it. Much ink is certainly spilled on the subject by education professionals and by journalists, but it remains very much at the margins of political analysis.[1]

In the United States, of course, education is largely a state and local responsibility. A federal Department of Education has existed only since the late 1970s, and its powers do not begin to approach those of education ministries in other advanced democracies. Yet the phenomenon we are considering has much deeper roots. Ultimately, it reflects a fundamental shift at the origins of modern liberalism from education to institutions as the central mechanism of regime management.

In traditional political science, education loomed large as a topic of interest. It is the central theme in the greatest document of that tradition,

Plato's *Republic*, and Aristotle deals with it extensively in his *Politics*. Both writers were deeply concerned with developments in the culture of their day that they felt were negatively affecting the education and outlook of potential political leaders and the political class generally. The spurious instruction offered by itinerant sophists and rhetoricians helped fuel the political ambitions of the young but lacked all moral compass. Plato's "philosopher-kings" provided one kind of response to this challenge. Another, more practical and palatable, was Aristotle's reform of tradition-al aristocratic education—a forerunner, it can be argued, of the idea of "liberal education" as we know it today. Still another was the reform of rhetorical instruction associated with the names of Isocrates and Cicero, an important (if now largely forgotten) source of modern humanistic education.[2]

In *The Prince*, Machiavelli announces a fundamental break with this entire mode of thinking. Claiming that it is "more fitting to go directly to the effectual truth of the thing than to the imagination of it," he tells us, "And many have imagined republics and principalities that have never been seen or known to exist in truth; for it is so far from how one lives to how one should live that he who lets go of what is done for what should be done learns his ruin rather than his preservation. For a man who wants to make a profession of good in all regards must come to ruin among so many who are not good. Hence it is necessary to a prince, if he wants to maintain himself, to learn to be able not to be good, and to use this and not use it according to necessity."[3]

The "imagined republics and principalities" of the past—the Chris-tian as well as the classical past—were, Machiavelli means to say, utopian constructs. They presumed that the one thing most needful for human life is moral or spiritual improvement, that such improvement is possible, and that the state can contribute importantly to furthering it. Machiavelli focuses attention on the dangerous effects of such a view on the fortunes of princes: leaders who take an idealistic view of human nature are setting themselves up for political failure. Note, however, that Machiavelli does not subscribe to the vulgar Machiavellian notion that a prince's behavior should be consistently self-seeking or immoral. He says only that the prince needs to remain flexible enough to employ immoral methods if or when they prove necessary. Nor does he deny that princes can actually be motivated by idealistic impulses. Indeed, that is an important part of the problem. Princes who understand "soulcraft" as the essence of statecraft may well prove ineffective leaders—but they can also be dangerous. Their imagined utopias can turn into very real dystopias when an attempt is made to impose them on necessarily imperfect—and resisting—human beings. It is both safer for princes and better for peoples to aim lower, taking men as they are but at the same time controlling their worst impulses through the checking and balancing of powerful leaders—or, better yet, impersonal institutions.[4]

The development of liberal constitutionalism in the centuries following Machiavelli is an aspect of a larger movement of thought that set out to remove the religious issue once and for all from politics. It did so through the nationalization of religious loyalties, the promotion of religious "toleration," the secularization of educational ideas and practices, and not least, the juridical separation of church and state.[5] All of these things, now so much taken for granted in the West, were once among the weightiest issues of statecraft. With the eruption of a newly militant Islam at the end of the twentieth century, they can no longer be taken for granted. But our leaders (and for that matter, leaders in the Muslim world today) are no longer in the habit of dealing with them.[6]

There can be little better illustration of the potency of education as a tool of statecraft than the role played over many years by some thousands of Islamic theological seminaries (*madrassas*) in Pakistan and Afghanistan as centers of indoctrination and training of young warriors bent on *jihad*. The new and more dangerous Islamic terrorism that has emerged in recent years, with its suicidal capabilities and global reach, is unthinkable apart from the ideological impetus provided by these schools. They have also been a major factor fanning militant Islamism in the Pakistani armed forces and security services. Former president Pervez Musharraf showed considerable courage and a farsighted appreciation of this domestic threat in supporting American actions against the terrorist-supported government in Afghanistan, cracking down on Islamic extremism in the army and the mosques, and instituting major reforms of the *madrassas* (including sweeping changes in their curricula); but such actions can come at a high political price. Similar choices will face the leaders of other Muslim nations over the next few years—particularly Saudi Arabia, which has played a significant if indirect role in bankrolling the *madrassas* in their current malign form.

There are signs that the new Saudi leadership is finally awaking to the magnitude of the problem.

Even in the United States, the classical liberal solution to the religious question has hardly proven universally satisfactory. By way of what many consider an extreme interpretation of the First Amendment by the courts, government is enjoined from showing a preference not only for a particular religion but for religion generally. Troubling moral issues such as abortion and human cloning have proven difficult or impossible to address as purely political matters outside a coherent religious or philosophical framework, and thus remain potentially very divisive. To what degree presidents and other politicians can or should provide real leadership on such matters is a difficult question. The least that can be said is that recent presidents have been unwilling simply to abdicate a role here but have also been unwilling to accept the potential risks of aggressive public advocacy. At the same time, it is worth noting that recent presidents have not hesitated to register symbolic commitment to religious beliefs and practice. In this respect, at any rate, the United States seems distinctly more traditional than most other advanced democracies. The growing presence of Muslims in the West, particularly in Europe, poses a special challenge, as not only radical Islam but Islam as such fundamentally rejects the very notion of the separation of church and state.

If the scope for leadership in today's liberal democracies in matters of religion or culture broadly is highly circumscribed, this is less so with respect to education itself. Again, contemporary publics look to politicians to improve the educational system—partly because of long-standing expectations they have placed in it, partly because of growing unhappiness with its perceived deficiencies. And fixing the problems of public education is a genuinely political problem, not merely an administrative one, especially given the enormous political strength of teachers' unions in the United States and elsewhere and the troublemaking potential of the higher professoriate. For this reason, however, contemporary leaders have not always been eager to involve themselves deeply in educational issues; and even when they do, the results are frequently unimpressive.

Consider the case of Margaret Thatcher. Thatcher had been minister of education in a previous Tory government before becoming prime minister in May 1979. She was therefore well acquainted with the British educational scene and had developed firm convictions concerning the need for change. Education issues figured prominently in the elections of 1987, and the new Thatcher cabinet could thus plausibly claim a popular mandate for a sweeping reform program. The education minister (Ken Baker) was committed to reform and a persuasive public advocate. The program had two distinct and indeed faintly contradictory components, reflecting the government's twin aims of decentralizing the educational system and of improving national standards. The decentralizing component, which sought to weaken the hold of local education authorities on the schools and enhance parental choice, was in the end reasonably successful. But the centralizing component, particularly the attempt to develop a national core curriculum, faltered under the pressure and bureaucratic maneuverings of the educational establishment and the inability or unwillingness of Baker to stand up to it.

In July 1989, Thatcher herself intervened when a History Working Group produced its interim report. She was unhappy with its emphasis on interpretation as distinct from factual knowledge, its insufficient attention to British history, and its neglect of chronology. While Thatcher regarded the document as comprehensively flawed, Baker wanted only minor changes. A final report proved to be little improvement. Thatcher's exasperation led her to air her views in a newspaper interview that predictably raised the hackles of the education ministry.[7]

Thatcher's complaints (like those of American education critics) have several distinct targets: the hyper-bureaucracy, mediocrity, and trade union mentality of the education establishment; its educational theories and methods; and its moral-political orientation. She demonstrates in particular that politicians need not defer automatically to faddish approaches to education that defy not only traditional and proven methods but also elementary common sense. And her emphasis on the need for more British history in the schools can hardly be criticized as inappropriate interference in the business of professional educators. Political leaders have every right to form and express judgments about the teaching of national history and to take action to shape public school curricula in this area. More generally, they have every right to expect that the schools will provide at least the rudiments of a civic education, promoting not only patriotism but an understanding of democratic principles and the fundamentals of personal and civic morality. Thatcher's own experience with Britain's education establishment suggests the distance between such expectations and the reality, even (or perhaps particularly) in the most advanced democracies today.

But let us not overlook higher education. In many countries, certain major universities, whether public or private, are virtually integral components of the regime by the fact that they create or validate a national elite: consider Oxford and Cambridge in England or Tokyo University (particularly its law school) in Japan. Yet it is very hard to hold them politically accountable.[8] In Latin America and elsewhere in the third world, large public universities have often served as little more than breeding grounds for leftist counter-elites. In Europe, hide-bound teaching methods, rigid curricula, cronyism, and corruption are widely recognized problems, with concrete penalties paid in terms of national economic performance. It is surprising how little real effort is expended by political leaders to improve such institutions.

In the United States, colleges, universities, and professional schools remain for the most part beyond the reach of the national government, although federal policy (for example, concerning student aid or funding for scientific research) has a very significant impact on their viability as businesses. Even state legislatures are not often disposed to interfere in substantive curricular matters in state-supported universities. The tenure system effectively protects faculty everywhere from official pressures, while administrators are able to pursue their own (sometimes fanciful) visions of governance free from significant political interference or even scrutiny. The alternately lunatic and sinister pursuit of the agenda of political correctness that pervades contemporary university life in America raises fundamental issues, including ones of legal due process.[9] Universities have suffered little from abolishing reserve officers' training programs (ROTC) on campus or barring recruiters from the military or the Central Intelligence Agency. And at least until recently, they have resisted cooperation with the federal government in tracking foreign students who are in the country illegally or may be pursuing dubious courses of study (such as nuclear physics).[10]

Finally, it is worth considering the role of governments and leaders in establishing and controlling schools of professional education, particularly those relating to public administration and public policy as well as certain technical subjects such as engineering or military science. Charles de Gaulle founded the École Nationale d'Administration in 1945 as part of a broader project to remake the regime of the Fourth Republic. This step, little noted at the time, laid the groundwork for the emergence of a national administrative elite that would effectively supplant the fractious legislature as the key policy-making body in France.[11] Military professionalism is a direct function of educational requirements and the *esprit* that is formed in elite military schools (St. Cyr in France or the old German Kriegsakademie). Such institutions can be all the more politically important in countries where educational levels are generally low and national cohesion questionable. They are, to be sure, not an unmixed blessing. But there is no reason in principle why they cannot be monitored and managed as necessary by political leaders to ensure that they continue to serve the interests of the state as a whole.

XVI

ECONOMICS

As we saw earlier, citizens in the advanced democracies tend to accept in theory the desirability of free markets while in practice looking to the state as the ultimate guarantor of their prosperity. Accordingly, democratic leaders cannot escape responsibility for the performance of their economies, even where it is clear that larger forces are at work over which they have little control. In this sense, at any rate, prosperity has to be considered a fundamental task of modern statecraft. But what exactly is it that leaders should know or do to achieve or maintain it?

Economics is unique among the social sciences today. It is more genuinely scientific in the sense that it rests on a cumulative body of technical knowledge that is widely accepted by its practitioners and has real predictive value. As a result, it enjoys extraordinary prestige. At the same time, because of its technical character, economics is difficult for the layman to understand and for politicians to master. Not unlike the soothsayers of ancient times, economists claim to be sole guardians of a kind of secret lore that leaders can use to divine and manipulate unseen forces. But this means that politicians are uniquely dependent on economists. The problem is that economists tend to be insensitive to the requirements of politicians and to lack political judgment.

Economists certainly have legitimate grounds for complaint against politicians. Many politicians today lack even rudimentary economic knowledge. Many are unwilling to take measures that are politically risky in the short run no matter how essential they may be for the overall health of the economy. And some are simply captive to a set of private interests. On the other hand, politicians know things economists do not. They understand instinctively that economists employ a model of man as rational calculator or profit maximizer—"*homo economicus*"—that departs significantly from man as he is in the real world. As Alexander Hamilton once observed, "Experience teaches that men are often so much governed by what they are accustomed to see and practice, that the simplest and most obvious improvements, in the [most] ordinary occupations, are adopted with hesitation, reluctance, and by slow gradations."[1] Economists tend to overlook the impact on economic choices of historical experience, habits, and culture. Moreover, they implicitly discount or deny the importance of non-economic motives such as honor, envy, or love. As a result of all this, they tend to overestimate the extent to which human behavior is predetermined by calculations of individual interest—and by the same token, underestimate the scope for political leadership. Economists are metaphysical individualists. The preferences of individuals are the fundamental starting point of their analyses; these are assumed to be somehow fixed and not legitimately subject to challenge by economists or anyone else. The function of politics and politicians is, therefore, not to shape or elevate such preferences but simply to "aggregate" them—in other words, to figure out how to reconcile them and reduce them to a set of policies to be pursued. Politics on this understanding is a purely instrumental activity, and politicians are leaders only by courtesy.[2]

As late as the eighteenth century, reflecting among other things the lingering influence of Aristotelian thought in Europe, "economics" (the word derives from the Greek term for "management of the household") was considered an integral component of political science.[3] The development of the discipline of economics in the intervening centuries has emancipated it from the tutelage of political science and thus encouraged the claim that what we now call "the economy" is a fully autonomous dimension of social reality that operates or should operate under its own laws. The decisive step in this development is generally traced to Adam Smith's *Wealth of Nations* (1776). In his great work, Smith, a Scottish philosopher steeped in the principles of liberal constitutionalism, systematically attacked the assumptions of the so-called mercantilist school of political economy then prevailing throughout Europe and laid out the fundamental arguments in favor of free trade. It is not coincidental that modern economics arose and has since flourished in the cultural matrix of Anglo-American liberalism, with its guiding ideas of limited government and personal freedom. Unfortunately, economists today too often fail to recognize the extent to which this legacy has hardened into a set of dogmas concerning the nature of economic phenomena and the role of the state, both historically and prescriptively, in economic matters.

A key question is the relationship between prosperity and security or national defense. Even Smith is less categorical on this issue than many of his followers today: as he memorably observed, "defense is much more important than opulence," and he favored discriminatory legislation supporting the British merchant fleet and domestic military industries.[4] The importance of economic development for national defense is a major theme in the writings of Alexander Hamilton, the foremost economic thinker among American statesmen, as well as in the German school of "national economy" inspired by Friedrich List (who was himself influenced by Hamilton). Hamilton supported a diversified national economy with a strong manufacturing sector that would provide at least a measure of self-sufficiency in military production. List also focused attention for the first time on the strategic importance of national railway systems. He played a significant role in shaping elite economic thinking in the later nineteenth century not only in his native Germany but also in Japan. "Rich country, strong army"—this maxim of the Meiji reformers is not as alien to our own traditions as it might sound.[5]

While they were by no means enemies of free trade, Hamilton and List argued on behalf of the importance of limited protectionist measures designed to support domestic industries in an early stage of their development.[6] In this and other respects, their economic thought has an illuminating kinship with the practices of "late modernizers" of the contemporary era such as Japan, Taiwan, or Singapore. Hamilton, the first secretary of the Treasury of the United States and a close adviser to President George Washington, had a profound influence on the economic future of the young nation. His innovative scheme to fund the American war debt helped create an entire financial system out of nothing or worse than nothing, with a sound currency, an expanding supply of money and credit, and a national bank. And his active encouragement of manufacturing was farsighted at a time when it was widely believed that land was the only real source of national wealth. Hamilton looked not merely to the narrowly economic impact of these measures but to their wider political and human effects as well. They strengthened the new nation and gave it reputation in the world. They encouraged honest industry and improved not only the material lot but the moral and mental well-being of the people.[7]

A common misconception concerning economic statecraft is that it pursues narrowly economic ends. Economic statecraft properly understood is the use of economic means in pursuit of any of the ends sought by states and leaders.[8] Through coinage of money, it validates symbolically the unity and independence of the state. It contributes to national security through the financing of armies and fleets, support for allies, and other measures. And it is a vital tool of regime management. Economic statecraft can be an instrument at the service of the class interests of a ruling elite; it may also be employed by princes to check the political power of elites and maintain the favor of the general population. Machiavelli, in spite of his reputation as indifferent to economic questions, shrewdly counsels aspiring princes to suppress the instinctive liberality of their noble natures and husband their resources in order to spare the people the harsh exactions that become unavoidable once their treasuries are empty.[9]

It is worth dwelling on the regime management function of economic statecraft because it is so generally neglected today. Aristotle pointed out long ago that relatively small changes in economic circumstances, such as fluctuations in the value of money, can have large consequences for the political standing of a particular social class and hence also for the overall political stability of a regime. Such changes can be foreseen and sometimes remedied precisely because they are small; but often they simply escape the notice of political leaders until it is too late. At other times, the politico-economic ills of a society may be so massive and regime-threatening that the only effective remedy is leadership intervention of a revolutionary sort. In the ancient world, both Athens and Sparta were spared civil conflict early in their history by such intervention by the founder-statesmen Solon and Lycurgus. The Greeks well understood the political dangers involved in grossly unequal distribution of property:

land reform was a central feature of the Lycurgan reforms that created the class of "peers" making up the formidable Spartan citizen army.[10] Even in the contemporary world, land reform has proven a potent tool of statecraft in traditional societies such as Taiwan (following its occupation by the Nationalist Chinese in 1949) and El Salvador (during the Communist insurgency of the 1980s). In these cases, the point of land reform is not simply to improve the efficiency of the agricultural sector; indeed, its immediate results can be economically disruptive. Rather, it is to change underlying power relationships and, above all, to break the political monopoly of the large landholders.

Even in the industrial democracies, however, economic statecraft can play a significant role in managing regimes. Every democracy must contend with its "oligarchs." This term has gained a new lease on life in recent years as applied to the super-rich of post-Communist Russia; in that context, it is meant to suggest wealth that has been acquired by dubious means and is being used for questionable ends—especially meddling in the political arena.[11] It is possible to debate whether figures like Vladimir Gusinsky or the media magnate Boris Berezovsky really did pose a serious threat to Russian democracy, as the Kremlin has claimed. But it would be hard to argue that the accretion of vast wealth and power by individuals, or their use of it to advance a political agenda, is not in principle a legitimate concern of democratic leaders. Even in the United States, which many throughout the world persist in seeing as a bastion of unreconstructed capitalism, the government has long been sensitive to concentrations of capital or market power in a few hands, and the political influence of wealthy campaign contributors remains a major concern with the public and the Congress. Particularly given the overt excursions of the Russian oligarchs into national politics, it is not easy to criticize the measures taken against Berezovsky and Gusinsky by President Vladimir Putin as part of his larger campaign to recentralize and consolidate the Russian state.[12]

The case of contemporary Russia is a particularly instructive one, because it shows as clearly as anything the baleful influence of social science on statecraft today. The collapse of the Soviet Union following the abortive putsch of August 1991 left Boris Yeltsin at the head of a newly democratic Russia and in a position to make fateful decisions about the political and economic future of that country and indeed of the entire former Soviet space. For economic advice Yeltsin turned primarily to Yegor Gaidar, a young and strongly Western-oriented liberal economist. Partly from conviction, partly believing it would open the way to very large infusions of cash and other material assistance from the West and from the international financial institutions, Gaidar embarked on a program of economic "shock therapy" designed to bring about a rapid transition from the communist command economy to capitalism. The main features of this program were price liberalization and the privatization of commercial and industrial enterprises. Unfortunately, the political preconditions for successful reform were lacking, and the government did little to create them. It sought to effect a top-down revolution not altogether unlike that begun by the Bolsheviks in 1917, one that simply ignored the concerns of Parliament or public opinion. As a result, Russia ended up with the worst of both worlds. The liberalization of prices created rampant inflation, which in short order wiped out the savings and pensions of ordinary Russians and essentially destroyed the nascent middle class as a political force. At the same time, in order to buy support for this and other reforms, the government had to make an accommodation with the bureaucrats and managers of the old communist order. Hence a privatization process that favored the Soviet-era *nomenklatura*, transforming it in effect into a new oligarchic class. Quite apart from the disastrous economic outcome (in the space of a few years, Russian industrial production would contract more than that of the United States at the height of the Depression of the 1930s), these reforms virtually crippled Russia's democratic development. Over the decade following, the reality of the Russian regime would become the uneasy balance between an increasingly autocratic Yeltsin and a new elite of oligarchs and regional political bosses. Nor is that all. Although the question is rarely considered, it seems very likely that a more prudent approach to managing the post-communist economic transition could have held at least some of the non-Russian Soviet republics in a new federal Russia.

It would be one thing if the ill-conceived Gaidar reforms were simply the result of flawed political leadership and poor advice from a young and inexperienced economist. In fact, however, the reform program was strongly pushed not only by prominent Western economists (some of whom became closely involved in the internal deliberations of the Russian government on these matters) but also by senior officials in the U.S. Treasury Department and the international financial institutions, particularly the International Monetary Fund. The precise role and responsibility of these outsiders for the ensuing fiasco remains controversial. But there can be little question that their influence contributed significantly to what has to be accounted one of the great failures of contemporary statecraft.[13]

Economic statecraft remains severely understudied both as a historical phenomenon and in terms of policy analysis. This is a function partly of the tendency of contemporary economics and historiography alike to pay attention to the play of impersonal economic forces rather than the actions of statesmen; partly too, however, it reflects the secrecy that has generally enveloped the economic dealings of governments at the highest level.[14] Statesmen have always recognized that there is a large psychological component to men's economic behavior, and hence have made particular efforts to manage appearances in the measures they undertook in this area. In a free society, as Hamilton for one well understood, leaders need to engage in a significant effort of public education in order to maintain the necessary confidence in the government's handling of the economy. In earlier times, though (and the same is true of parts of the world even today), leaders often went to great lengths to hide or misrepresent economic information in order to improve their relative position in dealing with recalcitrant parliaments or foreign bankers. Even in the United States today, however, with all its stated commitment to "transparency" and accountability in government everywhere, the Treasury Department and the Federal Reserve remain probably the most opaque organizations in the federal system—far surpassing the intelligence bureaucracy.[15]

Economic statecraft of course has an international as well as a domestic component. The repertoire of "sanctions" imposed on countries in an effort to modify their behavior through measures short of war is familiar today, and it has a long history. It has been a favored tool in the kit bag particularly of liberal statesmen who have sought by such means to avoid the moral burdens and political risks of war itself.[16] Sanctions in this sense include trade embargoes, boycotts, blacklists, quotas, asset freezing, suspension of air travel, and the like. In their strongest form, these measures are intended not simply to dissuade but to do direct damage to a nation's economy; as such, they may be viewed as economic warfare. It is one of the great commonplaces of contemporary social science that economic sanctions and similar measures rarely "work." In fact, this is far from clear.

Much depends on what is meant by "work," that is, what objectives such measures are intended to serve and how success is defined relative to other statecraft tools.[17]

Less familiar is a range of other economic measures involving trade, aid, investment, international financial flows, energy and other natural resources, and critical technologies. Some of these measures are relatively benign, designed to offer positive inducements for cooperation rather than threats of punishment. Foreign economic assistance falls in this category. So do trade concessions like the lowering or elimination of tariff barriers. Others are less benign than they are often assumed to be by economists and others accustomed to making sharp distinctions between pure or market-driven economic exchange and the politically driven exercise of economic power. Foreign trade is a tool governments have sometimes used with great effectiveness in schemes to extend their political influence. A classic case is Nazi Germany's economic penetration of Eastern Europe in the 1930s.[18] Even foreign aid has its darker side— strings attached in an effort to position the donor country favorably for future trade deals and investment projects (a specialty of contemporary China).

There is probably no better illustration of contemporary foreign economic statecraft than the endgame of the Cold War, when the United States set out on a deliberate campaign of virtual economic warfare against the Soviet empire. This campaign was orchestrated by President Reagan and a few key advisers, notably CIA director William Casey (a former New York investment banker) and National Security Adviser William Clark. The main components of this campaign were as follows. Reagan sought to reduce Soviet hard currency earnings by driving down (in collaboration with Saudi Arabia) the price of oil, as well as by blocking construction of a natural gas pipeline from the Soviet Union to Western Europe; to block Soviet efforts to manipulate the international banking system in order to finance this and other strategic requirements; to reduce Soviet access to strategically important Western technologies, particularly high-speed computing capabilities; to reduce the value of such capabilities to the Soviets through a program of clandestine disinformation and sabotage; and finally, to impose further strains on the Soviet economy through an aggressive military buildup and the threat of neutralization of Soviet nuclear forces through advanced ballistic missile defenses (the so-called Star Wars program). Though little noted at the time or indeed later, this campaign was a direct result of the strategic leadership shown by Reagan in the final confrontation with the USSR. Later testimony from various former Soviet officials suggests that it played an important if not decisive role in the collapse of Soviet power at the end of the 1980s.[19]

The global war against terrorism in which the United States presently finds itself engaged offers much scope for the creative employment of economic tools of statecraft. The ability to shift significant sums of money around the world is critical to any form of terrorism that has true "global reach," but such transfers are subject to tracing and interference by intelligence agencies and financial institutions. Money is also a strategic weapon that can be used to divide and demoralize the leadership of terrorist organizations. At the same time, it has not been sufficiently appreciated to what extent the vulnerabilities of Western societies to terrorism lie in the economic sphere rather than simply in the realm of physical destruction. Necessary as they may be, homeland security measures can be extremely expensive, especially when accompanied by the zero defects mentality that is so common among democratically responsible politicians and agencies today, or when driven by panic in the circumstances of an actual attack. The cost-benefit tradeoffs involved in all such measures must be coldly analyzed to ensure reasonable societal protection at an affordable level—and to maintain a proper balance between expenditures on defensive measures as distinct from the offensive capabilities that are essential to the ultimate liquidation of the threat. There is as yet little reason to believe that the United States (or other potentially threatened nations) has made any serious effort to address such issues.

XVII

DIPLOMACY

The conventional distinction between domestic and foreign affairs has less meaning for statesmen than it does for social scientists. At the highest reaches of government, compartments of information and expertise tend to break down, as leaders are constantly faced with issues that ramify in unexpected directions and potentially affect a wide range of diverse policy decisions. The interpenetration of domestic and foreign economic issues is a notorious case in point. In general, leaders must always calculate the effects of their deeds and speeches on audiences abroad as well as at home.

This needs to be kept in mind as we turn to consider the role of diplomacy in statecraft. Because diplomacy today is still widely regarded as an arcane art practiced by a professional guild whose expertise derives entirely from its dealings with foreign governments, we tend to lose sight of the unique and necessary perspective political leaders bring to this field. In fact, the beginning of wisdom in thinking about diplomacy is to see that there is an inescapable tension between statesmen and diplomats, just as there is between statesmen and soldiers. This tension, which can be very damaging to the national interest yet may also prove fruitful, cannot be abolished. It can only be managed, in much the same way leaders manage the civil-military relationship.

It is surprising and striking how recently diplomacy has come into its own as a distinct profession. In Europe, permanent ambassadors made their appearance in Italy around the time of Machiavelli, but it was only after the Napoleonic Wars that European states developed formal diplomatic organizations operating under agreed rules. As is clear from one of the earliest treatises on the subject, François de Callières's *On the Manner of Negotiating with Princes* (1716), the prestige of diplomacy was low in comparison with the soldier's art.[1] Much of the reason for this was that statesmen continued to function for the most part as their own chief diplomats, whereas battlefield command had been yielded (though with some conspicuous exceptions) to professional soldiers by the end of the seventeenth century. Diplomats, therefore, often had little scope to act on their own and tended to be employed only for specified and occasional missions. After the establishment of permanent diplomatic establishments in far-flung corners of the world, this situation changed, and ambassadors sometimes came to rival their own foreign ministers in their ability to influence the behavior of other nations—or even the policies of their own government. Ironically, the advent of instantaneous global communications in our own age has once again increased the diplomatic role of leaders at the expense of professional diplomats.

De Callières tells us that the model ambassador must possess a set of personal qualities that include the ability to penetrate the motives of others, firmness, patience, self-control, and good manners; in addition, he requires comprehensive knowledge of recent history and current international events. It is not obvious that political leaders will necessarily lack such qualifications. The case is stronger if one is speaking of democratic leaders whose breeding, education, political outlook, and exposure to the world may be relatively limited. At the same time, it is important to appreciate the limitations typical of career diplomats. Where political leaders are especially sensitive to the domestic context of foreign policy, diplomats are apt to know and care little about it. Where political leaders necessarily take a comprehensive view, diplomats often develop a picture of the world distorted by their own experience and by the well-known tendency of an ambassador to become a partisan of the country to which he is accredited (the phenomenon of "clientitis"). Diplomats, because of the nature of their job, tend to overvalue agreements, compromise, and conciliation while tending to undervalue the coercive instruments of power. Where political leaders appreciate the power of public communication, diplomats tend to undervalue and shun it. Political leaders sometimes apply considerable vision and strength of will to the pursuit of a strategic design; diplomats tend to be allergic to strategy.

These generalizations need to be qualified by at least some reference to the differing styles of diplomacy associated with particular regime types and cultures. In his classic treatise of 1939, the British diplomat Harold Nicolson usefully distinguishes between two very different traditions of diplomacy.[2] One tradition, the heritage of the trader-states of modern Europe, views diplomacy as an arena of negotiation and compromise in which national differences can and should be composed for everyone's greater good. The other sees it rather as a form of political struggle, where there can be only winners and losers. This tradition is perhaps best exemplified by the Byzantine Empire, which specialized in a diplomacy of maneuver, deception, bribery, and subversion designed to confuse and divide its many enemies. Byzantium succumbed to the Ottoman Turks in the fifteenth century, but its legacy is visible not only in the adroit maneuverings of Turkish diplomacy over the centuries but also in the paranoid and cutthroat diplomatic style of Russia, Iran, and indeed the present-day Middle East as a whole.

The conventions of contemporary diplomacy derive from the first of these traditions; but the persistence of the second cannot safely be ignored by today's leaders. In the first half of the twentieth century, the Western democracies had great difficulty adjusting to the unconventional diplomacy of the Soviet Union and Nazi Germany. Had the Nazi leadership been other than it was, the British strategy of "appeasement" of its expansionist ambitions would not have been so fatally wrong-headed. Hitler skillfully exploited this British failure in a sustained and spectacularly successful campaign of political warfare—one of the best demonstrations in recent times of the use of diplomacy as an integral tool of national strategy.

Contemporary diplomacy has its roots in the "cabinet diplomacy" practiced by the European great powers of the nineteenth century, and in some respects remains highly traditional. With the notable exception of the United States, foreign ministries in the advanced democracies tend to be monopolized by national elites and operate largely in secrecy or without serious public accountability, while foreign policy decision-making remains the reserved domain of a few senior ministers. At the same time, the great upheavals of the last century and the spread of liberal democratic regimes and ideas have clearly brought significant change. World War I put an end to the system of agreements by which governments had secretly committed their populations to go to war on behalf of other states. The growth of the popular press and the increasing role of domestic and international public opinion brought diplomacy out of the palace and imposed powerful constraints on the ability of governments to make foreign policy decisions on the basis of cold calculation of the national interest. Finally, the growth of a liberal internationalist outlook and of international institutions and regimes has given diplomacy not only a new focus but a new sense of mission and purpose. Increasingly, it has brought into question the principle—central to traditional diplomacy—of non-interference in the affairs of sovereign nations. Especially since the end of the Cold War, states, coalitions, and international organizations have been readier than in the past to employ the tools of statecraft to shape the internal policies of states in areas such as human rights, civil conflict, or management of the economy.

Whether democracies are good at diplomacy is a much-disputed question. In a well-known passage in his *Democracy in America*, Tocqueville states the negative case: "Foreign policy does not require the use of any of the good qualities peculiar to democracy but does demand the cultivation of almost all those which it lacks. . . . [A] democracy finds it difficult to coordinate the details of a great undertaking and to fix on some plan and carry it through with determination in spite of obstacles. It has little capacity for combining measures in secret and waiting patiently for the result. Such qualities are more likely to belong to a single man or to an aristocracy. But these are just the qualities which, in the long run, make a nation, and a man too, prevail."[3] To the extent to which democratic diplomacy is determined by the people at large, Harold Nicolson tells us, it will reflect a characteristic set of failings—irresponsibility, ignorance, hasty generalization or stereotyping, delay, and lack of precision.[4] In the view of "realists" such as George Kennan and Henry Kissinger, democracies are prone to approaching foreign policy questions in a legalistic and moralistic spirit. In a word, democratic diplomacy is incapable of prudence.

That there is something to all this is undeniable. On the other hand, it is possible to overstate the fecklessness of democracies in the face of external threats.[5] The United States may serve as the extreme example in the contemporary world of a democracy in which foreign policy is not made by a narrow elite and where public and legislative opinion carries (at least some of the time) considerable weight. Yet over the course of the Cold War, the United States pursued a remarkably consistent and tenacious (and of course ultimately successful) foreign policy geared to the overriding goal of containing Soviet power and the threat of global Communism. In spite of the apparent advantages possessed by the Soviet Union with respect to the making and executing of foreign policy, especially freedom from public opinion, Soviet diplomacy in practice was regularly ham-handed, inconsistent, and blundering, while the Americans were able to organize and sustain a formidable anti-Soviet coalition that held together in spite of many strains for some forty years.

There are a number of lessons to be drawn from this. First, it is a mistake to confuse successful diplomacy with the elaborate and subtle intrigues of courts or cabinets of the past. Otto von Bismarck, the undisputed virtuoso of nineteenth-century European diplomacy, wove an intricate web of treaties and understandings that in the end proved too difficult for others to grasp and too fragile to sustain politically. A better model for today is perhaps Bismarck's contemporary and counterpart Lord Salisbury, who held Britain aloof from unnecessary entanglements and believed in the value of truth-telling in diplomacy.[6] For all its subtleties, diplomacy in the end is a relatively blunt instrument, one that demands clarity and simplicity in concept and execution.

A second lesson is that diplomacy is not or ought not be a solo performance. The vice of great diplomatists is the belief that they alone are capable of keeping in hand and manipulating the various strands of national policy. To be sure, successful diplomacy needs the discipline of a single mind and will—"unity, activity, secrecy, dispatch," to cite again Hamilton's formula for executive leadership. At the same time, however, successful diplomacy depends critically on the diplomats—amateurs and professionals alike—who help formulate it and carry it out. There can be no substitute for the capable ambassador who develops relations of intimacy and confidence with the key leaders of a foreign state, or for the special envoy who delivers a request or a threat with authority and aplomb.[7]

This brings us back to the fundamental question of the role of political leaders in diplomacy. There are probably quite a few people today who hold the view that if the leaders of nations would only sit down together, they could resolve their mutual problems. And leaders themselves are by no means immune to the charms of personal diplomacy. The modern constitutional executive, aware as he must be of the sharply limited nature of his powers, is apt to see attractive opportunities for creative statesmanship in his dealings with foreign leaders. There are certainly international circumstances that legitimately invite or require the personal involvement of heads of state or foreign ministers. On the other hand, such high-level diplomacy has its problematic aspects and at the extreme (consider again the Munich summit of 1938) can lead to disaster.

"Summitry" is the primary mode of personal diplomacy but not the only one. Particularly in recent years, the telephone has become increasingly popular as a way for the leaders of major countries to manage crises or simply to stay in regular touch. Telephone diplomacy came into its own at the time of the Gulf War of 1991, when President Bush used it to rally the coalition against Iraq and raise funds to underwrite the war effort; but dedicated phone links between heads of government go back at least to the U.S.-Soviet "Hotline" established in 1963. The advantages of these forms of diplomacy are obvious. It is much more difficult to deny another nation's request or ignore its point of view when these issue directly from the mouth of its leader. Leaders are uniquely positioned to overcome impasses in negotiations stemming from domestic politics or bureaucratic inertia, as well as to force decisions in crisis situations. What is more, the personal "chemistry" of leaders can become a truly strategic factor in the relations of nations. (A case in point: the surprisingly close relationship that developed between American secretary of state James Baker and his Soviet counterpart Eduard Shevardnadze during the last years of the USSR.) In this perspective, leaders have to be considered a national resource or strategic asset—one, indeed, that is too often wasted.

Yet the dangers in such diplomacy should also be apparent. Unscripted conversations between leaders (particularly where barriers of language and culture exist) lend themselves readily to miscommunication and misinterpretation. It is difficult to persuade leaders to prepare adequately for such meetings; hence standing policy is not always well stated or defended. Leaders may make impulsive commitments or may simply leave wrong impressions through a desire to please. Moreover, they may reveal more than they intend. Leaders are the repositories of vast amounts of information of varying degrees of sensitivity and are likely to have difficulty making appropriate distinctions in such situations; they may also demonstrate damaging personal weakness.[8] Even their body language may betray them.[9]

The long history of U.S.-Soviet summit meetings is rich in examples of the promise and perils of personal diplomacy. The most trenchant critic of the practice of summitry by American presidents, ironically enough, is Henry Kissinger, himself one of the foremost practitioners of the art during his tenure in the Nixon administration.[10] For Kissinger, summits are hazardous in the first instance because of the tendency of their "atmospherics"—powerfully amplified by the international media—to overshadow substantive results. Secondly, they tend to disadvantage democratic leaders in their encounters with an autocratic adversary like the Soviet Union. Summits arouse expectations that they will advance the cause of peace through radical improvements in superpower relations; these expectations can then be exploited by the other side to leverage Western public opinion and extract additional concessions. Moreover, the focus on personalities that is inevitable on such occasions helps humanize otherwise unappealing leadership figures.

Politicians have large egos. There is always the danger that they will overinvest their own prestige in a summit encounter. This can lead them to become too involved in the tactics of a negotiation, losing sight thereby of its larger impact on national policy. It encourages them to push for agreement as an end in itself; to push for agreement on trivia—on what is most negotiable rather than what is most important; and to push for a quick agreement, because the time they can remain engaged in such an exercise is necessarily limited. All of this provides the other side with significant leverage to strengthen its own position at the other's expense. Finally, leaders can develop an irrational attachment to agreements that they have helped negotiate, willfully neglecting, for example, evidence of violation of the agreement by the other side or simply changing circumstances.

XVIII

FORCE

"**A** prince should have no other object, nor any other thought, nor take anything else as his art but that of war and its orders and discipline; for that is the only art which is of concern to one who commands. And it is of such virtue that not only does it maintain those who have been born princes but many times it enables men of private fortune to rise to that rank; and on the contrary, one sees that when princes have thought more of amenities than of arms, they have lost their states."[1] This comment may have seemed a pardonable exaggeration in Machiavelli's day; from the perspective of our own, it appears unsustainable. Yet it points to a ground truth of statecraft that is not always sufficiently appreciated. War is less a part of everyday experience than it once was, at least throughout much of the world. Perhaps there are large historical forces at work that will someday make it obsolete. Yet for the foreseeable future, at any rate, war shows few signs of going away. It is capable of erupting in unexpected places and unpredictable forms, as we have witnessed in the wave of Islam-inspired terrorist attacks against the United States and others of the last two decades. And in some ways, although it may not be as central a preoccupation of statesmen as was once the case, it offers political challenges at least as great.

In the premodern past, and even into relatively recent times, war, with all its horrors, was seen not merely as a legitimate instrument of statecraft but as a natural and ordinary aspect of human life.[2] Republics have hardly been more peace-loving than empires or primitive tribes, in spite of a common belief to the contrary. Indeed, Rome, the most successful empire in world history, grew out of a republic whose citizen-soldiers took the field against their enemies virtually every year over many centuries.[3] War has been a major factor in the founding and consolidation of states and the growth of state power.[4] Historically, it has been a central preoccupation of societies and in particular of their rulers and ruling elites, who have generally been accustomed to bearing arms and leading armies in the field. Where political leaders neglect the imperative of "good arms" and entrust their security to others, as Machiavelli complains of the Italian princes of his own time, they court disaster.

In our era, there can be no question that war has lost in some measure both its centrality as an element of statecraft and its perceived legitimacy. National power is now measured as much by economic resources and performance as by military capability. At the same time, the use of force by one state against another is no longer simply accepted as a fact of life but is seen rather as a violation of fundamental norms of international behavior. While the community of nations (if such there is) has never been able to agree on a satisfactory definition of aggressive war, it is nevertheless true that aggressive war has become relatively rare, particularly among the major powers. This cultural allergy to the resort to war has been greatly reinforced, of course, by the growing destructiveness of modern warfare, and especially by the development of nuclear weapons in the period following World War II. The prospect of an apocalyptic nuclear exchange between the United States and the Soviet Union led many to question whether war altogether could any longer be considered a rational enterprise.[5] Yet in spite of all this, Machiavelli's larger point remains valid. Contemporary politicians cannot afford to neglect the art of war.

States live in more or less dangerous neighborhoods. Some neighborhoods are favored by their geography or by particularly benign neighbors (consider Canada). In more dangerous places, disparities in relative power among states can also act to discourage serious attention to the military instrument of statecraft. Even for states not subject to a plausible external threat, however, the failure to maintain credible military forces exacts a price in terms of their international standing and diplomatic voice and creates a psychology of dependency that is difficult to reverse. As for the problem of small nations menaced by greater ones, such states always have options for their defense that can at least raise the costs to a potential attacker and make an attack seem unattractive. Of course, small nations can simply seek the protection of other friendly powers. But allies can be more or less reliable. In the contemporary world, Sweden, Switzerland, Singapore, and Israel have all conspicuously chosen to rely on their own arms rather than the arms of others.[6] They are in the front rank of states serious about war.

As for more consequential states, there can be little cause for complacency. Those who believe that war in general is on the decline today face a significant burden of proof. Throughout the Cold War, while internal or revolutionary war was a persistent phenomenon in the third world, wars between states in the traditional manner were rare and for the most part short, and war in Europe seemed virtually unthinkable. Over the last thirty years, to cite only major developments: Iraq invaded Kuwait, thus precipitating the largest conventional conflict since the Korean War of the 1950s; war returned to Europe in the form of a protracted struggle over the Yugoslav succession; Africa saw its first interstate war of the postcolonial era (between the former good neighbors Ethiopia and Eritrea), as well as brutal internal conflict in western Africa, Congo, Sudan, Libya, Nigeria, and elsewhere; the United States invaded Afghanistan and then reinvaded Iraq—the first steps in what has proven to be a lengthy campaign to destroy Islamic terrorism and its state sponsors; India and Pakistan came to the brink of a major (and potentially nuclear) clash over Kashmir; and North Korea stands poised to field nuclear-armed strategic missiles aimed at the United States and its allies. As for the other major powers: Russia, after a period of military decline and retrenchment following the collapse of the Soviet Union, has entered upon an ambitious program of military modernization, has not hesitated to use force against Ukraine and Georgia, including annexation of the Crimea in contravention of international norms, or to intervene in the ongoing Syrian civil war; at the same time, China continues and accelerates an unprecedented military buildup and displays increasingly provocative behavior toward its neighbors. In Asia and throughout the Muslim world, where cultural inhibitions against the use of force seem distinctly weaker than in the West, the prospects for warfare at all levels are almost certainly better than at any time during the Cold War. This includes warfare involving so-called weapons of mass destruction, the use of which has become more thinkable and potentially more lucrative as fears of a world-ending superpower war have waned.[7] Indeed, there is good reason to think that states generally—not to speak of non-state actors—are more persuaded of the utility of force today than at any time in the postwar era.

War is important to leaders not simply because of its physical destructiveness. War is an intensely political phenomenon, and its political effects can be and indeed frequently are more dramatic than any actual damage inflicted. The loss of a handful of soldiers in a firefight in Mogadishu essentially ended the American intervention in Somalia in 1994 by eroding political support for it at home. The humiliation of a nation's arms—for example, the American failure in Vietnam—can have far-reaching consequences for its international standing and lasting influence on foreign perceptions of both its military capabilities and its political will.[8]

At the extreme, war is hazardous to a state's political health. For democracies above all, war concentrates the minds of the people and forces them to decide how much they like the government they are living under and, in particular, whether they are prepared to die for it.[9] Defeat in war can undermine or destroy not only the authority of governments but the essential legitimacy of regimes, paving the way for revolution. The experience of Tsarist Russia in 1905 (the Russo-Japanese War) and 1917 (World War I) is perhaps the classic case. An instructive example from more recent history is the Falklands conflict of 1982. Here, the failure of the ruling military junta in Argentina to prosecute effectively its war against Britain compromised the very basis of its claim to power, making its fall inevitable.

The relationship between war and politics is a major theme in the study of statecraft. There is a marked tendency on the part of politicians and political scientists, particularly in our unwarlike democracies, to look on war as a realm apart and hence as the business of others—namely, military professionals. In the conventional understanding, civil-military relations are in good order when politicians provide basic political and strategic guidance to the generals but defer to professional military judgment for the management of modern defense establishments as well as the actual conduct of war.[10] But let us listen to Carl von Clausewitz: "When whole communities go to war—whole peoples, and especially *civilized* peoples—the reason always lies in some political situation, and the occasion is always due to some political object. War, therefore, is an act of policy." Or more precisely, war "is not a mere act of policy but a true political instrument, a continuation of political activity by other means."[11]

It is important not to misunderstand Clausewitz's famous formula. In the first place, it is not meant to imply that the political aim should never be adjusted to the reality of the military means available or to evolving circumstances. Nor does it imply that war is an instrument that can be wielded with surgical precision by politicians. On the contrary, he emphasizes that war represents a complex interplay of rational direction, chance, and "primordial violence, hatred and enmity"—war's "remarkable trinity."[12] The peculiar task of political leaders is to harness the professionalism and creativity of military commanders, the courage of their soldiers, and the passions war engenders in the people at large to a strategically sound and politically sustainable goal.

What this does imply is that the perspectives of political and military leaders inevitably—and legitimately—diverge. Military commanders are preoccupied with the means of war and the methods by which they can be combined to carry out effective military operations. Politicians worry about the effects of these operations on public opinion at home and on the nation's allies and adversaries abroad. It may well be the case that some wars are lost by feckless politicians who care more for their own political standing than for military realities on the ground (some would argue this happened to the United States in Vietnam). That the conduct of any war is subordinated to policy or politics (the German word *Politik* carries both meanings) does not mean that the policy is necessarily wise. A sure recipe for disaster, however, is for politicians to assume that deferring to professional military judgment will necessarily lead to the optimum result. This is certainly true of the complex peacetime planning and management required of modern military forces. It is even truer of actual combat. World War I is perhaps the most compelling example of the dangers of excessive civilian deference to military commanders. But the lessons of recent history are that the most successful wartime leaders generally have been those who relentlessly challenged their military subordinates in matters of military judgment and were unafraid to cashier them when the response proved unsatisfactory.[13]

Ensuring a proper balance between policy and military requirements is significantly more difficult today than it was in the past. It is important to understand why this is so. Civil-military relations is a central problem for contemporary statecraft in the first instance because it presupposes the existence of a professional military establishment that scarcely existed prior to the nineteenth century. This establishment includes an elite officer corps that is socially distinct from the political class, and institutions and a set of traditions that encourage the growth of a potent and enduring military subculture. What is more, especially in today's liberal democracies, this subculture tends to be out of step with the dominant culture. In Samuel Huntington's classic analysis of civil-military relations in the United States, the "conservative realism" characteristic of the outlook of military officers differs sharply from the "business liberalism" that dominates American culture as a whole. Elsewhere, military elites are sometimes even more sharply at odds with their nation's civilian leadership, and not always from a conservative direction. This fundamental instability is at the root of the distinctively modern phenomenon of military coups and military regimes.

The popular tendency in the West to link military involvement in politics with "fascism" is understandable yet misleading. The glorification of war and the promotion of national or racial crusades historically associated with German or Italian fascism has little to do with the "conservative realism" that Huntington plausibly ascribes to the military mind generally. Some military regimes in recent times (in Argentina or Turkey, for example) have certainly engaged in harsh repression of domestic opponents. But their purpose in doing so was not really to reshape their societies according to some ideological ideal but rather to defend the "nation" against "subversion" by radical movements of one sort or another. A sense of the armed forces as the ultimate guardian of a vaguely understood national interest is typical of modern military regimes generally. Such professions can certainly be hypocritical or self-serving. On the other hand, they may also reflect legitimate frustration with an irresponsible or kleptocratic civilian leadership.[14]

In the advanced democracies, civilian leaders have little to fear from military coups, or even from military adventurism.[15] Contrary to a certain cartoonish misconception, pressures on the American government to take military action rarely come from the Pentagon. Tocqueville's prediction that a democratic officer corps would agitate for war out of career ambition has proven wholly unfounded.[16] On the contrary, as many critics complain, the military leadership in the United States sometimes seems overly concerned with the risks of military action and routinely overestimates the forces needed for success in order to discourage adventurism by the civilian leadership. In any case, civil-military tensions in the United States—a test case in any such discussion because of its uniquely potent military establishment—take a subtler form. They are not for that reason to be simply dismissed.

The American military is a vast bureaucracy that commands immense resources. Its presence around the country (both directly and by way of the defense industry) is of strategic economic importance for many states and localities and exercises a large influence thereby on congressional decision-making. But perhaps more importantly, the uniformed military today enjoy a certain moral authority in the popular mind that mere politicians generally don't. Especially at a time when few legislators or executive branch officials can lay claim to significant military experience, their ability to challenge strongly held military views is distinctly limited. At the same time, a case can be made that senior military officers have become overly willing to challenge the judgment of their civilian superiors. The point is not that this is wrong in itself; on the contrary, failure to do so was one of the great errors of the American military leadership during the Vietnam War.[17] But such challenges have increasingly involved matters that are plainly in the domain of political leaders—above all, key policy questions concerning the circumstances in which military forces may properly be used, the purposes to which they may legitimately be put, and conditions for terminating their employment. Indeed, it is primarily with this development in mind that some have spoken of an emerging "crisis" in American civil-military relations since the end of the Cold War.[18]

What is the proper relationship of civilian and military authority in a modern democracy? The classic answer is Huntington's notion of "objective control," a kind of bargain by which the military renounce involvement in policy in exchange for freedom from civilian interference in the sphere of professional military judgment. (By contrast, "subjective control" is a system relying on direct penetration of military organizations by politically appointed officers—in the Communist variant, "commissars.") The problem, of course, comes from the difficulty of defining with precision the sphere of professional military judgment. It is easy to agree that tactics is uniquely a military responsibility, less easy when it comes to strategy or even operational art, the discipline that links them. Clausewitz himself admits that political considerations can rightly influence the planning not merely of a war but of a campaign or even a battle, and he suggests including the military commander in chief in cabinet deliberations in order to facilitate the cabinet's shaping of military decisions—not the other way around.[19] It must also be kept in mind that military commanders are frequently as inexperienced as their political superiors in facing a particular set of circumstances or, indeed, in encountering actual combat. Finally, the nature of contemporary conflict makes a difference. In a world like ours, where force is often used in very limited and unconventional ways and in close combination with other elements of statecraft, greater interpenetration of the spheres of military and civilian responsibility seems inevitable if not actually desirable, at least up to point.

In modern democracies with a wholly professional (that is to say, volunteer) military, there will always be room for concern over the relationship of the armed forces to the wider society. Machiavelli warned princes against the dangers of defending their states with mercenary troops. Today's professional armies are of course native ones, but the potential for estrangement from the general population remains.[20] Some commentators have noted an apparent drift to the political right in the American armed forces over the last half century or so, but its significance is far from clear.[21] What is certainly worrisome is the general decline of knowledge or experience of military affairs in the civilian leadership ranks of the American government, including the Congress.

Some remarks may be added on the institutional context of civil-military relations and military decision-making in the United States. Civilian control of the American military is complicated by the constitutionally mandated separation of powers and the role explicitly given the Congress to fund and equip the armed forces. In practice, while the president has at least in theory plenipotentiary power to command the armed forces in time of war, his authority in peacetime is doubtful and frequently contested. The result is that the military establishment is able to gain considerable room for maneuver between the two branches, thus enhancing its freedom of action. Presidents are unable to prevent senior military leaders from talking to congressmen and thereby promoting in more or less subtle ways their institutional agendas. A second point has to do with rivalry among the military services themselves. For reasons of history and geography (and unlike most countries), the United States has separate land, air, and naval services of comparable institutional weight and with very distinct traditions and cultures. Managing the tensions between these services has long been one of the greatest challenges to American military and civilian leaders alike. The Reagan-era (1986) reform of the Joint Chiefs of Staff organization was a congressional initiative designed to make progress on this intractable problem by strengthening the role of the chairman of this body (made up of the chiefs of the Army, Navy, Marines, and Air Force) and designating him the principal military adviser to the president. In spite of concerns in some quarters that this step would fatally weaken civilian control by forcing the military to speak with a single voice, there seems to be general agreement that it represents an improvement and has resulted in genuine progress toward interservice cooperation without clear adverse consequences for the existing civil-military balance.

Institutional reform of this kind is at least as important an aspect of defense statecraft—in this case, one brought about by legislative rather than executive leadership—as the exercise of actual command. Also noteworthy in this regard was the congressional intervention establishing at this same time a new unified command for special operations forces, traditionally a branch of the military that is disliked and distrusted by senior officers from the conventional branches. Civilian patronage of the special operators has paid large dividends, making possible the rapid conquest of Afghanistan by small numbers of these troops on the ground directing highly precise air power in support of local conventionally armed allies; today, they bear a disproportionate role in the global war against terror. A similar argument can be made in favor of aggressive civilian intervention in the ongoing "transformation" of American military forces and technology to meet the challenges of the new century.

XIX

INTELLIGENCE

"The reason the farsighted ruler and his superior commander conquer the enemy at every move, and achieve successes far beyond the reach of the common crowd, is foreknowledge. Such foreknowledge cannot be had from ghosts and spirits, educed by comparison with past events, or verified by astrological calculations. It must come from people—people who know the enemy's situation.... Intelligence is of the essence in warfare—it is what armies depend upon in their every move." Thus Sun Tzu, a Chinese general of the sixth century BC and author of what is arguably the greatest treatise on the art of war after Clausewitz. For Sun Tzu, the importance of intelligence transcends the function often assigned it today as (in American military jargon) a "force multiplier." For as he tells us, the highest excellence in war is not to win a hundred battles but to subdue the enemy without fighting at all; and this is possible, at least under certain circumstances, through the judicious use of intelligence in a larger campaign to deceive and demoralize the enemy's forces. Even where it is not possible, "he who knows the enemy and himself will never in a hundred battles be at risk."[1]

Intelligence can be conceived as an instrument of statecraft in a narrow and a broad sense. In the narrow sense, it involves the collection, analysis, and application of specialized information relating to the various operational components of statecraft. In the larger sense, intelligence itself may be viewed as an operational form of statecraft, one possessing considerable if not complete autonomy and directly answerable to the supreme political authority. Intelligence in this latter sense combines intelligence in the first sense with an array of dark arts that may be conveniently grouped under the rubric "psychological-political warfare"—covert political action (influence operations, subversion, or assassination), psychological warfare, and deception. Historically, these arts have flourished mainly in wartime. As noted earlier, however, they have also occupied a preferred place in the peacetime foreign relations of certain nations from at least the time of the Byzantine Empire; they played a major role on both sides in the Cold War, as the United States and the Soviet Union jockeyed for advantage around the world while avoiding a direct military confrontation that could have led to nuclear catastrophe; and they hold an honored place in the toolbox of Chinese statecraft today.[2]

The two senses of intelligence are analytically distinct, and some would prefer to regard psychological-political warfare as being not intelligence at all but something else—a mode of warfare or diplomacy. Still, it is far from accidental that such functions tend to be performed by organizations whose primary responsibility is intelligence in the narrow sense, since they depend so directly for their effectiveness on accurate knowledge of the adversary as well as an ability to operate in the shadows. For this reason, they will be treated here as part of a single whole.

Intelligence is probably the least well understood of the instruments of statecraft. This is so not just for the obvious reason that the activities associated with it are pursued in secrecy, but also because it is surrounded by so many prejudices and misconceptions. The flood of popular novels and films on intelligence in recent years is, to say the least, of limited value as a source for understanding the subject. Serious study of the history of intelligence is barely fifty years old and remains severely hampered by the absence or inaccessibility of records. What is more, the effort to understand the real impact of intelligence on political and military events, and in particular its influence on political leaders, has only recently begun.[3]

It is customary in the United States to distinguish among four so-called elements of intelligence—collection, analysis, covert action, and counterintelligence. Domestic intelligence has much in common with foreign intelligence but tends to be regarded more as a police than an intelligence function, and in contemporary democracies (though not necessarily elsewhere in the world) it is handled by different organizations. Collection and analysis form the core of intelligence in the narrow sense of the term. Covert action is a term of art (and now of law) covering a diverse range of intelligence operations, including assistance to foreign intelligence organizations, clandestine propaganda, influence activities, and paramilitary support for foreign guerrilla organizations. Not surprisingly, it remains controversial, especially after a congressional investigation in the 1970s exposed much of its checkered history, and it is now subject to careful oversight by both branches of government. Counterintelligence (and related passive defenses generally referred to as security countermeasures) is the discipline charged with safeguarding the nation's own secrets and countering foreign intelligence operations against the United States. This is also viewed by many as a discipline distinct from intelligence (it is mostly the responsibility of a separate agency, the domestically oriented Federal Bureau of Investigation), yet the two are intimately related, as counterintelligence operations can provide a unique window on what foreign governments know or would like to find out.[4]

There can be no question that much of the intelligence business is unsavory, raising fundamental questions not only about the moral side of statecraft generally but also about the proper place of such activities in a democratic society. That "gentlemen don't read each other's mail" is a deeply felt sentiment among traditional as well as liberal elites and points to the cultural obstacles that need to be overcome in creating an effective intelligence service.[5] If secrecy is essential to intelligence, how are intelligence officials to be held accountable for their behavior? It is easy to say that they must be carefully monitored by the nation's political leadership; in practice, however, many difficulties arise. Leaders are very likely to want to distance themselves from intelligence operations or to maintain (to use the American term of art) "plausible deniability" about them. And in fact, of course, it would be hard for them to track fully or to manage such operations even if they wanted to. Because of their very nature, intelligence organizations are extraordinarily hard to control, and yet at the same time they are particularly prone to going astray. Indeed, they pose a serious danger to a nation's leadership because of their potential for causing scandal or embarrassment or engaging in political intrigue—if nothing more.[6] All of this should be borne in mind in any assessment of the saga of Donald Trump's relationship with the American intelligence community, particularly the Federal Bureau of Investigation—an overt manifestation of dysfunction in the leader-intelligence relationship that is unprecedented in our history.

Organized intelligence work is a recent development in the modern West.[7] Military establishments have typically held intelligence in low esteem and thus have been slow to embrace and institutionalize the intelligence function. Espionage has been for the most part the preserve of amateurs, often acting virtually alone, often in direct contact with a head of state or his spymaster. During the American Revolution, General George Washington personally ran intelligence agents against the British. Some of the most effective intelligence networks in Europe were organized privately, notably by the Rothschild banking empire; during the American Civil War, the Union relied for its intelligence needs on the Pinkerton detective agency. As late as World War II, the United States had no permanent intelligence establishment. The Office of Strategic Services (OSS), the predecessor of the Central Intelligence Agency (CIA), was created virtually single-handedly by a brilliant New York lawyer, William J. Donovan, who personally recruited much of its talented staff from his own social circle.[8]

Part of the reason intelligence organizations are hard to control has to do with the kinds of people who tend to work in them. Spies tend to be highly individualistic (hence difficult to discipline), highly operational (hence frequently insensitive to the larger picture), adventurers and risk-takers, and not least, con artists—including in their dealings with superiors. They work in an environment that is on the margins of the law and hence tends to erode respect for regulations and other legal or moral constraints. Their chief occupational hazard is a certain blurring of personal identity and loyalty that can make them surprisingly vulnerable to recruitment by foreign intelligence agencies, sometimes to catastrophic effect (the Hansen and Ames cases are recent American examples). Finally, the closed nature of their world creates a clannish sensibility that makes it difficult or impossible to police these problems effectively from within.

In short, intelligence organizations are as much in need of civilian control as military organizations, if not indeed more so; yet in some ways they are even more resistant to it. There seem to be three modes of exercising such control. Objective control (to borrow Huntington's term) maximizes the autonomy of these organizations in return for formal deference to civilian authority and non-interference in the policy process. This may be said to be the preferred Anglo-Saxon model.[9] Subjective control minimizes their autonomy through directly subordinating them to political officials, as the Soviet Union subordinated its Committee for State Security (KGB) to the Communist Party, while at the same time permitting them a greater say in policy formulation. Finally, there is what might be called the checks and balances approach. This involves pitting various intelligence agencies against one another in a competitive environment that serves to keep them tolerably honest and protect the leader's freedom of action (and for that matter his person). Nazi Germany is the historical model here, but this approach is also common in much of the less developed world today for managing security services generally.[10]

Are intelligence agencies more trouble than they are worth? What vital tasks of statecraft do they perform that could not be performed as well or better in other ways? These questions are not raised as frequently as they might be. The CIA was created by the United States Congress in the aftermath of World War II largely in reaction to the failure of American military intelligence to predict or provide warning of the Japanese attack on Pearl Harbor in December 1941. Anticipating unpleasant and possibly fatal security surprises is perhaps the single strongest argument for a standing intelligence capability in peacetime. Yet the CIA's track record over this period is hardly inspiring in this regard. The United States was taken essentially by surprise by the North Korean invasion of South Korea in June 1950, and then by Chinese intervention in the ensuing war later that same year; by the Soviet nuclear buildup in Cuba in the summer of 1962; by Saddam Hussein's invasion of Kuwait in August 1990; and not least, by the terrorist attacks on New York and Washington in September 2001. Whatever avoidable errors may have occurred in each of these cases, a larger argument can be made that the singular character of such events as well as the dynamics of the intelligence assessment and warning process itself make it unlikely that surprise attacks can ever be reliably predicted. More generally, in spite of the emphasis the CIA continues to give to producing "estimates" of the future security environment, skepticism seems to be in order about the very possibility of policy-relevant intelligence predictions of this sort. To say nothing of other considerations, how can you credibly predict the future policy courses of other states when their own leaders may well have no idea what they will do next week?[11]

A good argument can be made that the primary utility of intelligence analysis lies not in predicting the future but rather in educating policy makers in the realities of the present and recent past. Understood in this way, however, intelligence competes with many other sources of information for the attention of a nation's leaders. Especially today, with the advent of the internet and the ready availability of data of all kinds, it is far from clear that intelligence organizations can provide real value added, except perhaps against that (shrinking) set of nations or organizations that are willing to impose the kinds of internal controls necessary to keep vital information secret. Since the end of the Cold War, some in the United States have actually called for an evolution in the intelligence world away from the traditional preoccupation with secret information and toward more comprehensive and academic-style analysis, much of which could be made available to the public (we shall return to this issue shortly). But then why not simply subcontract such work to contractors or university professors?

Plainly, it would be irresponsible for statesmen simply to ignore or discount intelligence. Certain types of intelligence information (for example, satellite images of inaccessible military facilities) are genuinely useful and unobtainable from other sources. The use of intelligence by adversaries is a weapon that needs to be countered like any other. Even the disciplines of psychological-political warfare have their place, providing a nation advantages in economy of force that are defensible not only strategically but in moral terms. On the other hand, statesmen ignore at their peril the pathologies of the intelligence world. Intelligence needs to be seen not just as another bureaucratic asset but as one existing in an intimate relationship with the leader, with much potential both for good and ill. Unfortunately, the highly institutionalized character of contemporary intelligence organizations tends to obscure this truth.

Leaders—including great ones—have varied enormously in their appreciation and use of intelligence. Great conquerors have been both assiduous processors of intelligence (Napoleon) and despisers of it (Hitler). Occasionally, leaders emerge from the intelligence world itself (Putin in contemporary Russia, Manuel Noriega in Panama); their policies and operating styles need to be evaluated accordingly. Democratic politicians tend to be temperamentally alien to the culture of intelligence. Yet without doubt the greatest consumer of intelligence among modern political leaders was Winston Churchill. When he was out of office in the 1930s, Churchill adroitly used his carefully preserved access to British intelligence documents to warn of German rearmament and criticize the government publicly for the inadequacies of British defense policy. During World War II, he was involved in every aspect of wartime intelligence. He created the Special Operations Executive, an unconventional warfare organization that was the model for the American OSS and later CIA; and he personally managed the sensitive technical collection program that provided what may well have been the vital margin of Allied victory.[12] Of recent American presidents, Eisenhower, with his exposure to intelligence at the highest levels during the war, was similarly an avid promoter both of covert action and of the development of sophisticated technical reconnaissance systems.[13]

It is worth dwelling for a moment on the vexed question of the merits of a centralized intelligence system or organization. The Central Intelligence Agency was created in 1947 by the United States Congress for a number of reasons. The CIA would, it was believed, provide better coordination of the intelligence products of the various (mostly military) entities engaged in these activities; provide a counterweight to the institutional biases often seen in military intelligence; and ensure that intelligence would be collected and analyzed from a truly strategic perspective, thus better serving the needs of the national leadership and, in particular, the president. From the beginning, therefore, the CIA was designed to play a direct supporting role to the White House's intelligence needs. Yet it never proved possible to centralize and fully coordinate intelligence through the CIA, owing primarily to the bureaucratic weight of the military intelligence establishment and its overriding mission of intelligence support to the military services. Instead, governance of the intelligence community has been handled by a kind of confederal arrangement, with authority nominally in the hands of the CIA director acting in a second capacity as Director of Central Intelligence (DCI). Over the years, this arrangement has been routinely criticized and proposals advanced for further consolidating the DCI's control. The question is whether moving in this direction would in fact have the advertised effect of strengthening intelligence collection and analysis in support of the requirements of national strategy and the president's policies. Recently, in partial acknowledgment of the problem, a Director of National Intelligence has been established independently of the CIA, but it remains unclear whether this institutional solution will prove effective.

There are reasons for doubt. While there is certainly merit in the original argument for a centralized analytic intelligence function, it must also be recognized that the CIA has over time developed a powerful institutional identity and culture of its own that prevents it from serving simply as an extension of presidential needs. A key element of the agency's culture is a certain view of the relationship between intelligence and policy. According to this view, the chief danger facing intelligence professionals is the corruption of the analytic process by policy officials who seek to use intelligence assessments to advance a certain policy agenda. In practice, therefore, any questioning of intelligence judgments by such officials tends to be seen as illegitimate interference in the business of the intelligence community, which accordingly must do its best to keep decision-makers at arm's length. A second key element of this culture is a certain philosophy of intelligence.[14] Reflecting the strongly academic orientation of the original OSS and CIA analytic staffs, this philosophy holds that the primary task of intelligence is not so much to ferret out the secrets of adversaries as to build a comprehensive picture of the world using the tools of contemporary social science. Implicit in all this is the assumption that policy officials lack an adequate understanding of their operational environment. More than that, in spite of formal acknowledgment of the right of policy makers to establish their own intelligence "requirements," it is often assumed that these officials in fact do not really know what they need to know: at the end of the day, intelligence analysis must supply not only the answers but the questions too.

This attitude—an odd mixture of wariness and condescension—can hardly endear intelligence officials to their policy superiors. But is it justified? In a system like the American one, where political appointees as well as elected officials can find themselves in leadership positions for which they have little real preparation, the condescending approach might at first sight seem reasonable. In fact, however, many political appointees (whether academics, lawyers, or congressional staffers) are very capable people who come to their jobs with a wealth of relevant knowledge and experience—frequently more than the typical intelligence analyst. Even politicians should not be treated simply as slow pupils.[15] Many of them are highly intuitive and perfectly capable of grasping the essence of a political situation in another part of the world in short order and without mastering all its details. Moreover, the politician who occupies high office quickly develops alternative sources of information and hence perspectives that are not necessarily available to the intelligence analyst. In particular, policy makers have one great advantage over intelligence analysts: they know what their own side is doing.

Further, the notion that policy makers have no standing to criticize intelligence judgments is inherently implausible. Such judgments represent an amalgam of what might be called hard secrets and soft analysis. Secrets need to be placed in an analytic context to be truly useful, but there is no particular reason why this task has to be performed by an intelligence organization. The reasoning that goes into such analysis is often little different from the reasoning underlying policy deliberations, and could well be performed (and historically often has been) by policy staffs. This brings us back to the broader issue of the scope of intelligence analysis. As long as the goal of intelligence is the creation of a sort of universal social science, intelligence is bound to be fundamentally at odds with the policy world. To define intelligence in this way is necessarily to slight the information needs of leaders and to underestimate their capacity for the exercise of prudential judgment.

That there are built-in tensions in the relationship of leaders and intelligence organizations is undeniable. Once leaders have made up their minds on a course of action, they are unlikely to want their decisions constantly second-guessed in intelligence reports, particularly when (as in the United States) such reports are routinely available to domestic political opponents. And in formulating policy, leaders may well believe that intelligence analysis constrains their options even as it provides little that is of real utility; they may be tempted simply to disregard intelligence when convinced of their own instinctive understanding of a situation; and at the extreme, they may try to force analysts to fall in line with their policy preferences. There is no simple solution to these problems. On the other hand, too much can be made of the problem of corruption of analysis or, more generally, the dangers of a close intelligence-policy relationship. Analysis can be corrupted or slanted in many ways, not least by intelligence analysts or managers themselves in an effort to curry favor with their superiors. But the key point is that the most objective intelligence is useless if it is not perceived to be relevant and is not in fact used. Intelligence is or should be viewed above all as an operational tool of leaders, not simply as an undifferentiated mass of information that someone someday might want to know about. From this perspective, presidents (as well as lesser policy officials) should work closely with intelligence personnel to shape collection and analysis to their own agenda and timetable. And they should be prepared to intervene in the institutional processes of intelligence if need be to ensure that this happens.[16]

This alternative approach—really, the traditional approach to the intelligence-policy relationship—implies a much more selective focus than in the CIA model. It implies that intelligence agencies should concern themselves after all with "secrets" more than with general knowledge. The kind of knowledge that is operationally useful to leaders might include, for example, information on the decision-making styles and processes of other world leaders, the policy orientations and strengths of factions within their government, or tensions in the relationship of their military establishment to civilian authority. It would not include such staple topics of the American intelligence community today as long-term demographic or environmental trends or the societal impact of the AIDS epidemic.

Unhappiness with the performance of the American intelligence community in recent years has been very generally shared across the political spectrum. A better case can almost certainly be made for fundamental organizational reform here than in any other sector of the American national security bureaucracy, with the exception of homeland defense. As indicated earlier, most proposals for change have favored further centralization of the sprawling intelligence establishment. The real problem, however, is not the CIA's inability to coordinate the work of other intelligence entities; it is the CIA itself. An argument can be made for a drastic devolution of the intelligence analysis function from the CIA to the primary intelligence consumers; there is even a case to be made for the abolition of the Directorate of Operations (the agency's covert action component) in its current form.[17] There has been little sign as yet of stomach for such far-reaching reforms either in Congress or in the White House, in spite of the powerful pressures for change generated by the terrorist attacks of September 11. This is testimony to the power of permanent bureaucracies in the modern state; more to the point, however, it underlines the extent to which intelligence organizations are skilled at self-protection and how they are oddly immunized by the political sensitivity surrounding them.

XX

COMMUNICATION

We come finally to an area of statecraft that is both venerable and supremely important for leaders in our media-driven age. Political communication, like intelligence, involves the processing of information; both functions uniquely engage the intellectual faculties of statesmen. Political communication is also an inescapable leadership responsibility, one that is impossible to delegate (like war or diplomacy, for example) and that is increasingly seen in the advanced democracies as a key test of political competence. Yet the study of political communication, it is fair to say, remains at the margins of contemporary political science and tends to be neglected in mainstream historical research. The speeches of politicians are the last place contemporary scholars are apt to look in attempting to understand their behavior.

This is not altogether surprising or necessarily wrong, given the fact that our politicians rarely write their own speeches—indeed, sometimes scarcely read them. Political speeches today are typically seen as tactical exercises that lose virtually all significance once they are reported in the next day's press. On the rare occasions when politicians do feel compelled to reach for elevation of tone or expression, they are generally incapable of doing so. Moreover, as speeches are increasingly crafted for the television medium, their intellectual level tends to sink accordingly. What is surprising is not that democratic publics find political speeches uninspiring but that they are willing to listen to them at all.

It has not always been thus. In the republics of the ancient world, speaking ability was regarded as essential for any aspiring politician, and instruction in speech and debate in the public assembly and the courts was a central component of higher education. The earliest surviving treatise on this subject, Aristotle's *Rhetoric*, is a classic that continues to be widely read. Other Greek and Roman writers on the art of rhetoric, especially Isocrates and Cicero, sadly forgotten as they are today, helped lay the foundations of a tradition of liberal education in which rhetoric would have a central role. This tradition remained very much alive in the early modern period and indeed through the nineteenth century. It shaped the practice of parliamentary debate in England, America, and elsewhere, setting a standard of eloquence (in politicians like Edmund Burke, Daniel Webster, or Abraham Lincoln) matched in our own times only by the speeches and writings of the incomparable Winston Churchill.[1] The eclipse of rhetoric as a practical art and its displacement in higher education by modern social science is the primary factor underlying the decay of contemporary political discourse.[2]

Leaders communicate, however, as much through deeds as words. The actions of governments are themselves a communications tool, and sometimes they speak louder than words: they can communicate, for example, resolution or weakness, seriousness or fecklessness, commitment or the lack of it. Beyond this, however, there are certain institutions, policies, or actions of governments whose *primary purpose* may be said to be symbolic communication rather than operational effect. Let us recall again Walter Bagehot's distinction between the "dignified" and "efficient" components of the British constitution. Contemporary monarchs and certain other heads of state, for example, perform a largely symbolic function in the politics of their countries, yet one that is not for that reason unimportant. They serve as a symbol of national unity, regime legitimacy, and continuity of government amid potentially destabilizing political change.[3] This symbolic dimension of political leadership is also largely neglected in our political science.[4] Part of the reason for this certainly is that it seems to comment negatively on the rationality of ordinary people and hence of popular government. A deeper reason is that it contradicts the disdain for "forms" that Tocqueville long ago noted as a characteristic feature of democratic political culture.[5]

What exactly is rhetoric? Disregarding contemporary academic usages, we shall say simply that it is the art of persuading large audiences, especially in political matters broadly construed. Aristotle, who remains an indispensable guide to its fundamentals, distinguishes rhetoric from three related arts: logic, "dialectic," and "sophistry." In his day, much as in ours, a popular view of rhetoric tended to equate it with sophistry, that is to say, with the use of verbal trickery to sustain or defeat an argument. Aristotle defends rhetoric against this misconception. For him, rhetoric has or can have an argumentative component that, while falling short of the rigor of logic proper, nevertheless has an integrity of its own. Dialectic may be described as the art of debate. Its natural home is not the political marketplace but small private gatherings of those with an interest in intellectual issues.

Thus while the logical or argumentative component of rhetoric is necessary and important, it is not the whole of it. In persuading large and therefore relatively popular or less educated audiences, two other mechanisms of persuasion also need to be employed: "character" and "emotion." Character refers to the personal impression—the "image," as we might say—that the speaker creates or projects. Emotion is the speaker's appeal to the emotions of his audience. Together, these things may be said to be the source of a speaker's "charisma" in our current sense of that term. Aristotle does not deny that these aspects of rhetoric lend themselves to manipulation or misrepresentation. But he insists that they are nevertheless a fully legitimate element of the art when deployed in an appropriate way. That rhetorical skill is all that a politician needs to succeed is another notion widely accepted both by Aristotle's contemporaries and ours and rejected by him. According to him, rhetoric is dependent for the substance of the arguments it makes on "political science," and its persuasive effect will increase in proportion (or at any rate in some reasonable relation) to its being genuinely informed by political knowledge.[6]

Perhaps the single greatest failure of contemporary orator-politicians from this perspective is their incapacity for political argument. A typical political speech today is an amalgam of unsubstantiated assertions and appeals to authority, particularly the authority of the courts and of studies issued in one corner or another of the academic or public policy world. Rarely do politicians try to make their case through any substantive argumentation, let alone by sustained reference to political first principles or historical context. The contrast with American public oratory of two centuries ago is remarkable and disturbing. Nor is this merely an American problem.[7]

Aristotle draws useful distinctions between three kinds of rhetoric. Deliberative rhetoric, at home in the popular assembly, is concerned with the politically advantageous and harmful. Forensic rhetoric, the rhetoric of the courtroom, deals with the just and the unjust. And then there is "epideictic" ("display") rhetoric, the rhetoric of ceremonial occasions and oratorical contests, which is concerned with "the noble"—with the celebration of distinguished persons and of deeds performed in the service of the nation. Examples of this genre include Pericles's "Funeral Oration" and Lincoln's "Gettysburg Address"—probably the two greatest pieces of political oratory of which we have a record. These various types of rhetoric are all recognizably alive today. Forensic rhetoric, for example, comes naturally to the lawyers who play such a dominant role in contemporary American politics (it is perhaps most visible in congressional hearings). The area in which contemporary politicians are weakest, however, is almost certainly the last. With a few notable exceptions—Ronald Reagan's 1984 speech commemorating the fortieth anniversary of the Allied invasion of Normandy in World War II is one of them—politicians seem to neglect the occasions that could provide the context for symbolically powerful oratory, or in any event do not rise to them. This dimension of their activity is simply not taken seriously as having fundamental strategic or political importance.

Two rhetorical settings are generally seen as critical for contemporary leaders, providing opportunities for dramatic political gain but also for sudden political death. One is the debate; the other, what might be called the crisis speech. In the United States today, televised political debates, for all their importance, frequently turn on questions of image and style. But debates can also serve to crystallize substantive issues in ways that can have a lasting strategic effect. The classic case is the Lincoln-Douglas senatorial debates of 1858, on the eve of the American Civil War.[8] As for crisis rhetoric, there is no better illustration than the wartime speeches of Churchill. When Churchill stood up before the House of Commons on May 13, 1940, his first appearance there as prime minister shortly after replacing the discredited yet still popular Neville Chamberlain, Britain was deeply demoralized, sentiment in elite circles for a deal with Hitler was strong, and the mood in the chamber was less than friendly. When he sat down a few minutes later, amid tumultuous applause, the nation was united and committed to "victory—victory at all costs, victory in spite of all terror, victory, however long and hard the road may be."[9]

Symbolic political communication operates at a more elemental level than political speech. Its power is therefore especially great in traditional societies and among strata of the population with low literacy and limited contact with the state; but it would be a mistake to underestimate its impact even in the advanced democracies today. Like political speech, it delivers messages, creates or projects certain images, and evokes certain emotions. Flags and national anthems are perhaps the most potent embodiment of patriotic feelings for most people (hence the political sensitivity of the national anthem issue in the United States today). Public buildings, monuments, statuary, and burial sites can also serve as powerful symbols of a nation's identity and history (hence the current controversy over Confederate statues). At another level, symbols of various kinds can be important props of particular regimes. The physical domination of central Washington by the Capitol building sends a clear message about the republican character of the American regime. The swastika and Nuremberg-style mass rallies were effective advertisements for Nazi Germany, as were the hammer and sickle and May Day parades for the Soviet Union. When one of Russia's great cities again became St. Petersburg, it was clear that Communism had thoroughly collapsed there.

Leaders have significant opportunities for symbolic communication. Indeed, they communicate symbolically whether they like it or not, simply because everything they do tends to be invested with larger meanings by the attentive public. The private behavior of leaders, for example, sends powerful messages to the wider society and can help define an era (Victorian England). Ronald Reagan's natural dignity and simplicity, by contrast with his immediate predecessors in the Oval Office, struck a powerful chord with the American public and were an enormous political asset. Personal communication—with politicians, domestic elites, and foreign leaders—is an important aspect of political leadership especially (though not only) in democracies. And of course contemporary leaders can and do spend much of their time attending "events" that have little purpose other than creating and projecting images aimed at a particular political constituency. All of this can obviously be overdone. It is certainly possible to squander a leader's prestige when such actions are taken too often or inappropriately. The challenge is to think through their impact and associated costs and benefits within a strategic framework rather than simply in response to day-to-day political pressures. This means in particular paying attention to the impact abroad of actions decided on within a purely domestic context. (Communication to foreign audiences will be discussed in a moment.)

Leaders of course cannot do all these things by themselves. As with the other disciplines of statecraft, political communication requires support by a class of professionals. Even before the advent of mass communications or press secretaries, leaders frequently looked to others to project a desired message or image. Patronage of poets and artists might simply gratify a prince's vanity, but it also served this highly practical purpose. Political history too was often written at the behest of rulers. Today, all such functions and more are performed by journalists, the unheroic chroniclers of leadership in our democratic age. The problem, however, is that journalists today enjoy a prestige and independence that is without historical parallel. The mass media are well and truly a fourth estate of the contemporary democratic realm.[10] Not surprisingly, the relationship between political leaders and the powerful barons of this estate is a problematic one. At the same time, the dependence of politicians on journalists or ex-journalists for communication expertise brings substantial liabilities.

Freedom of the press is an article of faith in contemporary American politics, thought to be guaranteed by a basic provision of the Constitution.[11] Tocqueville was among the first to appreciate the important political role a free press could play in modern democracies.[12] There can be no question that the press performs a vital service in checking and balancing the formidable power of the contemporary administrative state and acting as a modern tribune of the people. The problem occurs when the press itself metamorphoses into a potent and monolithic institution in its own right. This is currently the situation in the United States. In spite of their superficial diversity, the print and visual media have increasingly come under the control of a handful of corporate empires; and what may be described as their opinion-forming components are relatively few and dominated by a single culture and political orientation. When it is convenient to do so, media organizations emphasize their public interest roles. At the same time, they adamantly refuse to be held accountable in the performance of these roles and resist any effort by government to limit or regulate their activities.[13]

That the American mass media have developed over recent decades a distinctive culture and political outlook would probably be widely agreed. Studies invariably show that journalists are well to the left politically of ordinary Americans. They tend to be instinctively suspicious of government and of traditional elites (politicians, businessmen, the military). To the extent that they look to any authority, it is the intellectual authority of the *bien-pensant* liberalism of the universities and of academic social science. At the same time, they have become increasingly bold in inserting themselves in the operations of government and interpreting the actions of government to the people. With the peculiar combination of cynicism and idealism that is their trademark, they condescend to and diminish the nation's political leadership in the eyes of the public. In all of these respects, they are a problem for politicians. They are an active impediment to prudential decision-making and effective governance.[14]

The extent to which the elite media are virtually an integral part of the policy-making process in the United States today is not well understood. It is practically impossible to hold a cabinet-level meeting in the White House without the results appearing in the *New York Times* or the *Washington Post* the next morning. Favored reporters are given unimaginable access to senior officials to produce books on the inner workings of the government in the most sensitive areas of war and peace—books that are often published even before an administration has left office. In the past, presidents and other senior officials would make careful use of a trusted reporter or columnist to float ideas or make an administration's case. Today, the press is in the driver's seat. The leaking of information by officials is no longer an art form; it is simply the way things are done. The result is that secrets can no longer be reliably kept and, more to the point, that deliberative processes and orderly staff work are short-circuited by the need to decide and act before the next news cycle.[15]

The United States is admittedly an extreme case. In other advanced democracies, the media are generally kept at a much greater distance from government and at the same time are more deferential to it, while in less democratic states the media tend to be dominated if not fully controlled by the government. Nevertheless, the global impact of the American mass media should not be underestimated, and there can be no question that

American-style journalism has become increasingly the fashion elsewhere (sometimes with unfortunate consequences for journalists). What, if anything, should responsible leaders think or do about these problems?

A good case can be made that the march of information technology will correct some of them, especially the institutional power of the major television networks, now giving way under the impact of proliferating cable channels as well as the internet. However this may be, there are certainly steps governments can take to encourage or ensure genuine competition among media outlets. Above all, governments should not let media organizations forget that the airwaves are a public good and subject as such to accountability and reasonable regulation. Such regulation might include, for example, mandating certain kinds of public service programming, including substantial free or discounted airtime for political debates and advertising (an attractive alternative approach to campaign finance reform)—something the broadcasting industry has fiercely resisted for years and the American political class has never forcefully pushed.

The heart of the matter, however, is the right of governments to regulate media access to themselves and to shape the substance of media coverage. Part of the problem is that those in government charged with relations with the media are almost always journalists themselves—people who want to be thought well of by their peers and eventually return to their profession. Such people often are tactically adroit in orchestrating good press for their bosses, but they are unlikely to want to challenge in any fundamental way the operating assumptions of the organizations they have to deal with or to administer serious discipline for misbehavior. Of course, leaders themselves generally have little stomach for such measures either, for the price of thwarting media desires can be political misery. At a certain point, however, leaders have to consider the consequences of a stance of continuing appeasement of their media tormentors.

Should leaders attempt actively to shape the news? The "spinning" of reporters—trying to influence their coverage of a story in your favor—is a well-known practice that, while not always savory, is sometimes a defensive necessity. The real question, however, is whether leaders or their senior aides should personally intervene with journalists (or their editors or publishers) to try to influence the handling of a story. The case for this is clearest—and the practice most common in the past—in the area of sensitive military or (particularly) intelligence information in media hands. Yet there is no reason why official complaints should not be registered in public or private about skewed media coverage of any important policy issue. The idea, tirelessly promoted by media spokesmen, that government is fair game for comment of all kinds while government is barred from defending itself because of a supposed "chilling effect" on free speech is hard to take seriously.

There is a certain parallelism between government-media relations and civil-military relations. The model of "objective control" in civil-military relations might be said to have its counterpart in a bargain whereby government respects media autonomy and facilitates its coverage of national issues in return for the media observing certain fundamental norms of behavior and respecting certain government requirements. The fundamental norms are political and ideological neutrality and a reasonable respect for the symbols and traditions of the nation. The government requirements are protection of sensitive information and the integrity of government operations. The alternative to this formula is a system of direct or indirect control of media outlets by political parties, if not by governments themselves. Failing both, government and media relations may be said to be in a state of crisis. Is there any other way to describe the situation in the America of Donald Trump?

We conclude with a discussion of political communication geared primarily to foreign audiences, or what has come to be called "public diplomacy."[16] When the Soviet empire in Eastern Europe, and soon afterward the Soviet Union itself, collapsed virtually without a shot being fired in defense of the old order, many in the West were at a loss for a plausible explanation. That the legitimacy of Communist rule had already been profoundly eroded not only in the satellite countries but in the Soviet homeland itself prior to the events of 1989–91 could hardly be doubted. Yet the possibility that the overseas information programs of Western governments, especially those of the United States, might have been instrumental in that development has rarely been entertained by our academic and policy experts. The causes of the Soviet collapse are still far from clear. Yet it is fair to say that the contribution of American information or public diplomacy programs has not been adequately assessed and is almost certainly undervalued.[17]

International information programs have been a permanent tool of American policy since World War II.[18] Shortwave radio broadcasting was long their centerpiece; American libraries and cultural centers abroad also contributed, as well as a variety of specialized publications and educational and cultural exchange programs. In the early years of the Cold War, such programs were viewed straightforwardly as a strategic instrument of American resistance to the global challenge of Communism—of a piece with political-psychological warfare as practiced by the Central Intelligence Agency. In the aftermath of the Vietnam War and the shift in the 1970s to a policy of détente with the USSR, however, these attitudes ceased to be fashionable, and public diplomacy (a term coined at this time as an alternative to the newly odious "propaganda") came increasingly to be seen as a kind of news service disinterestedly provided by the United States to the rest of the world and, accordingly, as increasingly marginal to the nation's real strategic interests.

Ronald Reagan came to the presidency uniquely equipped to engage in ideological struggle. A former actor and radio personality, he understood instinctively the power of modern communications media and the importance of theater in contemporary politics. He had had firsthand exposure to Communist political warfare as president of the Screen Actors Guild in postwar Hollywood. As president, his speaking and acting skills would justly earn him the title "the Great Communicator." It is not altogether surprising, then, that Reagan should set out to revitalize America's languishing public diplomacy capabilities—and more than that, take up the cudgels personally against the Soviet foe.

When Reagan spoke publicly of the Soviet Union as an "evil empire" whose last chapter was even then being written, he broke all the rules that had governed official American commentary on East-West relations for at least a quarter century. Though derided at the time by his domestic critics and international adversaries, the president spoke these and similar words with deliberation and to great effect. By couching the U.S.-Soviet conflict not merely in political or ideological but in moral terms, Reagan tapped a profound vein of anti-Communist sentiment in the East. At the same time, he issued a formidable challenge to Communist elites everywhere, putting them on notice that the United States in effect no longer recognized the legitimacy of their rule. To the extent that American public diplomacy as a whole came to be infused with this spirit, it represented a strategic threat of an altogether different order than the one to which the Soviets had become accustomed over the years. Among other things, the promotion of democracy in the East was put on the table as an operational aspect of American policy, not merely a pious wish.

All this having been said, it remains true that public diplomacy never lived up to its full potential in the Reagan years, not to speak of the post–Cold War period, when the basic rationale for it has seemed less compelling. The fundamental reason for this is that public diplomacy is still tarred for many by its lingering association with psychological-political warfare. In particular, journalists are viscerally hostile to it, seeing it (quite unfairly) as a perversion of the standards of their profession and a dangerous step in the direction of government control of information generally. Should the new security environment created by the global war against terrorism cause leaders to take a second look at what public diplomacy can offer, as it certainly should, they need to realize that it remains a domestic political minefield, with progress almost certainly dependent on forceful intervention from the highest levels of government.

XXI

ON STRATEGY

Mastery of the various instruments of statecraft is a formidable undertaking for the aspiring leader, but by itself it is not enough. The leader must also be able to use them in coordination with one another and in an operationally effective fashion. We turn next, therefore, to consider what might be called the modalities of leadership decision and action—strategy and planning; crisis management; and advice and the decision-making process. We will be primarily concerned, as throughout, with leadership in its contemporary democratic setting.

Today, crisis management in a pejorative sense of the term may be said to be the modus operandi of most of the world's democracies. A certain lack of seriousness in dealing with a world seen as less threatening than during the Cold War, the entanglements of multilateral diplomacy, the pressures of the global economy—these and other factors combine to encourage reactive and ad hoc approaches to international challenges. At home, domestic politics are always preoccupying and create short time horizons for most politicians. As a result, democratic leaders rarely think ahead, nor do they attempt to plan systematically for the future of their countries. This should not be altogether surprising. Let us recall again Alexis de Tocqueville's famous warning: "A democracy finds it difficult to coordinate the details of a great undertaking and to fix on some plan and carry it through with determination in spite of obstacles. It has little capacity for combining measures in secret and patiently waiting for the result. Such qualities are more likely to belong to a single man or to an aristocracy."[1] In short, democracies are not well suited to strategy.

That the United States should find strategy particularly challenging is also not surprising. Throughout much of its history, the nation's insular position relieved it from having to think seriously about potential adversaries. Moreover, its growing material abundance lent itself to a style of warfare favoring logistics and firepower over maneuver, already evident in the Union's victory over the arguably superior generalship of the Confederacy during the Civil War.[2] In more recent times, the nation's unprecedented economic might has helped insulate it again from external threats. It is also important to understand the influence of law in the cultural outlook of Americans. Those who look primarily to legal procedures to deal with malefactors, whether criminals at home or aggressor states or terrorists abroad, tend to think very differently from those who take a strategic approach.

What exactly is strategy? The tendency to use this term as virtually a synonym for the art of war remains strong today.[3] Particularly under modern conditions, however, strategy even in this sense must extend deep into the realm of statecraft generally. According to an authoritative Soviet definition, for example, strategy "studies the conditions and nature of future war, the methods for its preparation and conduct, the services of the armed forces and the foundations for their strategic utilization, as well as foundations for the material and technical support and leadership of the war and the armed forces."[4] Strategy spans war and the preparation for war, but this means it has an active role in peacetime as well. It encompasses not merely the actual use of force but also the development of the instruments of force and the implied or open threat of their use. Moreover, strategy is sometimes used in an even broader sense, to refer to the full panoply of instruments of national power that come into play in time of war or in support of a nation's security interests. The term *grand strategy* is often reserved for strategy in this sense.

The idea of strategy has at least three basic elements. It is a plan of action; it applies means or resources to achieve a certain end; and it presupposes an adversary.[5] Understood in such terms, strategy is really an element of common sense, something that pervades much of daily life. It provides much of the fascination of games. Its intellectual content is not necessarily high (children are often particularly adept at it), nor does it have to be complex either in concept or execution. Yet its presence or absence can make itself quickly felt. Looked at in this way, strategic action (as we may call it) would seem to have a wider role in statecraft than strategy in its narrower senses.

Edward Luttwak has argued that strategy in war has a "paradoxical logic" that is unique to itself because it involves the interaction of adversaries.[6] It is certainly salutary to be reminded of what is without doubt the cause of the commonest errors in war—the tendency to neglect what the enemy is doing or might do. Clausewitz himself thought that war and politics share the same "logic," if a different "grammar." But it is far from evident that an adversarial clash of wills is at the core of the strategic behavior of statesmen as such. This would only be true if the international system were always a "zero-sum game" in which one nation's gains are automatically another's losses. In fact, relations between nations are a complex mixture of competition and cooperation. But this does not mean that such relations cannot be handled in a properly strategic manner, any more than relations among business firms.[7] Indeed, even in most situations of military conflict there is a certain element of cooperation between the antagonists. That "victory" is the only intelligible objective of strategy is a ground truth that is sometimes forgotten. At the same time, "winning does not have a strictly competitive meaning; it is not winning relative to one's adversary. It means gaining relative to one's own value system; and this may be done by bargaining, by mutual accommodation, and by the avoidance of mutually damaging behavior."[8]

Let us examine the instructive case of U.S.-Japanese strategic interaction prior to World War II. It is customary to treat the Japanese attack on Pearl Harbor in December 1941 as a failure of American intelligence, not of American policy or strategy. In fact, it is not at all clear that war was the fated outcome of the U.S.-Japanese relationship of the immediately preceding years, or that the United States could not have managed that relationship so as to avoid hostilities on a basis consistent with its fundamental national interests. If in fact it was possible for the United States to achieve a satisfactory settlement of its outstanding disputes with Japan in order to address the more serious Nazi threat, its failure to do so must be seen as one of the greatest strategic errors of American policy in the twentieth century.

President Franklin Delano Roosevelt has long enjoyed a reputation as one of the greatest American presidents. A virtuoso of political maneuver, Roosevelt presided over an administration where power and responsibility were intentionally fragmented among competing officials so as to maximize his own freedom of action. In foreign affairs, FDR took a personal role, sometimes working directly through subcabinet officials in his government, sometimes bypassing the departments altogether. Even in hindsight, it is not easy to reconstruct his policy toward Japan. Some have come to the conclusion that he played a deep game, intentionally provoking the Japanese attack in order to swing an isolationist public to support war. This seems very unlikely.[9] Still, it is difficult to deny that from 1938 on, American policy was surprisingly provocative, given the continuing weakness of the nation's defenses. The truth of the matter seems to be that Roosevelt never pursued a consistent line toward the Japanese. In an effort to satisfy one set of domestic critics, he routinely denounced Japanese militarism in public speeches and applied economic pressures of increasing intensity; at the same time, to ward off criticism from other quarters, he pursued diplomatic initiatives and avoided threatening military measures. To the extent that he had an overall strategy, it seems to have been to bluff the Japanese into abandoning or scaling back their plans of expansion in Asia while waiting on events elsewhere to strengthen America's hand.[10]

Could Roosevelt have better handled the Japanese during these critical years? There are good reasons for thinking so. In August 1939, the liberal ministry of Nobuyuki Abe assumed power in Tokyo and pressed for a renewal of the vital U.S.-Japanese trade treaty, while fending off pressures for a deal with Hitler. Roosevelt's intransigence contributed directly to Abe's fall in December. The wild inconsistency of which Roosevelt was capable was particularly evident in the summer of 1940, when he launched a private diplomatic feeler concerning a possible Pacific non-aggression pact and spoke approvingly in public of a (Japanese) Monroe Doctrine for Asia, only to turn around and impose a partial trade embargo on Japan in July. Even after Japan joined the Tripartite Pact, Tokyo seems to have been prepared and even eager to strike a bargain with the United States. Japanese counsels were divided, but the ministry of Prince Konoye might well have succeeded in reconciling the Japanese army to an eventual withdrawal from China and effective neutrality in the struggle with

Germany; and in fact the Japanese, in the protracted Hull-Nomura talks of 1941, came very far in the direction of these essential American desiderata. But the president's refusal to meet Konoye at a Pacific summit and what can only be described as the lack of seriousness in Hull's conduct of these talks seem to have persuaded the Japanese that they had little to hope from diplomacy. This, coupled with the de facto oil embargo imposed by the United States in July as well as the continuing weakness of American defenses in the Pacific, set the stage for Pearl Harbor and a war the Japanese knew they were unlikely to win but thought unavoidable without a total abdication of their national honor.

This history underlines the importance of strategy for statecraft. Roosevelt's secretiveness, his chaotic management style, and his constant tactical maneuvers unconnected to any visible strategic design confused friends and enemies alike. His use of diplomacy (including private channels that could be easily repudiated) was devious to the point of unreliability and debased the coin of American power in ways that were particularly damaging in a time of world crisis. But perhaps the most serious flaw in FDR's prewar statecraft was his failure to understand, or to make an effort to understand, the adversary.[11] In fact, Roosevelt had little regard for the Japanese and tended to see them in broad caricature. He was tone-deaf when it came to Japanese cultural sensitivities. He made no apparent effort to appreciate the delicate internal politics of the Japanese cabinet and the exposure (to assassination, among other things) of ministers who tried to accommodate American interests, much less to attempt to influence cabinet deliberations in ways favorable to the United States. And while he seems to have assumed (at least after 1940) that war with Japan was inevitable, he may well have believed the Japanese would not prove especially formidable in battle. At any rate, it is not easy to account on any other assumption for Roosevelt's seemingly relaxed view of American military requirements in the Pacific.

Several lessons emerge from all this for the practice of strategy. The first is the importance of a clear vision of the desired objectives or end state. Another is the need for a realistic assessment of the adversary and the threat he poses or might pose under various circumstances. A third is the importance of having a good grasp of one's own strengths and weaknesses, as well as a sense of how an adversary might perceive them and try to take advantage of them. A fourth is the need to ensure that the objectives of policy can be supported by the means available. A final lesson concerns the need to coordinate these means and if necessary shape them so as to better serve the requirements of policy.[12]

In a peacetime setting, the adversarial aspects of strategy properly recede from the statesman's view, while other aspects come to the fore. Above all, the statesman needs to think strategically about the basic relationship between national goals and national means or resources; and he also needs to ensure that the institutions charged with developing and maintaining the various instruments of national power do so in a coordinated manner and without succumbing to the distorting effects of institutional imperatives and cultures. In the advanced democracies today, the fundamental impediment to strategic action and to prudent statecraft more generally is the state bureaucracy and the elites variously associated with it. Leaders, therefore, must remain the ultimate guardians of the strategic perspective.

Of course, leaders cannot perform this task effectively by themselves. The complexity of the contemporary policy environment and the need to insulate leaders from the pathologies of bureaucracy has led increasingly in recent years to the creation of central staff organizations (or in some cases, policy analysis groups affiliated with political parties) to support directly the strategic requirements of the top leadership. We will return shortly to the question of the relation of leaders to such advisory mechanisms.

Strategy is sometimes identified—wrongly—with long-range planning. Strategy is as much a continuous process as it is a fixed plan of action; it can never escape the need for adjustment to the moves of the adversary or to shifts in the strategic environment more generally. And strategic action can span relatively short as well as longer periods. Legitimate questions can certainly be raised as to the possibility and the desirability of attempting to plan over time, particularly in democracies, where such activities can easily be seen as a derogation of the sovereign will of the people or their representatives. Politicians themselves are often cool to such planning efforts, seeing them as infringing their own freedom of action and as a potential source of avoidable political and diplomatic problems; and the time horizons under which they typically operate are a major disincentive to expending energy or political capital on such matters. Planning, of course, has acquired a bad name in the recent past by way of its association with economic planning in the Communist bloc and the dubious *dirigisme* of states like France. All of this having been said, planning exercises can be useful and important if properly structured bureaucratically, judiciously focused, and flexibly utilized. This is especially true in the area of defense, given the very long lead times now required for the development of major military systems.[13]

Even in foreign affairs, however, systematic planning has more to be said for it than current fashion would appear to allow. From the establishment of the National Security Council (NSC) in 1947 through the decade following, the United States experimented with a novel system of policy development in foreign and military affairs that centered on formal planning across all the relevant agencies and deeply engaged senior officials, up to and including the president. During the years when Eisenhower was in the Oval Office, it was the president himself who gave this system its fundamental inspiration and direction. The contrast between Eisenhower and Roosevelt in this regard could not have been greater. Indeed, much of the impetus for the creation of the NSC system was precisely the negative example of Roosevelt. But Eisenhower's peerless military experience during World War II had led him to understand fully the importance of the strategic dimension of statecraft and the need to attempt to embed it in a new set of institutions that could sustain the United States and the West in the challenging environment of the Cold War.

XXII

ON CRISIS MANAGEMENT

Everyday life is full of crises—personal crises, family crises, financial crises, and the like. Governmental crises, whether caused by scandal, coalition politics, or unexpected international developments, are always preoccupying events for the leaders of states. Severe non-military crises (the Great Depression of the 1930s, for example) can pose challenges as fundamental as major wars. At the extreme, crises of the regime—the Bolshevik Revolution of 1917 or the collapse of the Soviet Union at the end of the 1980s—can lead to revolution, civil war, and vast and unpredictable changes on the international scene. Political scientists and historians today too often assume that such crises are the product of impersonal historical forces and thus not really within the control of political leaders or elites. In fact, crises of regime are prime opportunities for the display of political leadership—both for good and for ill.[1]

Crises in the relations of states can be equally dramatic and demanding of attention at the highest levels of government. During the Cold War, it was widely feared that any direct clash between the United States and the Soviet Union could end in cataclysmic nuclear war, quite possibly against the better judgment of the leadership of the two superpowers. When former American defense secretary Robert McNamara, reflecting on the Cuban Missile Crisis of October 1962, famously remarked that "today there is no longer such a thing as strategy; there is only crisis management," he was suggesting that traditional approaches to national security, with their straightforward assumptions concerning the use of force and the meaning of victory, had to yield to a new approach suited to the unprecedented circumstances of the age. "Crisis management," as practiced by President John F. Kennedy and his advisers in the most acute and dangerous confrontation of the entire Cold War, calling as it did for the transformation of the military instrument into a tool of superpower "brinksmanship" that sought diplomatic gains while at the same time minimizing the risk of war, promised nothing less than a revolution in statecraft.[2]

A case can certainly be made that the nuclear preoccupations of the past are a poor guide to the pressing security concerns of today. Time-consuming multilateral diplomacy and protracted low-level conflict (as in the global war on terrorism), not the dynamics of a rapidly developing confrontation between major powers, are our most interesting current challenges. Today, the term *crisis* seems to be used with great frequency and looseness to refer to virtually any problem that reaches the front page of major newspapers. Crises today seem increasingly difficult to distinguish from the ordinary course of international events. If this is so, however, it is not clear that political leaders need to think or act very differently in such situations than they do in the normal course of things. Is the very idea of crisis management perhaps obsolete?

It would be rash to leap to such a conclusion. The realities of modern technology continue to hold open the possibility of virtually instantaneous devastation, while at the same time facilitating very rapid decision-making by national and military authorities. There are still nuclear-armed adversaries on the international scene. The proliferation of nuclear and other so-called weapons of mass destruction (particularly biological weapons) to states that seem more inclined to use them than was the case during the Cold War adds another dimension of threat. And quite apart from extreme scenarios, there is much scope for classical crisis management in persistent strategic confrontations such as the Arab-Israeli conflict. There is a broad continuity in the requirements for managing crises. Crises call for a working mastery of an array of statecraft instruments, orderly processes of information gathering and analysis, a probing review of available options, sensitivity to the opponent, and rapid and timely decision-making under conditions of uncertainty and stress.

That said, it is no doubt the case that classical crisis management theorizing tended to overstate the discontinuities between crisis and non-crisis situations. While it would be going too far to say that crises exist only in the eye of the beholder, there is surely an important sense in which this is true.[3] Crises are constituted by the perceptions of political leaders—perceptions of both an objective threat and a more or less subjective set of national and personal values and goals. For leaders who lack judgment, vision, and nerve, ordinary problems balloon easily into crises. And—a point rarely remarked on—political leaders have both incentives and disincentives to identify situations as crises. Proclaiming a particular foreign threat a crisis may be politically useful in some ways; but it may also make it difficult or impossible to resolve outstanding issues through negotiation with the other party.[4] Casual talk of crisis may make a political leader look weak if not followed by commensurate action. All of this is to suggest that identifying crises properly is a more complex exercise than seems to be generally assumed and, indeed, needs to be viewed as an integral aspect of crisis management itself.

The original meaning of *crisis* (in classical Greek) is "judgment" or "decision." A crisis in its most general sense really is a defining moment—a point in a developing series of events where significant change becomes possible, and which therefore calls for decision by those in authority. In the political arena, what distinguishes a crisis mode of policy-making is the need for rapid judgment and decision by a nation's political leadership. Why this need? For two related reasons: because of the complexity of the issues raised in crises as well as the governmental instruments that handle them; and because of the consensus style of decision-making that is the norm in most contemporary democracies. Direct intervention by the highest political authority is essential under such circumstances in order to make difficult tradeoffs between policy goods or evils, to co-ordinate recalcitrant bureaucracies, and, not least, to effect a transition from a consensus to a command mode of leadership. Crisis management so understood—*pace* McNamara—is a preeminently strategic function.

Secretary McNamara's remark was meant above all to underline the importance of the handling of crisis situations by the president of the United States personally, rather than deferring to a military leadership presumed to be enamored of purely military approaches to dealing with them. Implicitly, it asserted the importance of asserting close political or civilian control of the military instrument of statecraft in a delicate game of posturing, signaling, and bargaining with the adversary—a game in which both had more to lose than either had to gain. Military forces themselves were pawns in a high-stakes test of wills between national leaderships. The objective was to maneuver the other leader into blinking first, thus avoiding war while at the same time demonstrating resolve and bolstering the nation's standing in the world.[5]

This classical paradigm of crisis management is open to a number of criticisms. Perhaps most importantly, it appears to overstate the severity and inevitability of tensions between civilian and military perspectives or between diplomacy and the use of force.[6] At the same time, it neglects other factors in crises. One need only glance at newly declassified records of White House deliberations during the Cuban Missile Crisis to realize how prominent intelligence issues can be in such circumstances.[7] A second factor is public opinion both international and domestic and the competing demands of secrecy and publicity. Public statements by government officials have usually figured prominently in the handling of crises; today, however, new technologies and global media organizations such as CNN have revolutionized not only the reporting of international crises but also the behavior and interactions of governments in crises. The economic and financial aspects of crisis are a third factor, rarely discussed yet of obvious importance; another is the legal dimension. Finally, there is the exercise of command as such, that is, the management of men and institutions. The Argentine junta might have won the Falklands War had it not made the fatal mistake of installing a military administrator instead of a strategist as the islands' governor.[8] President Harry Truman's toleration of the erratic and insubordinate behavior of General Douglas MacArthur during the Korean War illustrates the opposite error.

But perhaps the most enduring legacy of Cold War crisis management thinking is the assumption that the overriding strategic purpose is to minimize risk. This may seem self-evident in a context of nuclear brinksmanship. At a certain point, however, crisis management so understood begins to produce diminishing returns and slides toward appeasement. Particularly troublesome is the idea that visible preparations for war should be avoided in a crisis for fear it could lead to unwanted escalation. The United States entered two world wars in the last century with deficiencies in military preparedness that in retrospect are virtually beyond belief. Preparation for war should be seen as a critical strategic task of crisis management, not something to be improvised when diplomacy has failed.

There is a tendency today in some quarters to understand crisis management as a form of "conflict resolution," in which third parties set out to prevent or end violent conflict between other states. One need not question the value of such efforts in principle to caution against the dangers of overoptimism, overactivism, and misplaced humanitarianism. Some conflicts are stubbornly resistant to mediation by outsiders, and there may well be cases (consider especially the successful Croatian offensive against Serb-controlled areas in Croatia and Bosnia in 1995) where military action is the only realistic option for advancing the prospects for a political settlement and eventual lasting peace.

In a larger perspective, it is well to bear in mind that crises can have their positive side. They present opportunities not always available to policy makers to mobilize the country behind certain policies and to overcome bureaucratic obstacles to firm action.[9] The Chinese word for *crisis* contains the characters standing for both "danger" and "opportunity." Crises can actually provide an impetus for improved relations among adversaries (as happened notably after the Cuban Missile Crisis). They may also open avenues for skilled leaders to strengthen alliances, bolster the legitimacy of their regimes, and enhance their international prestige.

A further limitation of the classical crisis management approach is its narrow view of crises as periods of tension potentially leading to military hostilities. If one of the defining features of crises is the requirement for personal involvement by the nation's leader or leaders, it has to be acknowledged that such a requirement may exist not only on the outbreak of war but also during its course and at its end. Not every moment in war necessarily demands the intensive engagement of the political leadership. Such engagement *is* required on those occasions when a major political or military development offers an unexpected opportunity or threatens catastrophic defeat. Chinese intervention in the Korean War in the fall of 1950 is a good example; others include major battles that mark a fundamental shift in the fortunes of the combatants, such as Stalingrad or El Alamein during World War II. These are cases in which events call for a fundamental strategic reappraisal of a state's military or political objectives. The challenge of such periods is recognizing them as such, rather than treating them simply as part of the flow of military operations and hence not requiring special civilian scrutiny—the great American error in the Korean case.[10]

A similar logic applies to the endgame of a war. That the termination phase of a war could be a kind of crisis seems paradoxical, and there may well be situations in which this phase poses what are essentially administrative problems. Yet it is a mistake to equate intensity of violence with strategic significance. Both World War II and the Gulf War of 1990-1 provide clear evidence of the consequences of failure on the part of an American president to recognize the point at which considerations of the shape of the international political order should take priority over the perceived requirements of the military endgame.[11]

An illuminating case in point is American decision-making at the end of the Gulf War.[12] There is surely a legitimate argument to be made in favor of the broad strategy the United States pursued following its rapid defeat of Saddam Hussein's army in Kuwait and southern Iraq. Even if Baghdad had been occupied or threatened, it is not certain that Saddam's regime would have fallen; and there were political constraints imposed on U.S. action not only by the fragility of the anti-Iraq coalition but by the formal mandate bestowed by the United Nations Security Council. In addition, the implications of a breakup of the Iraqi state for the stability of the region could not simply be ignored, and the Saudis in particular were intensely concerned over the potential for a greatly expanded Iranian role. Still, it is hard not to conclude that the United States squandered significant opportunities in the aftermath of military victory. When the United States imposed a cease-fire on itself after "100 hours" of ground combat, it essentially bowed out of the conflict before any real pressures were brought to bear to halt military operations and before extracting anything of significance in return from the Iraqis. Moreover, by gratuitously permitting the Iraqis to continue operating helicopters within the country, it facilitated a crackdown on internal opponents who had taken up arms partly in response to perceived American encouragement. While no one knows whether added coalition pressure would have led to the much-desired downfall of Saddam, it is certain that the failure of the American leadership during this critical period to look beyond the immediate crisis contributed importantly not only to the survival of Saddam's regime but also to the contraction of the political space for American diplomacy throughout the region in succeeding years.

XXIII

ADVICE AND DECISION

Leadership engagement in the management of crises points to a more fundamental issue: How do or should leaders make decisions generally? Particularly in contemporary democracies, what exactly are the scope and character of executive decision-making, and what is its relationship to legislatures or public opinion? To what extent can leaders be expected to rely on their own knowledge or instincts in making important decisions, and to what extent should they depend on advice, whether personal or institutional? When one surveys the various instruments of statecraft and the requirements they levy on political leaders, it is plain that they amount to a very considerable burden and that few leaders—particularly given the other (political or ceremonial) demands on their time—are likely to be able to wield all of them effectively by themselves. As we have seen, however, there are hazards in simple reliance on the elites and institutions that act as the guardians of these instruments.

That "decision-making" is somehow at the center of political leadership is taken for granted today. Yet this term—itself a curious artifact of contemporary social science—introduces a bias into the way we think about statesmen or the exercise of leadership generally that is unduly limiting. It evokes an image of activism and decisiveness—of energetic, specifically executive leadership on the Hamiltonian model. It insinuates the idea that the most critical thing in leadership is the act of deciding or the need for decision rather than what is actually being decided. Leaders decide, it seems, not because of any superior wisdom, or for that matter on any considered view of the policy environment, but simply because issues are brought to them for decision by others—because (as President Harry Truman liked to remind visitors to his office) "the buck stops here."

Executive power, as we saw earlier, is a modern invention, and its lineaments are already visible in Machiavelli. When Machiavelli addresses toward the end of *The Prince* the question whether caution or impetuosity is a more valuable quality in leaders, he seems inclined initially to the plausible view that it depends on the nature of the times in which the prince operates. His final judgment, however, is that "it is better to be impetuous than cautious, because fortune is a woman; and it is necessary, if one wants to hold her down, to beat her and strike her down. And one sees that she lets herself be won more by the impetuous than by those who proceed coldly. And so always like a woman, she is a friend of the young, because they are less cautious, more ferocious, and command her with more audacity."[1] This epochal challenge needs to be seen for what it is. The model leader for Machiavelli is no longer the wise old king of folklore, prudently taking counsel from the great of the land and ruling with a benevolent hand. Rather, it is the brash young prince or aspiring prince, ambitious of glory and gain and willing to act ruthlessly to achieve it. Caution, calculation, and moderation are displaced by enterprise, energy, and daring. At a deeper level, the message is that princes cannot afford to follow cautious or passive courses because the world is more easily shaped to human purposes than hitherto believed. Energetic leaders project an image of strength that overawes and impresses, that succeeds by its own success.

This Machiavellian model of decision-making is no doubt more in evidence today in the business world than in politics proper. In the United States and throughout the new global economy, the stately (if arguably hypocritical) values of older economic elites seem to be in the process of succumbing to the impetuous spirit of a new age of risk-taking and acquisitiveness. At the same time, there can be little question that what might be called the entrepreneurial style in leadership has gained ground in recent years in the political arena as well. Successful business magnates with no political experience claim and apparently believe that their management skills are directly transferable to public service. This is not to suggest that such people are necessarily less principled or less intellectually equipped for politics than most career politicians. It is only to say that the decision environment to which they are accustomed in the business world is not the best preparation for engagement in politics. Nevertheless, it has to be added that the scandals that have recently rocked the American corporate establishment certainly raise the question whether this leadership model or style can be considered desirable even there.[2]

There are other possible approaches to the exercise of political judgment (to use the more traditional term for the phenomenon we are discussing). One might be called the fatalist or minimalist approach. Leaders taking such an approach might believe that the knowledge necessary for sound political judgment is rarely or never available, or that history is the plaything of blind forces (Machiavelli's "fortune") or a providential God and hence that their actions in the end matter little; on any such view, there is no reason to make decisions that are not absolutely necessary. A portrait of (and brief for) leadership so understood may be found in Tolstoy's classic novel *War and Peace*. It is perhaps more common historically than one might at first suppose.

Even in the context of contemporary organizational management, there is a case to be made for a more austere or restrained understanding of leadership decision. Instead of an approach to leadership focused on formal decision-making, it is perhaps preferable to understand its core function rather as the shaping of institutions and institutional cultures. On such an understanding, it is possible to imagine leaders making only a few decisions over an extended period of time. Moreover, the personal qualities required for such leadership might be quite different from that of the brash entrepreneurial executive.[3] Another approach—let us call it iterative consensus formation—also de-emphasizes the role of individuals in decision-making relative to institutions or communities. This is the leadership style above all of the Japanese. But approximations of it may also be found in political and organizational settings in Africa, the Middle East, and indeed the West itself.

A third alternative approach may be called simply deliberation. This bears some similarity to the one just described but puts greater emphasis on the rationality of the process and the importance and possibility of attaining genuine political knowledge. It is inseparable from political argument or rhetoric. Deliberation is the core of political judgment in Aristotelian political science. It was central to the American founders' understanding of political process, and the constitutional framework they devised was designed among other things to protect legislative deliberation from the inevitable pressures of public opinion in a democracy. In more recent times, it has become fashionable for political scientists simply to deny the reality of deliberation in American politics. Yet a compelling case can be made that it remains a key if neglected aspect of decision-making within the United States government—and not only within the legislative branch. Deliberation needs to be seen as a key feature not just of traditional cabinet government in modern Europe but even of the more robustly executive American model of constitutional governance.[4]

To emphasize the role of deliberation in decision-making is to acknowledge the centrality of *reasoning* to the exercise of leadership. The point may seem obvious. In fact, however, there are powerful tendencies at work in contemporary political science and in our democratic culture that tell against it. American presidents are regularly derided by our elites as intellectual lightweights. And journalists and political scientists alike incline toward a fundamentally cynical view of politics and the policy process that focuses on the play of group interests and personal motivations at the expense of serious political argument. The limitations of such perspectives are evident if one compares, for example, the popular image of the golf-playing Dwight Eisenhower with the reality that has emerged fully only in recent years of a highly intelligent president intensively engaged in deliberations with his cabinet on fundamental policy issues. Eisenhower holds a unique place among postwar presidents in his dedication to systematic policy analysis and planning. Yet many presidents have brought to bear very considerable intellectual gifts on the issues of the day, even if within a framework largely dictated by domestic political considerations. Indeed, what is most distinctive—and genuinely impressive—about skilled politicians is their ability to synthesize policy and politics in a seamless strategic and operational picture.[5]

Having said this, we hasten to concede that the status of reasoning or rationality in the decision process remains a precarious one. This is so for two reasons. The first has to do with the decision environment surrounding political leaders; the second, with the limitations of leaders themselves.[6]

The decision environment is one of imperfect information and great uncertainty, compounded by personal and institutional pressures of all kinds designed to shape or force policy choices. Advisers, staffs, and supporting bureaucracies exist in theory to supply the leader with policy-relevant information and reduce the uncertainties he confronts. In practice, they often compound his problem. Organizations—whether the small staff or the large impersonal department—have a dynamic of their own that can limit the leader's ability to make rational decisions. Small advisory groups are a permanent feature of political leadership at all times.[7] Though sometimes internally divided by personal ambition and intrigue, such groups are undoubtedly more dangerous to the ruler when united. And the psychology of small groups in fact moves them in this direction (the phenomenon of "groupthink").[8] Leaders need to be sensitive to this problem and prepared to take active steps to counter it, as was done, for example, by President Kennedy in forestalling premature closure of debate among his advisers during the tense days of the Cuban Missile Crisis.[9] In large organizations, the danger to be guarded against is that routinized patterns of behavior and generally unspoken institutional imperatives will distort the options presented to policy makers or skew the implementation of decisions made. In both of these cases, the remedy is broadly similar: ensure that competing voices, outside as well as within government, have some access to the ear of the ruler. Yet this is easier said than done—given the behavioral pathologies of leaders themselves.

Leaders are of course subject to the limitations of the human mind generally; but they also suffer from various cognitive and emotional disorders to which politicians are prone, even—indeed, particularly—as they gain experience and succeed. Leaders generally have enormous workloads, yet their precious time is often squandered in politically un-avoidable rituals of various kinds; fatigue, stress, and intellectual paralysis or willfulness can be the result. Moreover, they are surrounded by people—let us call them courtiers—who have agendas and interests of their own, are in constant competition for the prince's attention, and actively attempt to shape his decisions. These courtiers outwardly defer to the prince even as they attempt to manipulate him; they have few incentives to speak unpleasant truths to him and every incentive to flatter. Over time, the effects of such an environment are to inflate a leader's sense of his own wisdom and reduce his openness to reasonable advice.[10] Moreover, partly because leaders are not unaware of the problem of flattery and partly because of the loneliness of their position, a powerful emotional need can sometimes cause them to develop an unhealthy and politically damaging dependence on one or a few favored advisers.

Machiavelli offers this sound counsel: "There is no other way to guard oneself from flattery unless men understand that they do not offend you in telling you the truth; but when everyone can tell you the truth, they lack reverence for you. Therefore, a prudent prince must hold to a third mode, choosing wise men in his state; and only to these should he give freedom to speak the truth to him, and of those things only that he asks about and nothing else. But he should ask them about everything and listen to their opinions; then he should decide by himself, in his own mode." And once he makes up his mind, Machiavelli adds, "he should move directly to the thing that was decided and be obstinate in his decisions. Whoever does otherwise either falls headlong because of flatterers or changes often because of the variability of views, from which a low estimation of him arises."[11] Machiavelli's point regarding the danger of princes being seen as vacillating is an important one. Leaders must be concerned to husband their credibility even at the price of appearing egotistical or irrational; excessive responsiveness to advisers, or an inability to choose among them, can fatally undermine their authority. At the same time, leaders also have to recognize not only that they need advice but that they should be *seen to seek it*, and from wise counselors rather than time-serving flatterers or buffoons. Advisers hold a conspicuous mirror up to the prince himself. Accordingly, they must be managed with care.

Unfortunately, recruiting wise counselors does not end the matter. There are a number of problems with such advisers, as Machiavelli for one was only too well aware. As the old saying goes, no man is a hero to his valet. Advisers are exposed to all the limitations, vulnerabilities, and quirks of a leader's personality. Clever advisers are better equipped than others to penetrate these personality traits—and to exploit them. At the same time, much as they may value the counsel of clever advisers, leaders instinctively worry about the private agendas of such people, and they can develop a strong sense of rivalry with them. In our day, the worst a leader may have to anticipate is the tell-all book. In former times, the defective loyalty of court advisers could threaten the lives of princes and the fortunes of dynasties.

The rivalry between leaders and their advisers is a phenomenon that does not seem to have been much noticed, in spite of its exquisite psychological aspects. It is especially visible at a time when academic intellectuals have become more prominent in senior advisory positions in government, individuals whose self-esteem frequently exceeds that even of successful politicians. The relationship between President Richard Nixon and his National Security Advisor, former Harvard professor Henry Kissinger, is a recent classic case.[12] But the tensions between leaders and advisers do not end there. Advisers always tread a thin line between advising and lecturing the ruler: leaders generally have little tolerance for efforts by their staffs to educate them, even where there may be a plain need for it.

All of this helps to explain why leaders sometimes turn their backs on competent advisers and seek substitutes elsewhere. The gallery of such persons reveals many continuities over the centuries. Spouses, in the first place, are commonly turned to—very frequently with disastrous results, since they are so difficult either to discipline or to dispense with. (Consider, for example, the political damage inflicted by Hillary Clinton during her husband's first term as president of the United States.) The boon companion is another type, also with interesting recent incarnations (Boris Yeltsin's bodyguard, the semiliterate Anatoly Korchakov, traded on their relationship to make himself a major power in Kremlin politics). Spiritual mentors (Rasputin, to cite another Russian example), astrologers, and soothsayers of various kinds also have a long history, though they are less in evidence today. Instead, we have pollsters, media gurus, and other political experts adept at reading the moods of the great god of public opinion and advising leaders on the techniques of political survival. Such figures can also come to wield disproportionate power (consider Dick Morris, Bill Clinton's talented political consultant and strategist, prior to his inglorious fall).[13]

Perhaps the fundamental lesson of all this is that at the end of the day there is no substitute for prudence in political leaders. Inseparable from prudence (in the sense we have been using that term) are both substantive understanding of the principles of statecraft and good moral character. As goes without saying, leaders cannot and need not know everything. Without an appropriate intellectual foundation, however, even the best advice on particular policy issues is apt to be unappreciated or misapplied. And leaders will be unable to formulate the questions that will elicit what it is they need to know. At the same time, leaders must resist the tendency of power to corrupt the good judgment and moral sense of those wielding it. Experienced leaders surely do know many things; they rarely know how and when to admit error or to accept unwelcome advice courageously offered by the occasionally selfless adviser. If they are to make effective decisions, leaders need to preserve the ability to listen to subordinates and to engage in reasoned deliberation with peers—personal qualities that tend to atrophy in the executive-centered politics we have come to take for granted in our contemporary democracies.[14]

XXIV

LEADERSHIP AND POLITICS

E ven in the most autocratic of regimes, leaders are rarely able to rule through simple command. In today's democracies, where the powers of leaders are constitutionally circumscribed and subject to constant political challenge, leadership is very much an art of indirect rule. It is worth examining briefly the ways in which democratic leaders seek to shape the political environment in order to facilitate achievement of their policy ends. For by the use of these methods, modern princes can leverage the formal weakness of the modern political executive to create real, operational strength.

It is fashionable nowadays, particularly among political scientists, to disparage democratic politicians as wholly driven by public opinion polls and the quest for reelection. According to an extreme version of this idea, "We should not expect democratically elected politicians to be 'leaders.' Or more accurately, we should not expect them to defy public opinion. Such actions are likely to lead to unemployment. Before polls, politicians could in fact stumble into leadership because they did not know what the public wanted. But with the rise of surveys, we need to adjust our expectations."[1] No one will deny the vital role of public opinion in contemporary democracies. As Lincoln once said, "In this and like communities, public sentiment is everything. With public sentiment nothing can fail; without it nothing can succeed." Yet he also went on to add, "Consequently, he who molds public sentiment, goes deeper than he who enacts statutes or pronounces decisions."[2]

The fact of the matter is that leaders regularly seek to mold public opinion rather than simply reacting to it. And they do so for good political reasons. As politicians instinctively know, on many issues public opinion has an indeterminateness and lack of fixity that lends itself to political leadership. What is more, it often makes political sense for politicians to be more responsive to the concerns of narrow but hard-core constituencies than to the weakly held views of a majority. This is particularly the case if they are able to devise ways to obfuscate their real positions. The conventional wisdom is that democratic politicians are more poll-driven and pandering today than at any time in the past. In fact, however, a good case can be made that they are if anything insufficiently responsive to broad public sentiment because they are increasingly adept at manipulating it to their advantage.[3]

There are differing styles or strategies of leadership available to politicians in their efforts to shape the political environment. Let us distinguish three broad varieties: bargaining, opinion leadership, and what may be called hidden hand leadership.[4] These are not necessarily mutually exclusive and can be adopted or discarded by politicians as circumstances require. On the other hand, a powerful historical trend over the last century or so has tended to favor opinion leadership as the preferred strategy of American presidents—and increasingly, of other Western leaders as well.

Traditional political leadership in the United States and other democracies has centered around bargaining—the brokering of various clashing interests and the formation of political coalitions to gain and maintain power.[5] Leadership of this sort tends to be linked closely with political parties, and the arena in which it principally operates is the legislature. Opinion leadership represents a turn away from reliance on party and elected representatives to a more direct relationship between politicians and the public. The rise of opinion leadership toward the end of the nineteenth century is linked with the rise of modern mass media but is not fully explained by it. In the United States, the increased importance of popular presidential rhetoric during the administrations of Theodore Roosevelt and Woodrow Wilson reflects a profound shift in the way presidents themselves have come to look on the role of the office in the constitutional order. In the early republic, presidents rarely or never addressed the public directly on policy matters; to do so would have risked in their eyes an appearance of demagoguery. Debates in the Congress, rather, were the appropriate way to air political issues and shape popular opinion. In the face of the growing challenges of a modernizing nation about to step on the world stage, however, congressional leadership came to seem increasingly insufficient. "Some presidents have felt the need, which unquestionably exists in our system," wrote Wilson, "for some spokesman of the nation as a whole, in matters of legislation no less than in other matters, and have tried to supply Congress with the leadership of suggestion, backed by argument and iteration and by every legitimate appeal to public opinion." And again, famously: "The president is at liberty, both in law and conscience, to be as big a man as he can; and if Congress be overborne by him, it will be no fault of the makers of the Constitution—it will be from no lack of constitutional powers on its part, but only because the president has the nation behind him and Congress has not. He has no means of compelling Congress except public opinion."[6]

Opinion leadership—or simply "going public," as it is sometimes called—can be used in selective fashion as an adjunct to the bargaining approach, but it is fundamentally at odds with that approach. Staking out forceful public positions on issues restricts the leader's room for maneuver and compromise. It implicitly devalues the legitimacy of other politicians and thereby complicates relations with them; in particular, it tends to undermine the trust necessary to sustain political arrangements and alliances. On the other hand, there may be political circumstances that demand it. Whether the long decay of political parties in the West is a cause or consequence of opinion leadership can be debated, but it is clear that weak party systems encourage such leadership. And the contemporary media environment further contributes to a politics of individual performance and publicity seeking and devalues the old-fashioned arts of comity, compromise, and legislative craftsmanship. This encourages leaders to appeal directly to the public if only for defensive reasons. Other developments—notably, changes in the presidential nominating process—have also played a role in detaching presidents or potential presidents from traditional party discipline and opening the door to plebiscitary-style individual leadership.[7]

Opinion leadership is the natural approach of "transformational" presidents, that is, those seeking revolutionary change in policies or institutions; Ronald Reagan is a recent, Franklin Roosevelt a more distant exemplar. Yet there may be circumstances that call for a more cautious, yet not for that reason less demanding, style of leadership. The exemplar here is Dwight Eisenhower. During his own presidency (1953–60) and for several decades thereafter, the popular "Ike" was portrayed in the press and in academic analyses as a disengaged and mediocre leader who was not fully in command of his own administration. Only with the appearance of declassified records and other archival materials in recent years is it clear how far wrong this picture was. Eisenhower had no transformational agenda, but he was nevertheless a highly engaged and activist president with a self-conscious philosophy of leadership. Central to that philosophy was a keen appreciation for the differing demands of the "dignified" and the "efficient" components of the presidency. Eisenhower (originally courted as a candidate by both of the major parties) sought to project an image of the president as beyond partisan politics. He also cultivated a friendly and reassuring public style that did not fully reflect his intense and sensitive nature. Contrary to a common assumption that he ran the White House on the model of a military staff, Ike was mindful of the differences between military and political leadership and avoided both the appearance and the reality of command. He studied the psychology of his political peers and subordinates alike and was skilled at the arts of persuasion and suggestion. He was more than content to let others take credit for his own ideas or initiatives, even (remarkably) at the cost of being widely perceived as not in charge of administration policy in areas as central as foreign affairs. This could not have been further from the truth.[8]

Eisenhower's "hidden hand" approach to leadership served a number of purposes. By keeping the president above the political fray, it conserved his popularity and political clout. By maintaining some uncertainty as to the president's responsibility for particular policies, it enhanced his room for maneuver, especially with the Congress. But it also served larger strategic purposes relating to the political circumstances at the time. The Republicans had just regained control of the presidency and the Senate after decades out of power, and Eisenhower was determined to shore up the party's electoral position by moderating its hostility to the welfare state and other liberal policies, in spite of the fact that his own inclinations were generally strongly conservative. In the national security sphere, Ike was a fierce hawk in the unfolding Cold War. Among other things, he was fully prepared to use nuclear weapons in any conflict with the Soviets or the Chinese, and he personally approved highly intrusive intelligence-gathering operations against the USSR. Yet he also painted a very different public face on the administration through initiatives such as "Atoms for Peace" and a personal diplomacy designed to "relax tensions" with the Soviet bloc. Nor is it surprising that Eisenhower was a great aficionado of covert action.[9]

What lessons can be drawn from all this? Both Reagan and Eisenhower were popular and successful presidents, without doubt the most successful of the postwar era. It could be argued that the divergent leadership strategies they employed were in fact perfectly attuned to the times and to the different policy goals they pursued. On the other hand, there is no denying that each strategy has its limitations and potential dangers. The hidden hand approach comes up short at times when the leader faces a direct political challenge, as Eisenhower did at the hands of Senator Joseph McCarthy, for example.[10] And it always holds the risk of deteriorating into Machiavellian duplicity—a political tactic that, pushed to an extreme, rapidly defeats itself through the sowing of confusion and distrust.[11] Opinion leadership arguably holds even greater risks, however. Habitual appeals to the people by democratic leaders cannot but debase the coin of political argument and undermine the perceived legitimacy of the other branches of government. Just as the American founders feared, it agitates the passions of the broad public as much or more than it educates, for it tends to foster a political and media environment of manipulative competition for the people's attention and favor.[12] At the end of the day, it is dangerous fire for democracies to play with.

A final word is necessary, though. Donald Trump and his counterparts abroad, especially within the European Union, have been routinely excoriated for their "populist" politics by the political class and its media enablers. Whatever can be said of the propriety or wisdom of national leaders communicating with their publics directly on social media, or of the debased standards increasingly in evidence in such communications, it has to be said in Trump's defense that this sort of criticism is unconvincing—not to say grossly hypocritical. The American Left long ago forfeited any claim to being the guardians of deliberative discourse in politics, and the American media has thoroughly compromised itself by its open hostility to every facet of the Trump revolution. Under these circumstances, the president can hardly be faulted for a communications strategy that has proved essential both for his improbable election and for the unpredictable political success he has so far enjoyed.

XXV

WHY LEADERSHIP DEPENDS ON THE TIMES

Machiavelli offers a useful reminder of the variability of human affairs and the difficulty of predicting or shaping their course. At the same time, he cautions princes against taking this as a counsel of despair. "Fortune" can be likened to a violent river that from time to time overflows its banks and floods the surrounding countryside: while the flood itself cannot always be prevented, it can at least be contained and its effects mitigated by the construction of dikes and levees. A prudent prince will adjust his behavior to accord with the times in which he lives. But he will also take measures to protect his state and himself against sudden and unanticipated turns of fortune.[1]

No less than in the past, our statesmen exist in a certain strategic environment and in what may be called political time. Understanding the limitations and possibilities of their particular situation is one of the most critical tasks of statecraft. At the most general level, leaders preside over either good times or bad, prosperity or adversity. Those accustomed to good times are apt to hold a relatively minimalist view of the requirements of statecraft and to lack incentives to prepare themselves adequately for changed circumstances. Adversity, on the other hand, is the teacher of princes. Reflecting the key tasks of statecraft, adversity can take the form of political upheaval, external insecurity, economic hardship, or some combination of these.[2]

The strategic environment is a convenient term to describe the general security condition of a state. Broadly speaking, that condition may be one of peace, conflict, crisis, or war. Conflict may be defined as a protracted strategic confrontation between two or more countries, involving intermittent small-scale violence ("low-intensity conflict") or simply a militarily threatening standoff ("cold war"). Crises and large-scale war generally develop out of a matrix of conflict. Peace itself, of course, may be more or less stable or enduring.

Each of these strategic settings poses its own particular challenge to leaders. Times of profound peace (particularly in today's democracies) call for leaders who will sustain the institutions and practices of military preparedness, counter isolationist sentiment, and resist tendencies toward complacency and corruption. In periods of protracted conflict, the challenge for leaders is to reconcile the appearance of peace or normality with the reality of struggle and the need to mobilize public opinion for the long haul (consider the situation of the United States in its war against global terrorism). In crises, the challenge is to manage a suddenly compressed decision cycle, control domestic political and military pressures, balance competing requirements for firmness and conciliation with the adversary, and prepare for a possible transition to war without provoking it in the process. In war, finally, leaders are called on for qualities of command that are rarely apparent and hardly exercised by democratic statesmen in more normal times.

The political environments facing leaders are even more changeable and complex. As we have seen, the character and structure of states and regimes are not just a given of the statesman's situation but a key object of his concern, subject as they are to sudden revolutions as well as gradual alteration over time. States and regimes go through phases of founding, consolidation, growth, decay, and collapse; these phases impose very different leadership requirements. The great princes of history are often great revolutionaries ("founders"), but there are also impressive examples of statecraft in times of, for example, imperial decay.[3]

As Machiavelli himself indicates,[4] the variability of the times and hence of the requirements of leadership is a potent argument for republican government. It is easy to say that the ideal monarch is one capable of adjusting his leadership style to a changed political environment, but in practice this is too much to expect of individuals long at the pinnacle of power. In republics, however, new leaders can emerge and assume office in response to new challenges, displacing those too closely tied to an older order of things (consider FDR in 1932, Churchill in 1940, or Trump in 2016). This enhances both the stability and the efficacy of republican regimes. Of course, it is not always easy to assess before the fact a politician's leadership ability. Accidental leaders (Truman in 1945) sometimes rise to the challenge, while accomplished statesmen can fail badly in the highest office (John Adams or James Madison).

Even in the relatively stable constitutional democracies we now enjoy, politics is a volatile business. Parties rise and fall, institutions develop, new issues come to the fore, scandals erupt, and leaders struggle to define and legitimize themselves. The dynamics of this environment can therefore look very different over time, in spite of broad continuities. Nor is it safe to assume that these dynamics evolve in simply linear fashion. Contemporary political science tends to assume that the proper frame of reference for understanding leadership in the United States today is the "modern" presidency of the Progressive Era and beyond. It can be argued, however, that there are recurrent patterns throughout American history that better explain the character and impact of presidential leadership than simple temporal proximity. Presidents exist in "political time." Jefferson, Jackson, Lincoln, and Franklin Roosevelt had more in common with each other than each did with his immediate predecessor or successor. They were all transformative or "reconstructive" leaders who took power in periods of systemic failure in the political environment with an undisputed mandate for far-reaching change and went on to found a new political dispensation within the framework of the American constitutional order.[5] Even at this early stage in his presidency, there is reason to place Donald Trump in this select company.

XXVI

EXHORTATION TO PRESERVE DEMOCRACY FROM THE BARBARIANS

The requirements of leadership are diverse, today as always. The need for great founders has not been made obsolete by the march of history, as was evident in the wake of the collapse of the Soviet Union in 1990. As Lincoln for one insisted, however, the preservation of established regimes is in some ways an even greater challenge for leaders than their founding. Soaring political ambition finds greater outlets and opportunities in unsettled times; there is little glory in being seen simply as a steward of monuments erected by others. This is particularly so in our contemporary democracies, where (to continue the metaphor) constitutions seem to be hewn out of a kind of political granite that is hard to topple and highly resistant to erosion. Publics and political leaders alike tend to take for granted the permanence of these regimes—and of the liberal democratic dispensation more generally.

They are foolish to do so. History is littered with the wrecks of states that existed for centuries in apparently unchallengeable might. Even if it is true that the broad movement of history is in some sense favorable to liberal democracy, this cannot mean that all liberal democracies are immune to the evils of fortune and of human nature itself that in the past have regularly caused regimes to fall and states to disappear. But it would be rash in any case to assume that history holds no more political surprises for us. The emergence at the beginning of the twenty-first century of a potent Islamic terrorist threat to the West and in particular to the American homeland is a sobering lesson in this regard.

It is vital that democratic statesmen not underestimate the security challenges of our age. It may well be that the West's material and technical advantages will eventually prove decisive in the struggle against militant Islam, but Machiavelli himself reminds us that "unarmed prophets" are not always doomed to geostrategic defeat. The holy warriors of a radicalized Islam are in any case the obvious barbarians at the gates of the new Rome of Western liberalism. At the same time, it is prudent to assume that great power conflict has not disappeared from the earth with the end of the Cold War. Even under relatively benign circumstances such as we currently face, it requires little imagination to anticipate the emergence of China as a serious military threat to American interests in East Asia in the coming decades, or scenarios of a new Sino-American war. The same may be said of a Russia that seems increasingly intent on challenging the U.S.-led global order. And let us note, finally, that conflict in this century is not likely to be less deadly than conflict in the nuclear age. Nuclear weapons are with us still, as well as weapons (biological devices in particular) in some ways more fearsome; and they are in the hands of more states, not to mention their potential for terrorist use.

All of this is simply to say that the defense of liberal democracy will remain first and most urgently a security question, just as it has in the past. The instruments of statecraft that have traditionally safeguarded the security of nations will therefore remain indispensable for the modern prince, and prudent leaders will need to resist the many voices in our day that deny or deplore this state of affairs. At the same time, however, their greatest challenge lies elsewhere. The real problem facing the modern prince is not the barbarians at the gates; it is the barbarians within.

At one level, this is simply an aspect of the security challenge facing contemporary democracies. The porousness of borders and the fragility of the technological infrastructure of today's advanced societies make them vulnerable to various forms of unconventional warfare. Generous immigration policies that reflect these societies' liberal ideals have contributed to the problem, in some cases creating a breeding ground and favorable operating environment for terrorism and global organized crime. In Europe, the issue of immigration looms ever larger on the political radar screen, in the form of a popular backlash against the failure of political elites to take more seriously its costs and consequences. It is perceived increasingly as a threat not only to domestic order but to national and cultural identity as well. That demagogic politicians have taken advantage of shifting public attitudes on immigration is undeniable; that such attitudes are themselves simply unreasonable is hardly clear.

Perhaps more worrisome than the problem of unassimilated minorities as such, however, is the multiculturalist mentality that makes sensible public discussion of such issues virtually impossible today. This mentality, which finds special virtue in non-Western cultures and tends to favor preferential treatment for presumptively oppressed racial and sexual groups, represents at bottom an indifference or hostility to the values and traditions of Western liberalism that is dismaying, to say the least. With its dominating presence in our educational institutions and popular culture, it points up the broader failure of political and opinion-forming elites in the United States and elsewhere to mount an effective intellectual defense of liberal democracy under contemporary conditions.[1]

This is by no means to deny that practicing Muslims, for example, have legitimate grounds for complaint about the condition of society and culture in the West today. Nor is it to assert that Western liberal democracy in its current form is necessarily the perfect or final system of governance for the world at large. It is rather to suggest that contemporary elites are at once too critical and too complacent in their attitudes toward the liberal political dispensation under which they live and prosper. Too critical, because they measure the contemporary West against standards that are themselves unattainable and that they hypocritically fail to apply to others. Too complacent, because they fail to take sufficient account of the costs and consequences of the compassion-driven pursuit of individual and group rights or entitlements and neglect the impact of a culture of self-interest and self-assertion on the very foundations of a liberal polity—namely, the continuing decay of moral and professional standards, civic behavior, and political engagement that is so evident throughout the most advanced democracies today.[2]

Elites who lose touch with the sentiments of the people are a danger to regimes. What was obvious in the case of the French aristocracy in 1789 is no less true, for example, of the French political establishment today.[3] It is precisely in such circumstances that demagogues arise and prosper.

In the United States, national and local elites are more public spirited and less corrupt than in many other places. Nevertheless, the demonstrated inability of these elites to provide suitable intellectual and moral leadership for the nation is a growing scandal that should raise fundamental doubts about the future of American democracy.

The decay of democratic ideals and practice is equally visible at the level of politics. The deliberative processes that were seen by the American founders as central to democratic decision-making are in manifest decline. In virtually all of the advanced democracies, the executive is in the ascendancy at the expense of the legislative branch of government. Coupled with this development is the weakening and fragmentation of political parties in recent decades (or, in the new democracies, a failure to build them) and the rise of a plebiscitary style of leadership detached from parties and inclined to approach governing as an extension of the political campaign. Such leadership marks the triumph of politics over statecraft.

What direction, then, should democratic leadership take?

Contemporary leaders, we argue, are at once too strong and too weak, too assertive and too timid. They try to do too much, yet in some ways they do too little. On the one hand, the modern prince needs to be more wary of the elites who are his partners—and rivals—in government. Their characteristic limitations and private agendas must be factored into all of his policy decisions; he must be prepared to stand up to them—more than that, he must see them as a problem that needs continuous management (and on occasion, dramatic intervention) in the larger interests of the nation. On the other hand, he needs to use his potentially very substantial executive powers with more restraint and selectivity than is the case in many if not most democracies today. The tactical or retail-level leadership of a Bill Clinton is a waste of the resources of high executive office. Its little victories provide an illusion of competence but distract the leader from the large issues and the real challenges of governing. Instead, it can be argued, leaders should greatly *reduce* their involvement in day-to-day politics and decision-making. They should make an effort to encourage policy initiative on the part of legislatures, all the while reserving for themselves the strategic or regime-related functions that the executive is uniquely suited to perform. Indeed, like the Singaporeans, they should consider institutional and other measures to *strengthen* the deliberative capabilities of the legislative branch.

All three branches of government are concerned in their own ways with the strategic aspects of regime management that are central to the practice of statecraft. For reasons discussed earlier, however, the executive may be said to have a particular responsibility and aptitude for maintaining a strategic perspective on the state of the nation. In the first instance, leaders need to keep a keen watch on the overall institutional health of the regime. They should be alive to the dysfunctional tendencies of bureaucracy and the vagaries of institutional leadership, and should be readier to intervene in this sphere than is typically the case for presidents or prime ministers today. They should be especially attentive to the condition of the institutions dealing with national security, their particular area of leadership responsibility. They should be mindful, in this time of war, of the unique challenges involved in managing military and intelligence organizations; and they should assure themselves that processes are in place both for handling immediate crises and for developing longer-term strategies for safeguarding the nation and the civilized world more broadly.

In the second place, though, and most critically, leaders should work to ensure the proper functioning of the legal system and the broader constitutional order supporting it. This includes important rhetorical and symbolic measures designed to foster the "political religion" of constitutionalism that Lincoln thought essential for the preservation of liberal democracy. It may also include extraordinary political action intended to remedy potentially regime-threatening developments in the legislative or judicial branches, even where this might carry some risk of overstepping accepted boundaries of executive power (as in Roosevelt's "court-packing" scheme of 1937). As we have seen, it is precisely the weakness of the modern constitutional executive that enables it to be strong when such (rare) circumstances require it.

To stress the strategic role of leaders may seem an obvious point. But it is far from the reality of leadership in most contemporary democracies. Sadly, though understandably, authoritarian governments not infrequently perform better in this regard. War of course particularly concentrates the mind in strategic channels. At our current juncture in history, however, democratic leaders arguably need to begin to think and act strategically beyond the framework of traditional security issues. The war on global terrorism in which we are now engaged has provided an important object lesson in the strategic application of a variety of non-military instruments of statecraft—notably law enforcement and control of financial flows—to defeat an unconventional threat. Let us hope that success in this war will show the way to a more effective approach to using such capabilities against other global scourges that more directly sustain the barbarians within our gates. Narcotics trafficking is at the top of this list.

But perhaps the greatest challenges facing contemporary leaders lie in an area that resists political solutions and for that reason is uncongenial to liberal statesmen—science and technology. The ongoing and in many ways accelerating transformation of the contemporary world under the impact of high technology constitutes nothing less than a revolution in human affairs, and one with significant moral and political implications. Though there are good reasons for skepticism about the various visions of environmental calamity abroad today,[4] there can be little question that governments need to attend to the impact of human activities on the global environment. Space is an arena of commercial and (increasingly) military activity of great importance particularly to the advanced democracies, and managing human competition there will be a major challenge to statecraft in this century. The internet is revolutionizing global communications in ways that are both beneficial and sinister, and fundamental questions concerning its regulation remain to be addressed. Finally, and perhaps most problematic, recent advances in genetic engineering and biotechnology generally have opened up new possibilities for remaking human nature itself. We have seen only the beginning of the political battles that are certain to be waged over such issues.[5]

It would be comforting if politicians could simply take their cue in these matters from the presumed experts. Yet, of course, the experts are frequently divided on politically controversial issues and not infrequently have heavy axes to grind. There is thus no escaping the need for an active exercise of prudential judgment on such issues by political leaders. More generally, though, it could be that the time is fast approaching for leaders to take a less deferential approach to the scientific-technical establishment as a whole, insofar as it appears to have a vested interest in the essentially unchecked march of scientific-technical progress. If scientists are incapable of making the judgment that human cloning is a morally monstrous undertaking (as many of them evidently are), politicians will have to exercise bold leadership to ensure that we do not take that fateful step. But this means they will have to be prepared to rise to a level of intellectually and morally informed argument that is for the most part sadly lacking in our political leaders and elites alike. The preservation of our way of life may require no less.

NOTES

PREFACE TO THE SECOND EDITION

1 Niccolò Machiavelli, *The Prince*, 2nd ed., trans. Harvey C. Mansfield (Chicago: University of Chicago Press, 1998), ch. 6. Citations from this work will be by chapter.

2 See notably Juan C. Zarate, *Treasury's War: The Unleashing of a New Era of Financial Warfare* (New York: Public Affairs, 2013); and Robert D. Blackwill and Jennifer M. Harris, *War by Other Means: Geoeconomics and Statecraft* (Cambridge, MA: Harvard University Press, 2016).

PREFACE

1 James MacGregor Burns, *Leadership* (New York: Harper & Row, 1978), 1–2.

2 Niccolò Machiavelli, *Discourses on the First Ten Books of Titus Livy*, trans. Harvey C. Mansfield and Nathan Tarcov (Chicago: University of Chicago Press, 1996), preface (henceforth *Discourses*).

3 See notably Michael A. Ledeen, *Machiavelli on Modern Leadership* (New York: St. Martin's Press, 1999); Dick Morris, *The New Prince* (Los Angeles: Renaissance Books, 1999); Antony Jay, *Management and Machiavelli* (Amsterdam: Pfeiffer, 1994); and Alistair McAlpine, *The New Machiavelli: The Art of Politics in Business* (New York: John Wiley & Sons, 1998).

I – WHY LEADERSHIP IS STILL POSSIBLE

1 An argument can be made that political leadership altogether is of this nature: F.G. Bailey, *Humbuggery and Manipulation: The Art of Leadership* (Ithaca, NY: Cornell University Press, 1988).

2 Francis Fukuyama, *The End of History and the Last Man* (New York: Free Press, 1992).

3 Consider Michael A. Genovese, ed., *Women as National Leaders* (Newbury Park, CA: Sage Publications, 1993).

4 Clifford Orwin, "Compassion," *American Scholar* 49 (Summer 1980): 309–33.

5 Michel Crozier, Samuel P. Huntington, and Jôji Watanuki, *The Crisis of Democracy: Report on the Ungovernability of Democracies to the Trilateral Commission* (New York: New York University Press, 1975).

6 Lloyd Cutler, "To Form a Government," *Foreign Affairs* 59 (Fall 1980): 126–43.

7   A useful appreciation is Dinesh D'Souza, *Ronald Reagan* (New York: Free
    Press, 1997). See also Lou Cannon, *President Reagan: The Role of a Lifetime*
    (New York: Touchstone, 1991); John W. Sloan, *The Reagan Effect: Economics
    and Presidential Leadership* (Lawrence: University of Kansas Press, 1999);
    and more recently, Steven F. Hayward, *The Age of Reagan*, vol. 1, *The Fall
    of the Old Liberal Order, 1964–1980* (Roseville, CA: Prima, 2001), and vol. 2,
    The Conservative Counterrevolution, 1980–1989 (New York: Three Rivers Press,
    2009); and Thomas C. Reed, *The Reagan Enigma, 1964–1980* (Los Angeles:
    Figueroa Press, 2014).

8   Lester M. Salamon and Michael S. Lund, eds., *The Reagan Presidency and
    the Governing of America* (Washington, D.C.: Urban Institute Press, 1984);
    Sloan, *Reagan Effect*, ch. 4.

9   Machiavelli, *Prince*, 6.

10 "This should be taken as a general rule: that it never or rarely happens that
    any republic or kingdom is ordered well from the beginning or reformed
    altogether anew outside its old orders unless it is ordered by one individual."
    Discourses, I.9.

II – WHY LEADERSHIP IS STILL NECESSARY

1   Wolfgang J. Mommsen, *Max Weber and German Politics, 1890–1920*, trans.
    Michael S. Steinberg (Chicago: University of Chicago Press, 1984), esp. ch.
    10.

2   Josiah Ober, *Mass and Elite in Democratic Athens* (Princeton, NJ: Princeton
    University Press, 1989); Ronald Syme, *The Roman Revolution* (Oxford:
    Clarendon Press, 1960).

3   See, for example, Sidney M. Milkis and Michael Nelson, *The American
    Presidency: Origins and Development, 1776–1990* (Washington, D.C.: CQ Press,
    1990), chs. 1–4.

4   Jeffrey K. Tulis, *The Rhetorical Presidency* (Princeton, NJ: Princeton
    University Press, 1987), chs. 2–3.

5   Susan J. Pharr and Robert D. Putnam, eds., *Disaffected Democracies: What's
    Troubling the Trilateral Countries?* (Princeton, NJ: Princeton University
    Press, 2000).

6   "The Perpetuation of Our Political Institutions" (1838), in *The Collected
    Works of Abraham Lincoln*, 9 vols., ed. Roy P. Basler (New Brunswick, NJ:
    Rutgers University Press, 1953), 1:108–19.

7   Milkis and Nelson, *American Presidency*, chs. 8–9, 11–12.

8   A noteworthy exception is James Burnham, *Congress and the American
    Tradition* (Washington, D.C.: Regnery, 1959).

9   Useful accounts are Martin Wallace, *The President We Deserve: Bill Clinton:
    His Rise, Falls, and Comebacks* (New York: Crown, 1996); and Stanley A.
    Renshon, ed., *The Clinton Presidency: Campaigning, Governing, and the
    Psychology of Leadership* (Boulder, CO: Westview, 1995). To say that the
    Clinton administration represents the nadir of the contemporary presidency
    may seem contestable in the light of the Obama presidency. Yet while Barack
    Obama and other prominent Democrats in recent years have certainly
    resorted to demagogic methods, the stark decline of the Democratic Party
    nationally since 2008 suggests that its leadership has become increasingly

careless and inept in its deployment of such methods. This surely helps explain the surprising electoral success of Donald Trump in 2016.

10 Burns, *Leadership*, chs. 6–9.

11 This generalization needs to be suitably qualified: both Disraeli and Churchill played a noteworthy role in the founding of the British welfare state. For the latter see Paul Addison, "Churchill and Social Reform," in *Churchill*, ed. Robert Blake and William Roger Louis (New York: W.W. Norton, 1993), ch. 4.

12 Walter Bagehot, *The English Constitution*, intro. by R.H. Crossman (Ithaca, NY: Cornell University Press, 1966; originally published 1867), chs. 1–2.

13 On leadership in primitive or pre-state societies see, for example, Elman R. Service, *Origins of the State and Civilization* (New York: W.W. Norton, 1975), ch. 4.

III – LEADERSHIP AND STATECRAFT

1 Max Weber, *Economy and Society*, 2 vols., ed. Guenther Roth and Claus Wittich (Berkeley: University of California Press, 1978), vol. 2, ch. 14. Fundamental on this subject is Robert Eden, *Political Leadership and Nihilism: A Study of Weber and Nietzsche* (Tampa: University Presses of Florida, 1983).

2 Machiavelli, *Prince*, 6.

3 Aristotle, *Nicomachean Ethics*, X.9, 1181a12–18. Citations are by book, chapter, and Bekker pagination. All translations of Aristotle are my own. For *The Politics* see *The Politics of Aristotle*, trans. Carnes Lord, 2nd ed. (Chicago: University of Chicago Press, 2013).

4 A noteworthy exception is Charles W. Anderson, *Statecraft: An Introduction to Political Choice and Judgment* (New York: John Wiley and Sons, 1977).

5 See, for example, Richard Rosecrance and Arthur A. Stein, eds., *The Domestic Bases of Grand Strategy* (Ithaca, NY: Cornell University Press, 1993).

6 Carl von Clausewitz, *On War*, ed. and trans. Michael Howard and Peter Paret (Princeton, NJ: Princeton University Press, 1976), 605.

7 For statecraft as a strategic discipline, consider Colin S. Gray, *War, Peace, and Victory: Strategy and Statecraft for the New Century* (New York: Simon and Schuster, 1990). David A. Baldwin's *Economic Statecraft* (Princeton, NJ: Princeton University Press, 1985) is a valuable attempt to reclaim the field of statecraft for political science; but Baldwin goes too far (pp. 8–12) in restricting the meaning of the term to the merely technical or instrumental. The constant adjustment of means and ends is a central task of statecraft and strategy alike.

8 Aspects of this critique are usefully developed by Alexander L. George, *Bridging the Gap: Theory and Practice in Foreign Policy* (Washington, D.C.: United States Institute of Peace Press, 1993); and Daniel L. Byman and Kenneth M. Pollack, "Let Us Now Praise Great Men: Bringing the Statesman Back In," *International Security* 25 (Spring 2001): 107–46. See more broadly Herbert J. Storing, ed., *Essays on the Scientific Study of Politics* (New York: Holt, Rinehart, and Winston, 1961).

9 This is a principal theme of David M. Ricci, *The Tragedy of Political Science: Politics, Scholarship, and Democracy* (New Haven, CT: Yale University Press, 1984).

10 See Douglas Torgerson, "Policy Analysis and Public Life: The Restoration of *Phronêsis?*" in *Political Science in History*, ed. James Farr, John S. Dryzek, and Stephen T. Leonard (Cambridge: Cambridge University Press, 1995), 225–52.

11 See generally Ronald Beiner, *Political Judgment* (Chicago: University of Chicago Press, 1983); and Peter J. Steinberger, *The Concept of Political Judgment* (Chicago: University of Chicago Press, 1993).

12 Aristotle discusses prudence thematically in *Nicomachean Ethics*, VI.7–13; for the distinction between the general and special (political) types of prudence, see VI.8, 1141b23–42a11. On the character of Aristotelian social or political science generally see Carnes Lord and David K. O'Connor, eds., *Essays on the Foundations of Aristotelian Political Science* (Berkeley: University of California Press, 1991), 1–48.

13 Aristotle, *Rhetoric*, I.4, 1359b19–23.

14 Aristotle, *Politics*, I.1, 1252a1–5; *Nicomachean Ethics*, I.4, 1095a14ff.

15 Aristotle, *Nicomachean Ethics*, I.1, 1094a6–18; 2, 1094a26–b11. The phrase "architectonic and practical thinking" occurs in *Eudemian Ethics*, I.6, 1217a1–6.

16 Aristotle, *Nicomachean Ethics*, I.2, 1094b14–15; 7, 1097a15–1098a18.

17 Aristotle, *Politics*, III.9, 1280a31–b12.

18 Aristotle, *Nicomachean Ethics*, I.13, 1102a5–1103a10.

19 George F. Will, *Statecraft as Soulcraft: What Government Does* (New York: Simon and Schuster, 1983). See also Charles Murray, *In Pursuit of Happiness and Good Government* (New York: Simon and Schuster, 1988).

20 Aristotle, *Nicomachean Ethics*, I.3, 1094b11–1095a13.

21 "There are certain persons who, it being held to belong to a philosopher to say nothing randomly but rather to use reasoned argument, make arguments that are alien to the subject and empty (they do this sometimes out of ignorance and sometimes from charlatanry) and are not detected, thus taking in those who are experienced and capable of acting, though they themselves neither have nor are capable of architectonic or practical thinking" (Aristotle, *Eudemian Ethics*, I.6, 1217a1–6). For Aristotle's critique of sophistic political science see further *Politics*, II.8.

22 For this larger argument see James W. Ceaser, *Liberal Democracy and Political Science* (Baltimore, MD: Johns Hopkins University Press, 1990). Consider especially his telling critique (chs. 6, 8) of recent schemes for reform of the American political system advanced by prominent academic political scientists.

23 Michael Kammen, *A Machine That Would Go of Itself: The Constitution in American Culture* (New York: Random House, 1986).

IV – ON STATES

1 Clausewitz, *On War*, 88–9.

2 Owen Arthur (then prime minister of Barbados) concludes his insightful survey of this subject with a reminder of the family resemblance of such states to the city states of classical antiquity: "Small States in a Changing World," *Fletcher Forum of International Affairs* (Fall 2000): 3–14.

3 Jeffrey Herbst, *States and Power in Africa* (Princeton, NJ: Princeton University Press, 2000), is a fundamental analysis.

4 See Michael W. Doyle, *Empires* (Ithaca, NY: Cornell University Press, 1986), esp. ch. 1; and Barry Buzan and Richard Little, *International Systems in World History* (Oxford: Oxford University Press, 2000), ch. 8.

5 For a generally prescient survey see Robert Conquest, ed., *The Last Empire: Nationality and the Soviet Future* (Stanford, CA: Hoover Institution Press, 1986).

6 See the fine analysis of Alexander J. Motyl, "Thinking About Empire," in *After Empire: Multiethnic Societies and Nation-Building*, ed. Karen Barkey and Mark von Hagen (Boulder, CO: Westview, 1997), ch. 1.

7 For an extended discussion see further Carnes Lord, *Proconsuls: Delegated Political-Military Leadership from Rome to America Today* (Cambridge: Cambridge University Press, 2012), 6–17.

8 For the relevant history: Brian Harrison, *The Transformation of British Politics 1860–1995* (Oxford: Oxford University Press, 1996), ch. 3. It is possible that Britain's exit from the European Union in 2016 will accelerate Scotland's secession from the United Kingdom, though this is as yet far from clear.

9 See particularly Hendrik Spruyt, *The Sovereign State and Its Competitors* (Princeton, NJ: Princeton University Press, 1994); and Daniel J. Elazar, *Constitutionalizing Globalization: The Postmodern Revival of Confederal Arrangements* (Lanham, MD: Rowman & Littlefield, 1998). In the ancient world, federal states had a presence which for the most part has been completely unappreciated in contemporary historical scholarship. See now Hans Beck and Peter Funke, eds., *Federalism in Greek Antiquity* (Cambridge: Cambridge University Press, 2015).

10 An excellent recent account is Todd Huizinga, *The New Totalitarian Temptation: Global Governance and the Crisis of Democracy in Europe* (New York: Encounter Books, 2016).

11 Richard Rosecrance, *The Rise of the Virtual State: Wealth and Power in the Coming Century* (New York: Basic Books, 1999).

12 Not that this might be wholly unrewarding. Consider the scenario of global politics in Kim Stanley Robinson's epic trilogy about the colonization of Mars.

V – ON REGIMES

1 These are the opening words of the first chapter of *The Prince*.

2 See Machiavelli's own account in his *Florentine Histories*, with the commentary of Harvey C. Mansfield Jr., *Machiavelli's Virtue* (Chicago: University of Chicago Press, 1996), ch. 6.

3 On the meaning of "liberal democracy" see Ceaser, *Liberal Democracy and Political Science*, ch. 1.

4 Fareed Zakaria, "The Rise of Illiberal Democracy," *Foreign Affairs* 76 (November–December 1997): 22–43.

5 See, for example, Kishore Mahbubani, "The United States: 'Go East, Young Man,'" *Washington Quarterly* 17 (Spring 1994): 5–23.

6 Aristotle, *Politics*, IV.1, 1289a15–18; cf. III.6, 1278b6–10.

7 This argument is well developed, with extensive reference to the contemporary world, in Angelo M. Codevilla, *The Character of Nations* (New York: Basic Books, 1997).

8 Aristotle, *Politics*, IV.1, 1289a13–14. For the "governing body" (*politeuma*) see III.6, 1278b10–14.

9 On the rule of law, see *Politics*, III.15–16; on democracy, IV.4–6, VI.2–5.

10 *Politics*, III.7.

11 *Politics*, III.8.

12 *Politics*, III.9–15.

13 *Politics*, IV.14–16, VI.1.

14 *Politics*, IV.7–9, 11–13.

15 For Carthage, see *Politics*, II.11. For Rome as mixed regime and the theory of the cycle of regimes, see Polybius, *Histories*, VI, and Machiavelli, *Discourses*, I.2. For America, John Adams's extended analysis of the classical republican experience in *A Defence of the Constitutions of Government of the United States of America* (1787) is illuminating if not fully typical of the views of the American founders.

16 Aristotle, *Politics*, V; the example mentioned is at 1308a35–b10.

17 *Politics*, VII.4–12.

18 Juan J. Linz and Arturo Valenzuela, eds., *The Failure of Presidential Democracy* (Baltimore, MD: Johns Hopkins University Press, 1994).

19 Larry Diamond, *Developing Democracy: Toward Consolidation* (Baltimore, MD: Johns Hopkins University Press, 1999).

20 Graham Fuller, *The Democracy Trap: The Perils of the Post–Cold War World* (New York: Dutton, 1991), is a penetrating analysis by an experienced American observer of the developing world.

21 See Diamond, *Developing Democracy*, ch. 1, as well as, for example, the annual surveys *Freedom in the World*, compiled and published by Freedom House.

VI – ELITES AND HOW TO MANAGE THEM

1 Harvey C. Mansfield Jr., "Liberal Democracy as a Mixed Regime," in *The Spirit of Liberalism* (Cambridge: Harvard University Press, 1978), ch. 1.

2 Nelson W. Aldrich Jr., *Old Money: The Myth of America's Upper Class* (New York: Random House, 1988), is a useful account. For Alexis de Tocqueville, see *Democracy in America*, I.1.3, I.2.8, and II.2.20.

3 Thus the almost prurient appeal of Paul Fussell, *Class* (New York: Ballantine, 1983).

4 See notably Charles Murray, *Coming Apart: The State of White America, 1960–2010* (New York: Crown Forum, 2012).

5 Mikhail Voslensky, *Nomenklatura: The Soviet Ruling Class* (Garden City, NY: Doubleday, 1984).

6 Richard J. Herrnstein and Charles Murray, *The Bell Curve: Intelligence and Class Structure in American Life* (New York: Simon and Schuster, 1994).

7 Forcefully argued by Christopher Lasch, *The Revolt of the Elites and the Betrayal of Democracy* (New York: W.W. Norton, 1995).

8 Notably, the Cultural Revolution in Maoist China.

9 Tocqueville, *Democracy in America*, II.3.17–20. This phenomenon is the central theme of Stendhal's classic novel *The Red and the Black*.

10 Compare Fukuyama, *End of History*, ch. 5.

11 Contemporary postmodernism may be said to consider axiomatic the idea that all traditional forms of "discourse" are merely masks designed to

conceal and justify elite power; its central task then becomes the unmasking ("deconstruction") of elite discourse in its various manifestations. For a critical analysis see Thomas L. Pangle, *The Ennobling of Democracy: The Challenge of the Post-Modern Age* (Baltimore, MD: Johns Hopkins University Press, 1992), pt. 1.

12 Machiavelli, *Prince*, 9. See James Burnham, *The Machiavellians* (Chicago: Gateway, 1970 [1943]).

13 The argument of C. Wright Mills's influential *The Power Elite* (New York: Oxford University Press, 1956). On the history of "elite theory" in modern social science see, for example, Geraint Parry, *Political Elites* (London: George Allen and Unwin, 1969).

14 Machiavelli, *Prince*, 9.

15 *Prince*, 9.

16 See Rupert Wilkinson, *Gentlemanly Power: British Leadership and the Public School Tradition* (London: Oxford University Press, 1964), which includes extensive comparative material on Confucian China.

17 A first-rate account is Bruce A. Kimball, *Orators and Philosophers: A History of the Idea of Liberal Education* (New York: Columbia University Press, 1986).

VII – MODERN FOUNDERS

1 See Harvey C. Mansfield Jr., *Machiavelli's Virtue* (Chicago: University of Chicago Press, 1996), ch. 1.

2 Machiavelli, *Prince*, 6.

3 Gordon S. Wood, *The Radicalism of the American Revolution* (New York: Alfred A. Knopf, 1992).

4 "Publius" (Alexander Hamilton, James Madison, and John Jay), *The Federalist* (1788), no. 1.

5 Federico Chabod, *Italian Foreign Policy: The Statecraft of the Founders* (Princeton, NJ: Princeton University Press, 1996), is a magisterial work that has wider importance for the study of foundings and statecraft generally. See also Henry Kissinger's classic analysis, "The White Revolutionary: Reflections on Bismarck," *Daedalus* 97 (Summer 1968): 888–924; and Edwin O. Reischauer, *Japan: The Story of a Nation* (New York: Alfred Knopf, 1970), ch. 8.

6 These and comparable leaders throughout the developing world have for the most part been very inadequately studied by historians and political scientists. No modern biography of Atatürk was available until Andrew Mango's *Atatürk* (London: Overlook, 1999); see further Dankwart A. Rustow, "Atatürk as Founder of a State," *Daedalus* 97 (Summer 1968): 793–828; and Geoffrey L. Lewis, *Atatürk and His Republic* (Princeton, NJ: Princeton University Press, 1982). On the evolution of modern Ethiopia and its reforming emperor: Leonard Mosley, *Haile Selassie: The Conquering Lion* (Englewood Cliffs, NJ: Prentice-Hall, 1965).

7 Machiavelli, *Prince*, 12.

8 *Prince*, 14.

9 James Tatum, *Xenophon's Imperial Fiction* (Princeton, NJ: Princeton University Press, 1989). For the interpretation of the central theme of this complex and poorly understood work see W.R. Newell, "Tyranny and the

Science of Ruling in Xenophon's 'Education of Cyrus,'" *Journal of Politics* 45 (1983): 889–906.

10 Anthony James Joes, *From the Barrel of a Gun: Armies and Revolutions* (Washington, D.C.: Pergamon-Brassey's, 1986).

11 Carolyn McGiffert Ekedahl and Melvin A. Goodman, *The Wars of Eduard Shevardnadze* (University Park: Pennsylvania State University Press, 1997), ch. 11. It should be noted that Shevardnadze finally moved against Khitovani and Ioseliani, especially after the latter tried to assassinate him with a car bomb in August 1995. Machiavelli cautions against the use of "auxiliaries" in *Prince*, 13.

12 A conspicuous American example is Woodrow Wilson prior to the U.S. intervention in World War I: Robert H. Ferrell, "Woodrow Wilson: A Misfit in Office?" in *Commanders in Chief: Presidential Leadership in Modern Wars*, ed. Joseph G. Dawson III (Lawrence: University of Kansas Press, 1993), ch. 3.

13 This is the message of Machiavelli's highly entertaining account of Agathocles of Syracuse in *Prince*, 7.

14 Machiavelli, *Discourses*, I.1–13.

15 Machiavelli, *Prince*, 11.

16 *Prince*, 18.

17 Paul A. Smith Jr., *On Political War* (Washington, D.C.: National Defense University Press, 1989), esp. ch. 3.

18 See particularly Noel Malcolm, *Bosnia: A Short History* (New York: New York University Press, 1994).

VIII – EXECUTIVE POWER
AND CONSTITUTIONAL GOVERNMENT

1 It has been fashionable in recent years to emphasize the influence on the American founding of so-called classical republicanism at the expense of Locke and Montesquieu, but this interpretation is highly contestable. Thomas L. Pangle, *The Spirit of Modern Republicanism: The Moral Vision of the American Founders and the Philosophy of Locke* (Chicago: University of Chicago Press, 1988), is an outstanding account. Montesquieu's chief work is *The Spirit of the Laws* (1748).

2 For a lucid exposition of these issues see Ceaser, *Liberal Democracy and Political Science*, ch. 1.

3 For this history: M.J.C. Vile, *Constitutionalism and the Separation of Powers* (Indianapolis: Liberty Fund, 1998 [1967]).

4 John Locke, *Second Treatise*, 11–14. For the interpretation offered here see Harvey C. Mansfield Jr., *Taming the Prince: The Ambivalence of Executive Power* (New York: Free Press, 1989), ch. 8.

5 Locke, *Second Treatise*, 13, sec. 158.

6 Why the pardoning power? Most Americans today assume the rationale is purely humanitarian. While not denying this factor, Hamilton gives more emphasis to prudential calculation: "In seasons of insurrection or rebellion, there are often critical moments when a well-timed offer of pardon to the insurgents or rebels may restore the tranquility of the commonwealth" (*The Federalist*, no. 74).

7 Locke, *Second Treatise*, 14.

8 Consider too in this connection the Roman model of executive prerogative, the (elected and temporary) "dictator" (Machiavelli, *Discourses*, I.34).

9 For useful historical analysis see Leonard W. Levy and Dennis J. Mahoney, eds., *The Framing and Ratification of the Constitution* (New York: Macmillan, 1987).

10 Hamilton and Madison would later become bitter political enemies; in 1793, they publicly debated the question of the constitutional scope of executive power in a series of newspaper articles (the "Pacificus" and "Helvidius" letters) that signaled an emerging fault line in American political culture. Whatever their differences on this subject might have been in 1787, though, the overall argument of *The Federalist* is strikingly coherent. See notably David J. Epstein, *The Political Theory of The Federalist* (Chicago: University of Chicago Press, 1984).

11 Note, however, that Madison goes out of his way to include not only those "ambitiously contending for pre-eminence and power" but also those he delicately describes as "persons . . . whose fortunes have been interesting to the human passions"—that is to say, politico-religious figures of charismatic bent.

12 Karl-Friedrich Walling, *Republican Empire: Alexander Hamilton on War and Free Government* (Lawrence: University Press of Kansas, 1999), ch. 6, is an outstanding brief account.

13 *The Federalist*, no. 68.

14 "But the great security against a gradual concentration of the several powers in the same department, consists in giving to those who administer each department, the necessary constitutional means, and personal motives, to resist encroachments of the others. The provision for defence must in this, as in all other cases, be made commensurate to the danger of attack. Ambition must be made to counteract ambition. The interest of the man must be connected with the constitutional rights of the place. It may be a reflection on human nature, that such devices should be necessary to controul the abuses of government. But what is government itself but the greatest of all reflections on human nature? If men were angels, no government would be necessary. If angels were to govern men, neither external nor internal controuls on government would be necessary." *The Federalist*, no. 51.

15 *The Federalist*, no. 70.

16 The question is rarely asked whether the Twenty-second Amendment significantly compromises the founding vision of the constitutional role of the president, in large part because it is seen to address a non-problem. This is not so clear. Foreclosure of a third term option undoubtedly contributes to the "lame duck" effect in a president's second term. One could also argue that it unduly minimizes the possibility of a recurrence of the conditions that led to Roosevelt's prolonged stay in office, or else discounts unreasonably the benefits of staying with a proven leader in times of national crisis or war. Consider the impact on the course of the Cold War if Eisenhower had been able to serve a third term. Among other things, American involvement in Vietnam would almost certainly have had a happier outcome.

17 *The Federalist*, no. 72.

18 *The Federalist*, no. 72. See notably Gerald Stourzh, *Alexander Hamilton and the Idea of Republican Government* (Stanford, CA: Stanford University Press, 1970), ch. 3.

19 Consider Hamilton's sly allusion at the end of *The Federalist*, no. 75, to the coming expansion of the Senate. For the critical case of the first president: Glenn A. Phelps, *George Washington and American Constitutionalism* (Lawrence: University Press of Kansas, 1993), chs. 5–6.

20 This argument is ably developed with reference to recent American presidents by Terry Eastland, *Energy in the Executive: The Case for the Strong Presidency* (New York: Free Press, 1992).

21 *The Federalist*, no. 23.

22 For contrasting views of these issues: Louis Fisher, *Presidential War Power* (Lawrence: University Press of Kansas, 1995); and L. Gordon Crovitz and Jeremy A. Rabkin, eds., *The Fettered Presidency: Legal Constraints on the Executive Branch* (Washington, D.C.: American Enterprise Institute, 1989). See also Mark J. Rozell, *Executive Privilege: The Dilemma of Secrecy and Democratic Accountability* (Baltimore, MD: Johns Hopkins University Press, 1994).

23 This is the argument of Mansfield's *Taming the Prince*, a pathbreaking work of intellectual history to which the present study is much indebted. Consider particularly Mansfield's discussion (ch. 2) of the absence of the executive in Aristotelian political science.

24 Machiavelli, *Discourses*, I.4; Harvey C. Mansfield Jr., *Statesmanship and Party Government: A Study of Burke and Bolingbroke* (Chicago: University of Chicago Press, 1965).

25 Bagehot, *English Constitution*, ch. 1.

26 See Daniel D. Stid, *The President as Statesman: Woodrow Wilson and the Constitution* (Lawrence: University Press of Kansas, 1998).

27 Winston S. Churchill, *Marlborough: His Life and Times* (4 vols., 1933–8), and *The Second World War* (12 vols., 1948–53); consider especially his comment on Baldwin in the first volume of the latter (*The Gathering Storm* [Boston: Houghton-Mifflin, 1948], 32–3).

28 Consider the comment of Mansfield, *Taming the Prince*, 293–4: "That the separation of functions has not worked does not mean that the separation of powers should be abandoned. . . . But Locke's intended division of responsibility between generalizing by law and using discretion has been overcome—not surprising to anyone schooled by Machiavelli—to the advantage of the power closer to the deed. As a sign of this universal tendency, one may remark that it is quite possible to use the term 'leadership' without seeming to favor monarchy. In executive leadership, bygone partisans of monarchy do not quite have all they ever wanted, but they have enough to satisfy them that modern republicans have unwittingly admitted much truth in the monarchist cause."

IX – DEMOCRACY WITHOUT LEADERS

1 It is important nevertheless to appreciate the potential latitude for intervention by Emperor Hirohito in Japanese decision-making during World War II, as revealed in recently discovered documentary records.

Edward J. Drea, *In the Service of the Emperor: Essays on the Imperial Japanese Army* (Lincoln: University of Nebraska Press, 1998), ch. 12.

2 For a sensible account of these issues see Richard Katz, *Japan: The System That Soured—the Rise and Fall of the Japanese Economic Miracle* (Armonk, NY: M.E. Sharpe, 1998), ch. 13.

3 See especially Chalmers Johnson, *MITI and the Japanese Miracle* (Stanford, CA: Stanford University Press, 1982), and *Japan: Who Governs?* (New York: W.W. Norton, 1995); Eamonn Fingleton, *Blindside: Why Japan Is Still on Track to Overtake the U.S. by the Year 2000* (Boston: Houghton Mifflin, 1995); and Peter Hartcher, *The Ministry: How Japan's Most Powerful Institution Endangers World Markets* (Boston: Harvard Business School Press, 1998).

4 Karel van Wolferen, *The Enigma of Japanese Power* (New York: Alfred A. Knopf, 1989). Whatever its flaws, this controversial book is an impressive work of Tocquevillian-style social science.

5 As one scholar has written of the prewar era, "The Japan of which General Hideki Tojo became premier was operated by remote control. It was a country in which puppet politics had reached a high state of development, to the detriment of the national welfare. The ranking members of the military services were the robots of their subordinates. . . . They, in turn, were influenced by younger elements within the services at large." Robert J.C. Butow, *Tojo and the Coming of the War* (Stanford, CA: Stanford University Press, 1961), 308. See more generally Yung H. Park, *Bureaucrats and Ministers in Contemporary Japanese Government* (Berkeley: Institute of East Asian Studies, University of California, 1986), 3–4.

6 Eiko Ikegami, *The Taming of the Samurai: Honorific Individualism and the Making of Modern Japan* (Cambridge, MA: Harvard University Press, 1995).

7 As Johnson remarks, with particular reference to MITI. Johnson notes elsewhere the curious fact that there is no term in Japanese for "consensus." *Japan: Who Governs?* 228, 173.

8 See Machiavelli's reinterpretation of the classical virtue of liberality in *Prince*, 16.

9 See Johnson, *Japan: Who Governs?* ch. 9, and more generally Jacob M. Schlesinger, *Shadow Shoguns: The Rise and Fall of Japan's Postwar Political Machine* (New York: Simon and Schuster, 1997).

10 Van Wolferen, *Enigma of Japanese Power*, 146–54.

11 Johnson, *Japan: Who Governs?* ch. 10; Schlesinger, *Shadow Shoguns*, ch. 19.

12 Johnson, *Japan: Who Governs?* ch. 22.

13 Tomohito Shinoda, *Leading Japan: The Role of the Prime Minister* (Westport, CT: Praeger, 2000); see also Kenji Hayao, *The Japanese Prime Minister and Public Policy* (Pittsburgh, PA: University of Pittsburgh Press, 1993). A key finding of these studies is that prime ministers have historically enjoyed much greater latitude in foreign than in domestic policy decision-making.

14 Just how recalcitrant the bureaucracy remains was evident recently in the ultimately successful campaign mounted by senior Foreign Ministry officials to force the resignation of Koizumi's appointee, Makiko Tanaka (daughter of Kakuei Tanaka and also a strong-willed and unconventional personality), after she attempted to assert greater control over them. Calvin Sims, "Japan's Unceremonious Foreign Minister," *New York Times*, May 23, 2001.

248 / THE MODERN PRINCE

15 See, for example, Robert Elgie, *Political Leadership in Liberal Democracies* (New York: St. Martin's Press, 1995), ch. 7.

16 Van Wolferen, *Enigma of Japanese Power*, ch. 9. Consider, however, Sophie Coignard and Alexandre Wickham, *L'omerta française* (Paris: Albin Michel, 1999).

17 Van Wolferen, *Enigma of Japanese Power*, chs. 10, 12. For the key issue of elite recruitment and management see Fingleton, *Blindside*, ch. 4, and Hartcher, *Ministry*, ch. 1.

18 Consider the ancient Spartans. The Spartan citizen-class (the so-called Peers) was a highly cohesive warrior elite that was at the same time well known for its reverence for authority. The two Spartan kings, however, like their medieval Japanese counterparts, exercised very limited powers, mainly in military command.

19 See notably Arno J. Mayer, *The Persistence of the Old Regime: Europe to the Great War* (New York: Pantheon, 1981); John H. Kautsky, *The Politics of Aristocratic Empires* (Chapel Hill: University of North Carolina Press, 1982); and Andreas A.M. Kinneging, *Aristocracy, Antiquity and History: Classicism in Political Thought* (New Brunswick, NJ: Transaction, 1997).

X – AUTOCRATIC DEMOCRACY

1 Donald Kagan, *Pericles of Athens and the Birth of Democracy* (New York: Free Press, 1991).

2 On the origins of the Fifth Republic and de Gaulle's role generally, see Jean Lacouture, *De Gaulle: The Ruler, 1945–1970*, trans. Alan Sheridan (New York: W.W. Norton, 1992), ch. 16.

3 See, for example, Maurice Duverger, *La monarchie républicaine* (Paris: Robert Laffont, 1974).

4 Jean-François Revel, *L'absolutisme inefficace: ou contre le présidentialisme à la française* (Paris: Plon, 1992), 17. For a more sympathetic account of the Mitterrand regime see, for example, Julius W. Friend, *The Long Presidency: France in the Mitterrand Years, 1981–1995* (Boulder, CO: Westview, 1998).

5 See further Jean-Michel Bélorgey, *Le Parlement à refaire* (Paris: Gallimard, 1991).

6 Notably, the tendency of officials to hold multiple positions, to blur political and administrative roles, and to work around overly restrictive regulations. Yves Mény, *La corruption de la République* (Paris: Fayard, 1992).

7 Revel, *L'absolutisme inefficace*, 119–24. A striking parallel is the presidentialist regime of Boris Yeltsin in Russia. See especially Igor Klyamkin and Lilia Shevtsova, *This Omnipotent and Impotent Government: The Evolution of the Political System of Post-Communist Russia* (Washington, D.C.: Carnegie Endowment, 1999).

8 The classic study is Ezra N. Suleiman, *Politics, Power, and Bureaucracy in France* (Princeton, NJ: Princeton University Press, 1974).

9 Lee's recently published memoir of the post-independence era, *From Third World to First: The Singapore Story: 1965–2000* (New York: HarperCollins, 2000), especially chs. 4–5, is interesting and informative on this history. See also Garry Rodan, *The Political Economy of Singapore's Industrialization* (London: Macmillan, 1989).

10 This is a major theme of the first volume of Lee's memoir, *The Singapore Story: Memoirs of Lee Kuan Yew* (Singapore: Prentice Hall, 1998).

11 Lee, *From Third World to First*, ch. 12. International surveys consistently rank Singapore as one of the least corrupt countries in the world.

12 This involved the creation of several special categories of members of Parliament to give guaranteed representation to the opposition, to improve the electoral chances of minority ethnic candidates, and to encourage non-partisan criticism of the government (by distinguished citizens serving as so-called "nominated" MPs).

13 For a detailed history and analysis see Kevin Tan and Lam Peng Er, eds., *Managing Political Change in Singapore: The Elected Presidency* (London: Routledge, 1997).

14 Lee, *From Third World to First*, 664–8.

15 Aristotle, *Politics*, III.13.

XI – WHAT GOALS LEADERS PURSUE

1 Consider David Hume's defense of luxury against this still powerful prejudice: "Refinement in the Arts," in *Essays Moral, Political, and Literary* (1741–2).

2 Geoffrey Parker, "The Making of Strategy in Hapsburg Spain: Philip II's 'Bid for Mastery', 1556–1598," in *The Making of Strategy: Rulers, States, and War*, ed. Williamson Murray, MacGregor Knox, and Alvin Bernstein (Cambridge: Cambridge University Press, 1994), ch. 5.

3 See more generally Daniel J. Mahoney, *De Gaulle: Statesmanship, Grandeur and Modern Democracy* (Westport, CT: Praeger, 1996).

4 For this fundamental argument see further Elliott Abrams, ed., *Honor Among Nations: Intangible Interests and Foreign Policy* (Washington, D.C.: Ethics and Public Policy Center, 1998). The dynamics of honor, "face," and "prestige" in international conflict are well analyzed in Barry O'Neill, *Honor, Symbols, and War* (Ann Arbor: University of Michigan Press, 1999).

5 Such factors are too often ignored in the currently dominant "realist" school of international relations theory. Consider, for example, John J. Mearsheimer, *The Tragedy of Great Power Politics* (New York: W.W. Norton, 2001), in the light of Paul W. Schroeder, *The Transformation of European Politics 1763–1848* (Oxford: Clarendon Press, 1994).

XII – WHAT TOOLS LEADERS HAVE AVAILABLE

1 There is no accepted term to designate style or culture in the practice of statecraft. "Strategic culture" is a term usually used to refer to styles of warfare, though sometimes it is given a broader sense. See, for example, Alastair I. Johnston, *Cultural Realism: Strategic Culture and Grand Strategy in Chinese History* (Ithaca, NY: Cornell University Press, 1995).

XIII – ADMINISTRATION

1 "Though we cannot acquiesce in the political heresy of the poet who says—'For forms of government let fools contest—That which is best administered is best'—yet we may safely pronounce, that the true test of a good government is its aptitude and tendency to produce a good administration."

[Alexander Hamilton,] *The Federalist*, no. 68. The couplet is from Pope's *Essay on Man*.

2 The seminal discussion is Woodrow Wilson's paper "The Study of Administration" (1887). This and other relevant materials are usefully collected in Frederick C. Mosher, ed., *Basic Literature of American Public Administration, 1787–1950* (New York: Holmes and Meier, 1981).

3 This is the view taken in Sir Henry Taylor's *The Statesman* (1842), the earliest treatise on public administration and a minor classic of traditional political science.

4 See, for example, Herlee G. Creel, *The Origins of Statecraft in China* (Chicago: University of Chicago Press, 1970), ch. 1; and Hans Rosenberg, *Bureaucracy, Aristocracy and Autocracy: The Prussian Experience 1660–1815* (Boston: Beacon Press, 1958).

5 The American case is an instructive one: Stephen Skowronek, *Building a New American State: The Expansion of National Administrative Capacities, 1877–1920* (Cambridge: Cambridge University Press, 1982).

6 See generally Weber, *Economy and Society*, 1:212–26, 2:956–94.

7 Tocqueville, *Democracy in America*, II.4.6. See Paul Rahe, *Soft Despotism and Democracy's Drift: Montesquieu, Rousseau, Tocqueville, and the Modern Prospect* (New Haven, CT: Yale University Press, 2009).

8 Probably the single best treatment of the dynamics of bureaucratic organizations is Anthony Downs, *Inside Bureaucracy* (Boston: Little, Brown, 1966). See more recently James Q. Wilson, *Bureaucracy: What Government Agencies Do and Why They Do It* (New York: Basic Books, 1989).

9 See his comments on the Prussian and Russian monarchs—Weber, *Economy and Society*, 2:993–4—as well as the discussion of Rosenberg, *Bureaucracy, Aristocracy and Autocracy*, ch. 8.

10 Mayer, *Persistence of the Old Regime*, chs. 3–4.

11 See, for example, Hugh Heclo, *A Government of Strangers: Executive Politics in Washington* (Washington, D.C.: Brookings Institution, 1977); and Hugh Heclo and Lester M. Salamon, eds., *The Illusion of Presidential Government* (Boulder, CO: Westview, 1981).

12 FDR's remark is a classic: "The Treasury is so large and far-flung and ingrained in its practices that I find it almost impossible to get the action and results I want—even with Henry [Morgenthau] there. But the Treasury is not to be compared to the State Department. You should go through the experience of trying to get any changes in the thinking, policy, and action of the career diplomats and then you'd know what a real problem was. But the Treasury and the State Department put together are nothing compared with the Na-a-vy. The admirals are really something to cope with—and I should know [as a former secretary of the Navy]. To change something in the Na-a-vy is like punching a feather bed. You punch it with your right and you punch it with your left until you are finally exhausted, and then you find the damn bed just as it was before you started punching." Marriner S. Eccles, *Beckoning Frontiers* (New York: Knopf, 1951), 336.

13 FDR was also the first president to bring the doctrines of academic public administration to bear on questions of governmental organization. The Brownlow Report of 1937 led to several fundamental changes in the nature

of presidential governance, notably, the creation of the Executive Office of the President. See generally Barry D. Karl, *Executive Reorganization and Reform in the New Deal* (Cambridge, MA: Harvard University Press, 1966).

14 The Nixon case is particularly interesting for our purposes. See Joan Hoff-Wilson, "Richard M. Nixon: The Corporate Presidency," in *Leadership in the Modern Presidency*, ed. Fred I. Greenstein (Cambridge, MA: Harvard University Press, 1988), ch. 6. Jimmy Carter should perhaps also be mentioned, but his administrative tinkering seems to have lacked real strategic purpose.

15 Dwight D. Eisenhower, *The White House Years: Mandate for Change, 1953–1956* (Garden City, NY: Doubleday, 1963), 114.

16 For the evolution of this critical administrative mechanism see Carnes Lord, *The Presidency and the Management of National Security* (New York: Free Press, 1988).

17 See generally Fred I. Greenstein, "Dwight D. Eisenhower: Leadership Theorist in the White House," in Greenstein, *Leadership in the Modern Presidency*, ch. 3.

18 In spite of forceful warnings from many quarters, notably the blue-ribbon U.S. Commission on National Security/21st Century, *Road Map for National Security: Imperative for Change* (Washington, D.C., March 2001). The creation of a new Department of Homeland Security in the wake of the attacks represents the most ambitious reform of the American bureaucracy since the National Security Act of 1947.

19 A striking example is Admiral Hyman Rickover's nuclear Navy; for an illuminating account see John F. Lehman Jr., *Command of the Seas* (New York: Scribner's, 1988), introduction. For the business world see, for example, John P. Kotter and James L. Heskett, *Corporate Culture and Performance* (New York: Free Press, 1992).

20 Machiavelli, *Prince*, 17.

XIV – LAW

1 Blandine Kriegel, *The State and the Rule of Law*, trans. Marc A. LePain and Jeffrey C. Cohen (Princeton, NJ: Princeton University Press, 1995).

2 Stanton H. Burnett and Luca Mantovani, *The Italian Guillotine: Operation Clean Hands and the Overthrow of Italy's First Republic* (Lanham, MD: Rowman and Littlefield, 1998).

3 Alec Stone Sweet, *Governing with Judges: Constitutional Politics in Europe* (New York: Oxford University Press, 2000).

4 See Christopher Wolfe, *The Rise of Modern Judicial Review: From Constitutional Interpretation to Judge-made Law* (New York: Basic Books, 1986); and Sylvia Snowiss, *Judicial Review and the Law of the Constitution* (New Haven, CT: Yale University Press, 1990).

5 "Under the original Judiciary Act there were six Justices of the Supreme Court. As episodes in the Jeffersonians' struggle to control the judiciary, Congress changed the number to five in 1801, then back to six in 1802. The number was raised to nine in 1837 (to water down the influence of John Marshall), and to ten in 1863 (to prevent Andrew Johnson from making any appointments), and voted back to nine in 1869, when Grant could name the

new members—who, as expected, brought a reversal of the Court's previous finding against the Legal Tender Act." Burnham, *Congress and the American Tradition*, 133.

6 For a detailed account see Kenneth S. Davis, *FDR: Into the Storm, 1937–1940* (New York: Random House, 1993), ch. 2. For a defense of Roosevelt: Philip Abbott, *The Exemplary Presidency: Franklin D. Roosevelt and the American Political Tradition* (Amherst: University of Massachusetts Press, 1990), ch. 7.

7 David Herbert Donald, *Lincoln* (New York: Simon and Schuster, 1995), 199–202.

8 See the discussion of Tocqueville and political culture in Ceaser, *Liberal Democracy and Political Science*, chs. 3, 7.

9 Aristotle, *Politics*, II.8.

10 The expression is borrowed from the title of Montesquieu's classic study.

11 Aristotle's account of Athenian constitutional history (in the *Politics* as well as a treatise entitled *The Constitution of Athens*) stresses the progressive emancipation of democratic decision-making from traditional laws; Plato's *Laws* is a thought experiment designed to show how democracy and the rule of law can be made compatible.

12 Tocqueville, *Democracy in America*, I.2.8.

13 Lincoln, "The Perpetuation of Our Political Institutions." See Glen E. Thurow, *Abraham Lincoln and American Political Religion* (Albany: State University of New York Press, 1976).

14 James R. Stoner, *The Common Law and Liberal Theory* (Lawrence: University Press of Kansas, 1992), is valuable on the common law background of American constitutional and legal thought.

15 See Walter Berns, *The First Amendment and the Future of American Democracy* (New York: Basic Books, 1976); and Raoul Berger, *Government by Judiciary: The Transformation of the Fourteenth Amendment* (Cambridge, MA: Harvard University Press, 1977).

16 Consider Anthony T. Kronman, *The Lost Lawyer: Failing Ideals of the Legal Profession* (Cambridge, MA: Belknap Press, 1993).

17 Eastland, *Energy in the Executive*, chs. 17–18.

XV – EDUCATION AND CULTURE

1 A noteworthy recent exception: Orit Ichilov, ed., *Citizenship and Citizenship Education in a Changing World* (London: Woburn Press, 1998).

2 See Kimball, *Orators and Philosophers*; Carnes Lord, "Aristotle and the Idea of Liberal Education," in *Dēmokratia: A Conversation on Democracies, Ancient and Modern*, ed. Josiah Ober and Charles Hedrick (Princeton, NJ: Princeton University Press, 1996), 271–88.

3 Machiavelli, *Prince*, 15.

4 Whether or to what extent Machiavelli envisioned a thoroughly secular solution to the problem discussed here is controversial; see especially Vickie B. Sullivan, *Machiavelli's Three Romes* (DeKalb: Northern Illinois University Press, 1996).

5 John Locke played an important role here. See his *Letter on Toleration* and especially *Some Thoughts Concerning Education*, with the analysis of Nathan Tarcov, *Locke's Education for Liberty* (Chicago: University of Chicago Press, 1984).

6 As former president Musharraf of Pakistan put it, "I used to avoid discussing religion. I did not want to get distracted from economic and political reconstruction." Jim Hoagland, "Pakistan's Promises," *Washington Post*, January 23, 2002.

7 Margaret Thatcher, *The Downing Street Years* (New York: HarperCollins, 1993), 590–7.

8 Thatcher's perceived meddling in the affairs of Oxford and Cambridge (which included certain limits on faculty tenure) caused an uproar; see her comments in Thatcher, *Downing Street Years*, 598–9.

9 For illuminating reportage and analysis: "The Politics of Political Correctness," special issue, *Partisan Review* 60, no. 4 (1993); and Angelo M. Codevilla, "The Rise of Political Correctness: From Marx to Gramsci to Trump," *Claremont Review of Books* (Fall 2016): 37–43.

10 Federal policy toward foreign students is currently a shambles and a serious national security concern. George J. Borjas, "Rethinking Foreign Students," *National Review*, June 17, 2002, 38–41.

11 Suleiman, *Politics, Power, and Bureaucracy in France*, 42–52.

XVI – ECONOMICS

1 Hamilton, "Report on Manufactures" (1791), in *The Papers of Alexander Hamilton*, 27 vols., ed. Harold C. Syrett et al. (New York: Columbia University Press, 1961–79), 10:266–7.

2 For this overall argument see Steven E. Rhoads, *The Economist's View of the World: Government, Markets, and Public Policy* (Cambridge: Cambridge University Press, 1985), chs. 9–11.

3 The key text for Aristotle's economic ideas is *Politics*, I.3–13.

4 Adam Smith, *An Inquiry into the Nature and Causes of the Wealth of Nations*, IV.2. Donald Winch, *Adam Smith's Politics* (Cambridge: Cambridge University Press, 1978), is a valuable corrective to conventional interpretations.

5 See Edward Mead Earle, "Adam Smith, Alexander Hamilton, Friedrich List: The Economic Foundations of Military Power," in *Makers of Modern Strategy*, ed. Peter Paret (Princeton, NJ: Princeton University Press, 1986), ch. 8.

6 This so-called infant industries argument can be traced to Sir James Steuart's *An Inquiry into the Principles of Political Oeconomy* (1767), a work that strongly influenced Hamilton. See Forrest McDonald, *Novus Ordo Seclorum: The Intellectual Origins of the Constitution* (Lawrence: University Press of Kansas, 1985), ch. 4.

7 The definitive account of Hamilton's economic statecraft is Forrest McDonald, *Alexander Hamilton: A Biography* (New York: W.W. Norton, 1979).

8 For fundamental discussion see David A. Baldwin, *Economic Statecraft* (Princeton, NJ: Princeton University Press, 1985), ch. 3. According to Baldwin, "economic means" are "resources that have a reasonable semblance of a market price in terms of money" (p. 30).

9 Machiavelli, *Prince*, 16. See Clifford Orwin, "Machiavelli's Unchristian Charity," *American Political Science Review* 72 (December 1978): 1217–28.

10 Plutarch, *Life of Lycurgus*, *Life of Solon*. G.E.M. de Ste. Croix, *The Class*

Struggle in the Ancient Greek World (Ithaca, NY: Cornell University Press, 1981), is useful in spite of its Marxist orientation.

11 On this phenomenon see especially Thomas E. Graham Jr., "From Oligarchy to Oligarchy: The Structure of Russia's Ruling Elite," *Demokratizatsiya* 7 (Summer 1999): 325–40.

12 For a preliminary assessment of Putin's statecraft generally see Thomas E. Graham Jr., *Russia's Decline and Uncertain Recovery* (Washington, D.C.: Carnegie Endowment, 2002), ch. 4.

13 Peter Reddaway and Dmitri Glinski, *The Tragedy of Russia's Reforms: Market Bolshevism Against Democracy* (Washington, D.C.: United States Institute of Peace, 2001), ch. 5 (esp. pp. 245–7 and 280–6).

14 A striking example of this historiographical neglect is Bismarck's relationship with the Jewish banker Gerson Bleichröder, as reconstructed by Fritz Stern in his exemplary study *Iron and Gold: Bismarck, Bleichröder, and the Building of the German Empire* (New York: Random House, 1977).

15 See notably William Greider, *Secrets of the Temple: How the Federal Reserve Runs the Country* (New York: Simon and Schuster, 1988); and Zarate, *Treasury's War*.

16 The American case is highly instructive. See Robert W. Tucker and David C. Hendrickson, *Empire of Liberty: The Statecraft of Thomas Jefferson* (New York: Oxford University Press, 1990).

17 This is the fundamental argument of Baldwin's *Economic Statecraft*, a relentless exposure of the conceptual confusion that marks much of the literature on this subject.

18 Analyzed by Albert O. Hirschman in what probably remains the best overall study of this subject: *National Power and the Structure of Foreign Trade* (Berkeley: University of California Press, 1980 [1945]).

19 See particularly Peter Schweitzer, *Victory: The Reagan Administration's Secret Strategy that Hastened the Collapse of the Soviet Union* (New York: Atlantic Monthly Press, 1994); and Derek Leebaert, *The Fifty-Year Wound: The True Price of America's Cold War Victory* (Boston: Little, Brown, 2002), ch. 10.

XVII – DIPLOMACY

1 For a brief account see Gordon A. Craig, "On the Nature of Diplomatic History: The Relevance of Some Old Books," in *Diplomacy: New Approaches in History, Theory, and Policy*, ed. Paul Gordon Lauren (New York: Free Press, 1979), ch. 2.

2 Harold Nicolson, *Diplomacy* (New York: Harcourt Brace, 1939), ch. 2.

3 Tocqueville, *Democracy in America*, I.2.5.

4 Nicolson, *Diplomacy*, ch. 4.

5 Consider Jean-François Revel's ill-timed prediction of Western defeat in the Cold War, *How Democracies Perish*, trans. William Byron (Garden City, NY: Doubleday, 1984).

6 Henry Kissinger, *Diplomacy* (New York: Simon and Schuster, 1994), ch. 5; Anatole Lieven, "Lord Salisbury: A Model for Aspiring Imperialists," *National Interest* 53 (Fall 1998): 75–84.

7 For this neglected diplomatic subspecialty see Vernon A. Walters, *Silent Missions* (Garden City, NY: Doubleday, 1978). For an assessment of the

American diplomatic instrument today, see Kori N. Schake, *State of Disrepair: Fixing the Culture and Practices of the State Department* (Stanford, CA: Hoover Institution Press, 2012).

8 The impression of personal weakness conveyed by President John F. Kennedy at the Vienna summit shortly after assuming office in 1961 seems to have contributed significantly to the decision of Soviet leader Nikita Khrushchev to send nuclear weapons to Cuba in the summer of 1962.

9 This is the main reason direct video links between the American president and foreign leaders have never been seriously considered in Washington.

10 Henry A. Kissinger, *The Necessity for Choice* (New York: Harper, 1961), ch. 8. For what follows see further Charles H. Fairbanks Jr., "The Allure of Summits," in *FPI Policy Briefs* (Washington, D.C.: Johns Hopkins Foreign Policy Institute, 1988).

XVIII – FORCE

1 Machiavelli, *Prince*, 14.

2 Azar Gat, *War in Human Civilization* (Oxford: Oxford University Press, 2006), is a magisterial work of contemporary social science.

3 William V. Harris, *War and Imperialism in Republican Rome, 327–70 B.C.* (Oxford: Clarendon Press, 1979). Although Rome was not a democracy in our sense, this history creates massive difficulties for the "democratic peace" thesis so popular with political scientists today. In fact, Rome was incapable of waging war effectively without the support of the people as a whole. Consider Machiavelli, *Discourses*, I.6; [Alexander Hamilton], *The Federalist*, no. 6; and Zakaria, "Rise of Illiberal Democracy."

4 Bruce D. Porter, *War and the Rise of the State: The Military Foundations of Modern Politics* (New York: Free Press, 1994).

5 For these large issues see Martin van Creveld, *The Transformation of War* (New York: Free Press, 1991).

6 Angelo M. Codevilla, *Between the Alps and a Hard Place: Switzerland in World War II and Moral Blackmail Today* (Washington, D.C.: Regnery, 2000), chs. 1–2. See also Tim Huxley's eye-opening *Defending the Lion City: The Armed Forces of Singapore* (St. Leonard's, NSW: Allen & Unwin, 2000), esp. ch. 2.

7 This term is something of a misnomer, as it includes weapons (chemical and radiological devices in particular) that are unlikely to cause catastrophic damage—or to evoke an apocalyptic response if used.

8 The Vietnam precedent seems to have contributed significantly to Saddam Hussein's miscalculation of the American reaction to his occupation of Kuwait in 1990.

9 Paul Seabury and Angelo Codevilla, *War: Ends and Means* (New York: Basic Books, 1989), chs. 1, 4.

10 This is the argument of Samuel P. Huntington's highly influential *The Soldier and the State: The Theory and Politics of Civil-Military Relations* (Cambridge, MA: Harvard University Press, 1957). Whatever its flaws, this book has to be recognized as a classic of contemporary political science.

11 Clausewitz, *On War*, 87.

12 Clausewitz, *On War*, 89.

13 Eliot A. Cohen, *Supreme Command: Soldiers, Statesmen, and Leadership in Wartime* (New York: Free Press, 2002), demonstrates this convincingly through detailed analysis of the wartime leadership of Abraham Lincoln, Georges Clemenceau, Winston Churchill, and David Ben-Gurion.

14 See generally Amos Perlmutter, *The Military and Politics in Modern Times* (New Haven, CT: Yale University Press, 1977); and Amos Perlmutter and Valerie Plave Bennett, eds., *The Political Influence of the Military* (New Haven, CT: Yale University Press, 1980).

15 Charles J. Dunlap Jr., "The Origins of the American Military Coup of 2012," *Parameters* (Winter 1992–3): 2–20, is entertaining but hardly convincing. Its main point is to warn against undue involvement of the military in non-traditional activities such as counter-narcotics or "nation-building."

16 Tocqueville, *Democracy in America*, II.3.22 ("Why Democratic Peoples Naturally Want Peace but Democratic Armies Want War").

17 H.R. McMaster, *Dereliction of Duty: Lyndon Johnson, Robert McNamara, the Joint Chiefs of Staff, and the Lies that Led to Vietnam* (New York: HarperCollins, 1997); Cohen, *Supreme Command*, ch. 6.

18 The contemporary debate on these issues was initiated by Richard H. Kohn, "Out of Control," *National Interest* 35 (Spring 1994): 3–17; see more recently Peter D. Feaver and Richard H. Kohn, eds., *Soldiers and Civilians: The Civil-Military Gap and American National Security* (Cambridge, MA: MIT Press, 2001). Post–Cold War military allergies include "nation-building," civilian constraints on target selection, incremental commitment of forces, and commitment of forces without a (political) "exit strategy."

19 Clausewitz, *On War*, 608.

20 See generally Eliot A. Cohen, *Citizens and Soldiers: The Dilemmas of Military Service* (Ithaca, NY: Cornell University Press, 1985).

21 One plausible explanation is simply that the culture as a whole has become more hostile to widely shared military values—Huntington's "conservative realism." See, for example, Thomas E. Ricks, *Making the Corps* (New York: Scribner, 1997).

XIX – INTELLIGENCE

1 Sun Tzu, *Art of War*, trans. Roger T. Ames (London: Francis Lincoln Limited, 2015), chs. 1, 3, 13. On the nature of this text and its significance see Carnes Lord, "A Note on Sun Tzu," *Comparative Strategy* 19 (October–December 2000): 301–7.

2 See notably Michael Pillsbury, *The Hundred-Year Marathon: China's Secret Strategy to Replace America as the Global Superpower* (New York: Henry Holt, 2015).

3 See in particular Ernest W. May, ed., *Knowing One's Enemies: Intelligence Assessment Before the Two World Wars* (Princeton, NJ: Princeton University Press, 1984); Michael I. Handel, ed., *Leaders and Intelligence* (London: Frank Cass, 1989); and Michael I. Handel, ed., *Intelligence and Military Operations* (London: Frank Cass, 1990).

4 For a concise overview see Abram N. Shulsky and Gary J. Schmitt, *Silent Warfare: Understanding the World of Intelligence*, 3rd ed. (Washington, D.C.: Brassey's, 2002 [1991]), the best introduction to the conceptual aspects of this subject.

5 So famously commented American secretary of state Henry L. Stimson on abolishing the department's Cipher Bureau in 1929: G.J.A. O'Toole, *Honorable Treachery: A History of U.S. Intelligence, Espionage, and Covert Action from the American Revolution to the CIA* (New York: Atlantic Monthly Press, 1991), 337.

6 After the death of Stalin in 1953, the political ambitions and personal power of Soviet NKVD chief Lavrentii Beria moved the rest of the leadership to conspire to have him arrested and secretly executed. In 1979, South Korean president Park Chung Hee was assassinated in his office by the head of the Korean Central Intelligence Agency. More recently, consider the role played by intelligence chief Vladimiro Montesinos in the fall of the Fujimori regime in Peru.

7 This is not to say that intelligence has no prehistory. See, for example, Francis Dvornik, *Origins of Intelligence Services* (New Brunswick, NJ: Rutgers University Press, 1974).

8 Anthony Cave Brown, *Wild Bill Donovan: The Last Hero* (New York: Times Books, 1982).

9 In practice, it should be noted, management of the American intelligence community represents a much purer version of objective control than management of its military establishment. There are dozens of political appointees in the Pentagon, but only the Director of Central Intelligence and the Director of the Federal Bureau of Investigation (the FBI) are political appointees—and only very recently have they been chosen from outside the professional ranks. In 1981, DCI William Casey's attempt to bring in a political deputy to run the operations side of the CIA was foiled in a deft covert operation mounted from within. Robert M. Gates, *From the Shadows: The Ultimate Insider's Story of Five Presidents and How They Won the Cold War* (New York: Simon and Schuster, 1996), 208–10.

10 See, for example, John J. Dziak, *Chekisty: A History of the KGB* (Lexington, MA: D.C. Heath, 1978); and David Kahn, *Hitler's Spies: German Military Intelligence in World War II* (New York: Macmillan, 1978).

11 The classic analysis of this problem is Roberta Wohlstetter, *Pearl Harbor: Warning and Decision* (Palo Alto, CA: Stanford University Press, 1962).

12 David Stafford, *Churchill and Secret Service* (New York: Overlook Press, 1997).

13 Christopher Andrew, *For the President's Eyes Only: Secret Intelligence and the American Presidency from Washington to Bush* (New York: HarperCollins, 1995), ch. 6.

14 The classic statement of this approach is Sherman Kent, *Strategic Intelligence for American World Policy* (Princeton, NJ: Princeton University Press, 1949). Kent was director of the CIA's Office of National Estimates (the senior analytic post) for more than fifteen years.

15 "The director of intelligence would undoubtedly be considered presumptuous if his advice took on a pedantic, superior tone certain to alienate the leader. Having survived years of political struggles to reach his current position, the leader wants to feel like the master, not a student." Yehoshafat Harkabi, "The Intelligence-Policymaker Tangle," *Jerusalem Quarterly* 30 (Winter 1984): 125–31 (quoted in Handel, *Leaders and Intelligence*, 15).

16 For this argument see especially Kenneth E. deGraffenreid, "Intelligence in the Oval Office," in *Intelligence Requirements for the 1980's: Intelligence and Policy*, ed. Roy Godson (Lexington, MA: D.C. Heath, 1986), ch. 2.

17 Consider William E. Odom (a retired Army lieutenant general and former director of the National Security Agency), *Fixing Intelligence: For a More Secure America* (New Haven, CT: Yale University Press, 2003), esp. ch. 7. For a penetrating critique of the CIA's historical performance from a vantage point sympathetic to the intelligence function, see Angelo Codevilla, *Informing Statecraft: Intelligence for a New Century* (New York: Free Press, 1992).

XX – COMMUNICATION

1 On this history see Kimball, *Orators and Philosophers*; and Thomas M. Conley, *Rhetoric in the European Tradition* (Chicago: University of Chicago Press, 1990).

2 Kathleen Hall Jamieson, *Eloquence in an Electronic Age* (New York: Oxford University Press, 1988). It may seem surprising that Machiavelli has little to say about rhetoric, given the deceptive or manipulative approach to politics he endorses in *The Prince*. Actually, this silence (of a piece with Machiavelli's disdain for the rhetorical humanism of his day) is another sign of his proto-modernism.

3 On the British monarchy see especially Harrison, *Transformation of British Politics*, ch. 12.

4 An outstanding exception is O'Neill, *Honor, Symbols, and War*. See also Murray Edelman, *The Symbolic Uses of Politics* (Urbana: University of Illinois Press, 1964), esp. ch. 4 ("Political Leadership").

5 Tocqueville, *Democracy in America*, II.4.7; see further Harvey C. Mansfield Jr., *America's Constitutional Soul* (Baltimore, MD: Johns Hopkins University Press, 1991), ch. 14.

6 Aristotle, *Rhetoric*, I.1, II.1. For useful commentary: Eugene Garver, *Aristotle's Rhetoric: An Art of Character* (Chicago: University of Chicago Press, 1994).

7 The corrupting role of speechwriters has much to do with what Jamieson (*Eloquence in an Electronic Age*, ch. 8) aptly calls "the divorce between speech and thought" in contemporary American politics. Though British politicians have long honed their rhetorical skills in the famously challenging House of Commons environment, the decline in British political discourse in recent years is palpable. In Russia, democratic development since the end of the Cold War has clearly been hurt by the failure of politicians to find a rhetorical style free of Communist-era cant and thuggery.

8 For a full appreciation see Harry V. Jaffa, *Crisis of the House Divided: An Interpretation of the Lincoln-Douglas Debates* (Seattle: University of Washington Press, 1959).

9 Winston Churchill, "Blood, Toil, Tears and Sweat," in *Complete Speeches, 1897–1963*, 8 vols. (New York: Chelsea House, 1974), 6:6218–20. See more generally Robert Rhodes James, "Churchill the Parliamentarian, Orator, and Statesman," in Blake and Louis, *Churchill*, ch. 29.

10 The classic statement is Douglass Cater, *The Fourth Branch of Government* (Boston: Houghton Mifflin, 1959).

11 In fact, the Constitution's famous First Amendment was originally intended to limit only the actions of the federal government, not the states; and there is little reason to suppose that the founders would have subscribed to any sort of absolutist interpretation of its language in any case. See Leonard W. Levy, *Legacy of Suppression: Freedom of Speech and Press in Early American History* (Cambridge, MA: Harvard University Press, 1960).

12 Tocqueville, *Democracy in America*, I.2.3, II.2.6.

13 For the broad argument developed here, see more generally Timothy E. Cook, *Governing with the News: The News Media as a Political Institution* (Chicago: University of Chicago Press, 1998).

14 It is worth emphasizing that the problem is not so much the biases of individual journalists but rather "the very real possibility that journalism, as a collective enterprise across individuals and indeed across organizations, implicitly contains an entire series of assumptions about how the world works, and how the world should work, that bring with it a limited set of political interpretations. This homogeneity across news outlets and repetition over time makes for the political force of the news" (Cook, *Governing with the News*, 166).

15 Michael Ledeen, "Secrets," *National Interest* 10 (Winter 1987/8): 48–55; Cook, *Governing with the News*, chs. 6–7.

16 For what follows see further Carnes Lord, *Losing Hearts and Minds? Public Diplomacy and Strategic Communication in the Age of Terror* (New York: Praeger International, 2006).

17 See "The Strange Death of Soviet Communism," special issue, *National Interest* 31 (Spring 1993), especially Stephen Sestanovich, "Did the West Undo the East?" 26–34. For the reverse phenomenon—foreign attempts to influence the American political process—see Jarol B. Manheim, *Strategic Public Diplomacy and American Foreign Policy: The Evolution of Influence* (New York: Oxford University Press, 1994). This issue has gained an entirely new salience since the election of Donald Trump.

18 This is, however, hardly a new dimension of American statecraft. See, for example, Carl Berger, *Broadsides and Bayonets: The Propaganda War of the American Revolution* (San Rafael, CA: Presidio Press, 1976).

XXI – ON STRATEGY

1 Tocqueville, *Democracy in America*, I.2.5.

2 "During 1941–45 and throughout American history until that time, the United States usually possessed no national strategy for the employment of force or the threat of force to attain political ends, except as the nation used force in wartime openly and directly in pursuit of military victories as complete as was desired or possible. The only kind of American strategy employing the armed forces tended to be the most direct kind of military strategy, applied to war. The United States was not involved in international politics continuously enough or with enough consistency of purpose to permit the development of a coherent national strategy for the consistent pursuit of political goals by diplomacy in combination with armed force." Russell F. Weigley, *The American Way of War* (Bloomington: Indiana University Press, 1973), xix.

3 Its original meaning in classical Greek is "the art of leading the army." An

outstanding treatment is Colin S. Gray, *Modern Strategy* (Oxford: Oxford University Press, 1999); more recently, see Lawrence Freedman, *Strategy: A History* (Oxford: Oxford University Press, 2013).

4   V.D. Sokolovsky, *Soviet Military Strategy*, ed. Harriet Fast Scott (New York: Crane Russak, 1975), 11.

5   This draws on several well-known definitions: strategy is a "plan of action designed to achieve some end; a purpose together with a system of measures for its accomplishment" (J.C. Wylie); "the art of distributing and applying military means to the ends of policy" (Basil Liddell Hart); "the art of the dialectic of two opposing wills using force to resolve their dispute" (André Beaufre). See Gray, *Modern Strategy*, 17–19.

6   Edward N. Luttwak, *Strategy: The Logic of War and Peace* (Cambridge, MA: Harvard University Press, 1987).

7   For a game-theoretical perspective on contemporary business strategy along these lines, see Adam M. Brandenburger and Barry J. Nalebuff, *Co-opetition* (New York: Doubleday, 1996).

8   Thomas Schelling, *The Strategy of Conflict* (New York: Oxford University Press, 1960), 4–5.

9   The most recent version of this case is Robert B. Stinnett, *Day of Deceit: The Truth About FDR and Pearl Harbor* (New York: Free Press, 2000). Contrary to this book's central thesis, there is no reason to believe that decrypted Japanese communications relating to the attack on Pearl Harbor were available to U.S. officials *before* December 7.

10 For the larger view of Roosevelt taken here, as well as the specific argument concerning Japan, see Frederick W. Marks III, *Wind over Sand: The Diplomacy of Franklin Roosevelt* (Athens: University of Georgia Press, 1988). The standard interpretation is perhaps best represented by Robert Dallek, *Franklin D. Roosevelt and American Foreign Policy, 1932–1945* (New York: Oxford University Press, 1979).

11 Marks, *Wind over Sand*, ch. 7, provides a revealing analysis.

12 A key blunder in American policy toward Japan in the summer of 1941 concerned the way the oil embargo was understood and applied by the State Department. See Scott D. Sagan, "From Deterrence to Coercion to War: The Road to Pearl Harbor," in *The Limits of Coercive Diplomacy*, ed. Alexander L. George and William E. Simons (Boulder, CO: Westview, 1994), ch. 4.

13 See, for example, Perry M. Smith and Jerrold P. Allen, *Creating Strategic Vision: Long-range Planning for National Security* (Washington, D.C.: National Defense University Press, 1987).

XXII – ON CRISIS MANAGEMENT

1   See notably Mattei Dogan and John Higley, eds., *Elites, Crises, and the Origins of Regimes* (Lanham, MD: Rowman and Littlefield, 1998). For a suggestive analysis of the role of Gorbachev and the Soviet elite in the fall of the Soviet Union: Charles H. Fairbanks Jr., "The Nature of the Beast," *National Interest* 31 (Spring 1993): 46–56.

2   The McNamara remark is cited in Coral Bell, *The Conventions of Crisis* (London: Oxford University Press, 1971), 2, a seminal theoretical discussion of this subject. See also Richard N. Lebow, *Between Peace and War: The*

Nature of International Crisis (Baltimore, MD: Johns Hopkins University Press, 1981); and James L. Richardson, *Crisis Diplomacy: The Great Powers since the Mid-Nineteenth Century* (Cambridge: Cambridge University Press, 1994).

3 For this argument see Thomas Halper, *Foreign Policy Crises: Appearance and Reality in Decision Making* (Columbus, OH: Charles S. Merrill, 1971).

4 The Gulf of Tonkin incident of 1964 illustrates what might be called the constructed or pseudo-crisis, while the Cienfuegos submarine base episode of 1970 shows how a genuine or potentially serious crisis can be suppressed by conscious political choice. Patrick J. Haney, *Organizing for Foreign Policy Crises* (Ann Arbor: University of Michigan Press, 1997), 143–5.

5 See, for example, Alexander L. George, "Crisis Management: Political and Military Considerations," *Survival* 27 (September/October 1984): 223–34.

6 Joseph F. Bouchard's study of American naval operations during past crises, *Command in Crisis* (New York: Columbia University Press, 1991), provides a wealth of detail suggesting that military commanders from the 1950s onward have been more sensitive to political and diplomatic requirements and more prudent in handling local situations than crisis management theory would lead one to imagine. The notion that distortions in decision-making arising from bureaucratic interests and organizational routines constitute *the* problem of crisis management may be traced to the influence of Graham Allison's well-known study of the Cuban Missile Crisis, *Essence of Decision* (Boston: Little, Brown, 1971).

7 Ernest R. May and Philip D. Zelikow, eds., *The Kennedy Tapes: Inside the White House During the Cuban Missile Crisis* (Cambridge, MA: Harvard University Press, 1997).

8 Lawrence Freedman and Virginia Gamba-Stonehouse, *Signals of War: The Falklands Conflict of 1982* (Princeton, NJ: Princeton University Press, 1991), 147–9.

9 Richard G. Head, Frisco W. Short, and Robert C. McFarlane, *Crisis Resolution: Presidential Decision Making in the "Mayaguez" and Korean Confrontations* (Boulder, CO: Westview, 1978), 2–3.

10 The notion of an "intra-war crisis" is recognized by Michael Brecher and Jonathan Wilkenfeld, *A Study of Crisis* (Ann Arbor: University of Michigan Press, 1997).

11 "In part, governments tend to lose sight of the ending of wars and the nation's interests that lie beyond it, precisely because fighting a war is an effort of such vast magnitude. Thus it can happen that military men, while skillfully planning their intricate operations and coordinating complicated maneuvers, remain curiously blind in failing to perceive that it is the outcome of the war, not the outcome of the campaigns within it, that determines how well their plans serve the nation's interests. At the same time, the senior statesmen may hesitate to insist that these beautifully planned campaigns be linked to some clear ideas for ending the war, while expending their authority and energy to oversee some tactical details of the fighting. If generals act like constables and senior statesmen act like adjutants, who will be left to guard the nation's interests?" Fred Charles Iklé, *Every War Must End* (New York: Columbia University Press, 1971), 2.

12 Michael R. Gordon and Bernard E. Trainor, *The Generals' War: The Inside Story of the Conflict in the Gulf* (Boston: Little, Brown, 1995), ch. 20.

XXIII – ADVICE AND DECISION

1 Machiavelli, *Prince*, 25.
2 See, for example, David Leonhardt, "The Imperial Chief Executive Is Suddenly in the Cross Hairs," *New York Times*, June 24, 2002.
3 "It is the function of the leader-statesman—whether of a nation or a private association—to define the ends of group existence, to design an enterprise distinctively adapted to these ends, and to see that that design becomes a living reality. These tasks are not routine; they call for continuous self-appraisal on the part of the leaders; and they may require only a few critical decisions over a long period of time. . . . This basic contribution is not always aided by the traits often associated with psychological leadership, such as aggressive self-confidence, intuitive sureness, ability to inspire." Philip Selznick, *Leadership in Administration* (New York: Harper & Row, 1957), 39–40.
4 See Joseph M. Bessette, *The Mild Voice of Reason: Deliberative Democracy and American National Government* (Chicago: University of Chicago Press, 1994).
5 Consider Abbott, *Exemplary Presidency*, esp. ch. 1.
6 A useful recent analysis is Thomas Preston, *The President and His Inner Circle: Leadership Style and the Advisory Process in Foreign Affairs* (New York: Columbia University Press, 2001).
7 See, for example, John Crook, *Consilium Principis: Imperial Councils and Counselors from Augustus to Diocletian* (Cambridge: Cambridge University Press, 1955); and J.P. Mackintosh, *The British Cabinet* (Oxford: Oxford University Press, 1977).
8 Irving L. Janis, *Groupthink* (Boston: Houghton Mifflin, 1982 [1972]), Paul 't Hart, *Groupthink in Government: A Study of Small Groups and Policy Failure* (Baltimore, MD: Johns Hopkins University Press, 1994 [1990]).
9 May and Zelikow, *Kennedy Tapes*.
10 For this and what follows see especially Yehezkal Dror, "Conclusions," in *Advising the Rulers*, ed. William Plowden (Oxford: Blackwell, 1987), ch. 11.
11 Machiavelli, *Prince*, 23.
12 Walter Isaacson, *Kissinger: A Biography* (New York: Simon and Schuster, 1992), 139–51.
13 Morris's advice is on offer to the general public: Dick Morris, *The New Prince* (Los Angeles: Renaissance Books, 1999).
14 Particularly valuable on the connection between the intellectual and moral aspects of prudence is Alberto R. Coll, "Normative Prudence as a Tradition of Statecraft," *Ethics and International Affairs* 5 (1991): 33–51.

XXIV – LEADERSHIP AND POLITICS

1 John G. Geer, *From Tea Leaves to Opinion Polls: A Theory of Democratic Leadership* (New York: Columbia University Press, 1996), 182.
2 Abraham Lincoln, *Collected Works*, 3:27.

3 Lawrence R. Jacobs and Robert Y. Shapiro, *Politicians Don't Pander: Political Manipulation and the Loss of Democratic Responsiveness* (Chicago: University of Chicago Press, 2000).

4 A case could be made for subsuming "hidden hand leadership" under a larger rubric that might be called political manipulation or maneuver. The foremost theorist of this oddly neglected subject is William Riker; see his *The Art of Political Manipulation* (New Haven, CT: Yale University Press, 1986) and *The Strategy of Rhetoric: Campaigning for the American Constitution* (New Haven, CT: Yale University Press, 1996).

5 This is what James MacGregor Burns calls "transactional" as distinct from "transformational" leadership. Influential accounts in the political science literature are Robert A. Dahl and Charles E. Lindblom, *Politics, Economics, and Welfare* (New York: Harper & Row, 1953); and Richard E. Neustadt, *Presidential Power* (New York: John Wiley and Sons, 1959).

6 Woodrow Wilson, *Constitutional Government in the United States* (New York: Columbia University Press, 1908), 73, 70. See on this subject generally Jeffrey K. Tulis, *The Rhetorical Presidency* (Princeton, NJ: Princeton University Press, 1987); and Richard J. Ellis, ed., *Speaking to the People* (Amherst: University of Massachusetts Press, 1998).

7 Samuel Kernell, *Going Public: New Strategies of Presidential Leadership* (Washington, D.C.: Congressional Quarterly Press, 1997).

8 The seminal work is Fred I. Greenstein, *The Hidden-Hand Presidency: Eisenhower as Leader* (Baltimore, MD: Johns Hopkins University Press, 1994 [1982]).

9 See, for example, Christopher Andrew, *For the President's Eyes Only* (New York: HarperCollins, 1995), ch. 6.

10 See Greenstein, *Hidden-Hand Presidency*, ch. 5, with Jeff Broadwater, *Eisenhower and the Anti-Communist Crusade* (Chapel Hill: University of North Carolina Press, 1991), 137–66.

11 Consider the case of Franklin Delano Roosevelt, who may be said to have combined elements of the hidden hand with opinion leadership. Perhaps the best example of hidden hand leadership in earlier American history is Thomas Jefferson, who went to great lengths to disguise the new reality of party control of Congress.

12 Consider the notion of "crafted talk" developed by Jacobs and Shapiro, *Politicians Don't Pander*, ch. 2.

XXV – WHY LEADERSHIP DEPENDS ON THE TIMES

1 Machiavelli, *Prince*, 25.

2 Yehezkal Dror, *Policymaking Under Adversity* (New Brunswick, NJ: Transaction, 1986).

3 Consider, for example, Metternich's rear-guard defense of Austria-Hungary in the early nineteenth century: Henry A. Kissinger, *A World Restored: Metternich, Castlereagh, and the Problems of Peace, 1812–1822* (Boston: Houghton Mifflin, 1957).

4 Machiavelli, *Discourses*, III.9.

5 Stephen Skowronek, *The Politics Presidents Make: Leadership from John Adams*

to George Bush (Cambridge, MA: Harvard University Press, 1993). The term "political time" is borrowed from this pathbreaking book—probably the single best study of American presidential leadership.

XXVI – EXHORTATION TO PRESERVE DEMOCRACY FROM THE BARBARIANS

1 See, for example, Kim R. Holmes, *The Closing of the Liberal Mind: How Groupthink and Intolerance Define the Left* (New York: Encounter, 2016); and Ryszard Legutko, *The Demon in Democracy: Totalitarian Temptations in Free Societies* (New York: Encounter, 2016).

2 Consider again Christopher Lasch's prescient study, *The Revolt of the Elites and the Betrayal of Democracy* (New York: W.W. Norton, 1995), as well as Lasch's *The Culture of Narcissism: American Life in an Age of Diminishing Expectations* (New York: W.W. Norton, 1979).

3 Eric Zemmour, *Le suicide français* (Paris: Albin Michel, 2014), is a powerful indictment.

4 The politicization of climate science in the United States and elsewhere in recent years is an ominous development. For a critical discussion see, for example, Ian Plimer, *Heaven and Earth: Global Warming, the Missing Science* (Lanham, MD: Taylor Trade, 2009).

5 Francis Fukuyama, *Our Post Human Future: Consequences of the Biotech Revolution* (New York: Farrar, Straus and Giroux, 2002).

INDEX